THE HINDU DIASPORA

Hindus and Hinduism outside India represent a divergent diaspora. Among the estimated nine million Hindus scattered across the world, sets of beliefs, practices, identities and social formations have developed rather differently from each other as well as from those found in the subcontinent. Throughout the diaspora, Hindus and Hinduism have travelled along distinct historical trajectories significantly conditioned by a wide range of local factors.

In this theoretically innovative analysis, Steven Vertovec identifies key patterns and processes of change that have affected Hindu beliefs, practices and identities in diaspora. He examines the construction of the category 'Hinduism' in both India and abroad, while developments in two contrasting contexts – Trinidad and Britain – are given detailed historical and ethnographic attention. The notion of 'diaspora' itself is also critically discussed.

Providing a rich and fascinating view of the Hindu diaspora in the past, present and possible futures, this book will be of value not only to students of Hinduism and South Asian society but to those interested in the study of diasporas and transnationalism, religion, ethnicity and multicultural societies.

Steven Vertovec is Research Reader in Social Anthropology at the University of Oxford and Director of the Economic and Social Research Council's Research Programme on Transnational Communities.

GLOBAL DIASPORAS
Series Editor: Robin Cohen

The assumption that minorities and migrants will demonstrate an exclusive loyalty to the nation–state is now questionable. Scholars of nationalism, international migration and ethnic relations need new conceptual maps and fresh case studies to understand the growth of complex transnational identities. The old idea of 'diaspora' may provide this framework. Though often conceived in terms of a catastrophic dispersion, widening the notion of diaspora to include trade, imperial labour and cultural diasporas can provide a more nuanced understanding of the often positive relationships between migrants' homelands and their places of work and settlement.

This book forms part of an ambitious and interlinked series of volumes trying to capture the new relationships between home and abroad. Historians, political scientists, sociologists and anthropologists from a number of countries have collaborated on this forward-looking project. The series includes two books which provide the defining, comparative and synoptic aspects of diasporas. Further titles focus on particular communities, both traditionally recognized diasporas and those newer claimants who define their collective experiences and aspirations in terms of diasporic identity.

This series is associated with the Transnational Communities Programme at the University of Oxford funded by the UK's Economic and Social Research Council.

Already published:

THE
HINDU DIASPORA

Comparative patterns

Steven Vertovec

London and New York

First published 2000
by Routledge
11 New Fetter Lane, London EC4P 4EE

Simultaneously published in the USA and Canada
by Routledge
29 West 35th Street, New York, NY 10001

Routledge is an imprint of the Taylor & Francis Group

© 2000 Steven Vertovec

Typeset in Sabon by
Keystroke, Jacaranda Lodge, Wolverhampton
Printed and bound in Great Britain by
Clays Ltd, St Ives plc

British Library Cataloguing in Publication Data
A catalogue record for this book is available from the British Library

Library of Congress Cataloging in Publication Data
Vertovec, Steven.
The Hindu diaspora : comparative patterns / Steven Vertovec.
p.   cm. (Global diasporas)
Includes bibliographical references and index.
1. Hindu diaspora. 2. Hindus—Trinidad. 3. Hindus—West Indies.
I. Global diasporas (London, England)

BL1151.3 V47 2000
294.5′09–dc21   00-032305

ISBN 0–415–23892–7 (hbk)
ISBN 0–415–23893–5 (pbk)

FOR ASTRID, LIA AND NIKO

CONTENTS

ACKNOWLEDGEMENTS

First and foremost I express my sincere thanks to the numerous people in Trinidad, Great Britain, the United States, Canada and India who have kindly acted as my informants over some fifteen years. The work draws fundamentally from them – indeed without them there would of course be no book.

Academically I have benefited from the support and feedback of Robin Cohen (as Series Editor as well as a friend and colleague whose opinions and insights I value), Bhikhu Parekh, and Routledge's anonymous referees. David Gellner and Alisdair Rogers have provided invaluable criticism of the text, and I am especially grateful to them for their time and input. Mari Shullaw at Routledge has been an excellent and highly supportive Editor, while Anna Winton's wide-ranging help in Oxford has been of considerable assistance throughout the preparation of the book.

Finally, but certainly not least, I am grateful to my family for putting up with me while I spent time and energy on this project.

Most chapters in this book are refashioned versions of previously published articles: Chapter 2 stems from Vertovec (1994a), Chapter 3 from Vertovec (1990a), Chapter 4 from Vertovec (1996c), Chapter 5 from Vertovec (1994b), Chapter 6 from Vertovec (1992a), and Chapter 7 from Vertovec (1999).

INTRODUCTION

Hinduism is an ever-malleable thing. Indeed, to paraphrase Richard Burghart (1987a), the process of reforming beliefs and practices in light of shifting historical contexts is as old as Hinduism itself. What is much newer is that outside of India, over the past one hundred and fifty years or so (almost the wink of an eye relative to Hinduism's history over thousands of years), the forms and meanings of Hinduism have continued to change in ways that are curiously both distinct from, and continuous with, the still evolving forms and meanings in India itself.

Hinduism outside India represents a divergent diaspora, not simply in that beliefs, practices and social formations develop differently from – indeed, may emerge to be quite unlike – those in the subcontinent. Hindu socio-religious phenomena and the identities of Hindu people from place to place outside India are often highly unlike each other, having travelled along diverse historical trajectories conditioned by a wide range of locally contextual factors.

It is too tempting, and perhaps too easy, to observe overseas Hinduism and comment that it is different from Hinduism in India. A methodological shift is called for in the study of this – or for that matter, any – diaspora. It is often inherent in popular views of diasporas that the homeland is 'authentic' and that the diaspora represents but a deviation from the 'true' or presumed normative form. Joanna Lessinger (1995: xii), who has conducted research among Indians in Trinidad and New York, recounts the suspicions she faced from colleagues who thought that diasporic Indians 'lived a diluted, watered-down version of Indian culture'; indeed, while Lessinger was a graduate student, one of her professors advised that she should go to India to see 'the real thing'.

Dhooleka Sarhadi Raj (1997: 25) is not alone in urging researchers to 'resist understanding diasporic South Asians by going to South

1

Asia. We need to stop looking to India as the ideal culture, the fountainhead, or yardstick.' There is indeed a need for a shift in perspective and method. This should entail a change from constantly measuring socio-cultural transformation among diaspora communities against some presumed archetype (usually associated with a homeland), to analysing and accounting for the dynamics of cultural reproduction, innovation and change *in situ*. Therefore, in addition to providing accounts of social, cultural and religious developments among Hindus outside India, in this book I suggest a number of methodological approaches to understanding processes of socio-cultural change relevant to other kinds of diasporas. But is it appropriate to treat Hindus as a diaspora in the first place?

A Hindu diaspora?

In his masterly book which commences the series of which the present book is part, Robin Cohen (1997) questions whether religions can or should be described as 'diasporas' alongside the dispersed ethnic groups which conventionally comprise the term. For Cohen, religions generally do not constitute diasporas in and of themselves. He describes religions as posing phenomena 'cognate' to diasporas. This is largely because religions usually span more than one ethnic group and, in the case of faiths that have come to be widely spread around the globe, religions normally do not seek to return to, or to recreate, a homeland. Judaism and Sikhism are the obvious exceptions: as Cohen recognizes, members of these do represent diasporas since they are considered to comprise discrete ethnic groups, albeit marked by their religion, among whom many do indeed hold strong views about returning to or establishing homelands.

At best, from Cohen's (ibid.: 189) perspective, while religions do not constitute diasporas themselves, they 'can provide additional cement to bind a diasporic consciousness'. Other scholars are quicker to work with notions of 'diaspora religion', conceiving the notion simply as dispersed religious traditions existing in minority conditions away from a land of origin (see, for instance, Smart 1987; Hinnells 1997a; Ter Haar 1998).

Although I am in broad agreement with Cohen, I suggest that Hindus may represent a kind of special case akin to Judaism and Sikhism. Like these two latter faiths, and in contrast to religions like Christianity and Islam, Hinduism is generally not a proselytizing faith (while there are certain sects within the Hindu fold that do indeed proselytize). According to *Encyclopaedia Britannica Online* (which now has an entry on 'Hinduism outside India'), Hinduism does not seek converts from abroad 'because of its inextricable roots in the social system and the land of India'. Bhikhu Parekh (1993: 140), too, underscores an 'acute sense of rootedness' characterizing the relationship between Hinduism and India – a relationship that, Parekh believes, makes Hinduism 'an ethnic religion'.

Not all Indians are Hindus of course, but practically all Hindus are Indians (Nepalese and Balinese Hindus being obvious exceptions). By itself, this fact would fit with Robin Cohen's assertion above that religions tend mostly 'to provide additional cement to bind a diasporic consciousness' – in this case, Indian. Yet for many committed Hindus, the tie to India goes beyond ethnic (and its often conflated 'racial'/cultural) origins. For many, if not most, such Hindus India is a sacred space abounding with sacred places, from local shrines venerated by castes and clans to sites described in central religious texts like the Mahabharata, where the most widely recognized gods and legendary humans are believed to have undertaken some of their most significant deeds. It is mother India – Bharat Mata, conceived by many as a goddess herself. As Terence Thomas (1993: 175) explains:

> Bharat is a vital land for Hindus, especially for the twice-born [high-caste] classes and in particular the Brahmans. For such Hindus, Bharat is a sacred universe, the abode of Brahma, the creator divinity. This is the traditional Hindu view of the world and, though recently it has tended to become less important and less powerful, many Hindus still undergo purification rites on returning to the sacred soil of Bharat from abroad.

Indeed, it is the centrality of India's sacred geography that is emphasized and played upon by Hindu nationalists both in the subcontinent and abroad (Deshpande 1998). For instance, V.D. Savarkar, one of the most prominent Hindu nationalist leaders in the 1920s, declared, 'A Hindu means a person who regards this land of Bharat Varsha, from the Indus to the Seas, as his Father-Land as well as his Holy-Land that is the cradle of his religion' (in van der Veer 1994: 1).

Many Hindus outside India do not necessarily have any strong desire to return to India, whether it was they or their forefathers who had emigrated. Often Hindus outside India are appalled by that country's poverty or embarrassed (in the face of non-Indians) by some aspects of its cultural traditions such as caste. Nevertheless, among perhaps the bulk of nearly 9 million Hindus outside India – whether among people such as in the Caribbean who have been practically cut off from the subcontinent for 150 years, or among American and British-based Hindus who fly back and forth to India a number of times each year – sentimental respect if not spiritual reverence for that place and its civilizational heritage remains exceptionally strong. In this sense, then, (and despite all the problems associated with the term 'Hindu' that I will outline in the next chapter) I believe that it is expedient to speak of a 'Hindu diaspora'.

Categorizing Hinduism and constituting Hindus

This book explores questions and processes surrounding the reproduction and representation of culture, the construction of 'community' and identification as they have emerged in different periods and places among people who identify themselves as Hindus. It is suggested that the case of Hindus and Hinduism provides an exceptional view into such processes since the terms – and the social formations that they have fostered – are open to description as constructs of relatively recent history. As Friedhelm Hardy (1990: 145) puts it:

> It goes without saying that there are now people who refer to themselves as 'Hindus', using the label to define their own identity within a wider social context (both in India and in Britain). But when lining up the answers that different individuals and groups give us about their beliefs and practices, about what constitutes for themselves their 'Hinduness', the range and variety are staggering ... Although in popular writing the alleged content of 'Hinduism' is rapidly developing a monolithic and stereotyped character, this is no more than a fairly arbitrary abstraction from a random set of facts.

The book is comprised of chapters that provide analytical overviews of certain comparative processes and trends (Chapters 1, 2, 4 and 7) and ethnographic case studies (Chapters 3, 5 and 6). Chapter 1 presents some aspects of the historically constructed nature of the category 'Hinduism' in India. The discussion underlines the point that in India the category 'Hinduism' has always been conditioned by highly contextualized meanings and uses. This remains the case in diasporic situations as well. The background and breadth of the contemporary Hindu diaspora are introduced along with numerous examples of the ways in which Hindu traditions have continued to be retooled outside India. A number of perspectives are proposed through which we might come to understand better the factors affecting Hinduism's ongoing transformation overseas.

Material presented in the successive chapters of this book describes processes involving the construction, representation, and reproduction of Hinduism and Hindu identity in diaspora. Such phenomena succeed those produced during the course of transformation that occurred in the Indian subcontinent since the early nineteenth century. Yet outside of India processes of change affecting Hindus and Hinduism have been differentially conditioned by a host of factors unique to local contexts and conditions. These are explored in Chapters 2 to 6 mainly by examining divergent trajectories in the Caribbean and Great Britain. These chapters basically tell stories about some of the kinds of processes that have affected the evolution of Hinduism, as well as individual and community identities constructed around the religion. In a different way each chapter asks how and why Hinduism and Hindu identities have developed the way they have in these substantially different places.

Chapter 2 describes how an array of north Indian social and religious traditions were sieved, channelled and routinized – even politicized – in light of local conditions among nineteenth-century indentured labourers and their descendants in the Caribbean. Chapter 3 extends the story by way of examining 'the Hindu renaissance' in Trinidad and the role of a youth movement in constructing a highly 'ethnicized' understanding of Hinduism. In Chapter 4 the scene shifts to Great Britain, describing an altogether different set of migrations and exemplifying how a diversity of regional and caste-based Hindu traditions and communities have been reproduced (rather than homogenized, as in the Caribbean). One distinct Hindu community has experienced particular difficulties interacting with other groups of Hindus: these are Indo-Caribbeans who migrated from Trinidad and Guyana to Britain in the 1960s. Their situation is depicted in Chapter 5, noting how the historically produced version of Hinduism that they brought to Britain has, along with other cultural traits, influenced their relationships with Indians from the subcontinent and East Africa. Despite the truism that temples act as important 'community centres' among Hindu migrants in Britain, divergent patterns of temple use in London are summarized in Chapter 6. From mainly individual visits (reflecting the main pattern in India) through to wholly 'congregational' activities, the patterns indicate a number of things about the nature of the local Hindu communities which the temples serve.

Chapter 7 returns to a broader discussion of the category 'diaspora' and the burgeoning literature surrounding it. I suggest that much of the current writing on 'diaspora' can be grouped into three complementary 'takes' or ways of approaching diasporic phenomena – namely, as a social form, as a type of consciousness and as a mode of cultural production. Various contemporary Hindu patterns and activities overseas are raised to exemplify these three perspectives or understandings concerning 'diasporas'.

By way of conclusion, I draw from a number of points raised throughout the book to sketch a number of alternative – indeed, still divergent – paths along which Hindus and Hinduism in diaspora seem set to travel in the immediate future.

1

TRACING TRANSFORMATIONS OF HINDUISM

In a study on the development of Caribbean Hinduism, Peter van der Veer and I (1991: 149) premised our work with a view that

> to be a Hindu is neither an unchanging, primordial identity nor an infinitely flexible one which one can adopt or shed at will, depending on circumstances. It is an identity acquired through social practice and, as such, constantly negotiated in changing contexts.

This assumption holds as much in India as it does in the diaspora.

The following chapter outlines some of the ways in which, and influences by which, Hinduism and Hindu identity have been conceived, negotiated and modified in light of a variety of contexts – historically within the subcontinent as well as outside of it. The chapter sets the stage for the discussion of discrete, often divergent, processes presented in subsequent chapters.

Conceiving Hinduism

A considerable amount of scholarship concerning South Asian history, society and culture has involved detailing or commenting upon the tremendous diversity of what has come to be known as 'Hinduism' in India. Practically every overview of the category Hinduism commences with some comment to the effect that the term includes a vast range of disparate phenomena which – not least because they considerably vary regionally, locally, and in respect of specific caste hierarchies – appear wholly unintegrated with each other. On these grounds Hinduism is often considered to be fundamentally unlike most other 'world faiths'. For instance, W.C. Smith (1964: 61) famously saw 'Hinduism' as 'a particularly false conceptualization'. As Smith put it:

> my objection to the term 'Hinduism', of course, is not on the grounds that nothing exists. Obviously an enormous quantity of phenomena is to be found that this term covers . . . It is not an entity in any theoretical sense, let alone any practical one.
>
> (ibid.: 63)

In similar terms, Robert E. Frykenberg (1989: 29) states:

> there has never been any such thing as a single 'Hinduism' or any single 'Hindu community' for all of India. Nor, for that matter, can one find any such thing as a single 'Hinduism' or 'Hindu community' even for any one socio-cultural region of the continent.

Briefly, among the phenomena accounting for such diversity are the following. There is no single, central, or basic creed, doctrine or dogma from which all religious traditions of India derive; instead, 'animism and polytheism, pantheism, panentheism and henotheism, dualism, monotheism and pure monism exist side by side' among a plethora of traditions with 'different views of cosmogony, anthropology and the nature of salvation' (von Stietencron 1989: 14). In relation, there is no scripture that is authoritative for the mass of Indians or for all periods of history, and no central ecclesiastical body holds any parallel authoritative position. Ritual practice, especially, represents a sphere entailing a vast range of difference with regard to focus, intent, and actual undertaking.

Throughout virtually the entire history of Indian civilization, such differentiation of doctrine, authority, and practice has been particularly operative in the religions of relatively discrete social segments, particularly defined by caste, sub-caste and sect (or *sampradaya*, a tradition focused on a set of beliefs transmitted through a line of teachers). Moreover, language differences, regional histories and provincial customs throughout India combine to produce highly localized religious understandings and practices.

Given such a 'mosaic of discontinuities' characterizing Indian religious traditions (Frykenberg 1989: 41), a unitary category encompassing all or most of them could only be arrived at rather artificially.

The term 'Hindu' was used by Persians in the first millennium AD to designate generally the people of India (that is, of the region of the river Indus, after which the term derives). 'This all-inclusive term', Romila Thapar (1989: 223) suggests, 'was doubtless a new and bewildering feature for the multiple sects and castes who generally saw themselves as separate entities.' Yet centuries later, after the Mughal civilization had been introduced and developed in India, the indigenous peoples and the Muslim rulers did not see each other in terms of monolithic religious traditions, 'but more in terms of distinct and disparate castes and sects along a social continuum' (ibid.: 225). It was only after the arrival of, and colonization by, Europeans that subsequently the term 'Hinduism' was derived from 'Hindu' by way of abstraction. Hinduism denoted 'an imagined religion of the vast majority of the population – something that had never existed as a "religion" (in the Western sense) in the consciousness of the Indian people themselves' (von Stietencron 1989: 12).

The first attested usage of the word Hinduism in English was as late as 1829 (Weightman 1984). The form and content of the emergent 'ism' since the turn of the eighteenth century to the nineteenth century were variously conceived of or influenced by a number of agents. The most prominent factor in such conceptualization was doubtless the political presence of the British Raj; within this, we can point to at least three major sources which contributed to the construction of Hinduism and an India-wide 'Hindu community'.

The first was Christian missionary activity. Missionaries approached Indian religious traditions as a vast, primitive yet singular complex (Thapar 1989). This was reflected in the missionaries' techniques of preaching, which involved harsh critiques of an assumed 'other faith'. The assumptions and techniques were eventually adopted by Indians themselves struggling, for different reasons, to create a united 'Hindu' community (see Jaffrelot 1992).

Second, nineteenth-century foreign ('Orientalist') scholars assumed Indian heritage to be grounded in a single religion. These scholars worked with theoretical models and categories based on Semitic religions, further equating these categories with historical or evolutionary periods. Many Orientalist scholars were also strongly influenced by early racial theories which mistakenly posited that a single, ancient Aryan people and culture had conquered and had imposed their religion and culture over all of India. By the end of the nineteenth century, Heinrich von Stietencron (1989: 15) notes, 'The Indians had no reason to contradict this: to them, the religious and cultural unity discerned by western scholars was highly welcome

9

in their search for a national identity in the period of struggle for national union.'

The third factor in channelling the conceptual production of 'Hinduism' and a 'Hindu community' in the nineteenth century was the Raj itself. Robert Frykenberg demonstrates, for South India at least,

> [how] both the ideological and institutional reification of 'Hinduism', as we now know it (with all its boggy imprecisions), and the construction of something akin to a 'civic' or 'public' religion for India, were parts of a broader political process; and that, as such, when they first began to emerge during the early nineteenth century, they were integral parts of the imperial system engendered by the East India Company.
>
> (1990: 1)

This was effected mainly by way of British laws and other forms of subsuming colonial control (with the assistance of a Brahmin elite) over a range of religious institutions and practices. This, Frykenberg (ibid.: 33) suggests, in turn 'eventually gave rise to a distinct kind of "public" consciousness' among Indians as to what 'Hinduism' might consist of. A 'process of reification' ensued which amounted to 'the defining, the manipulating, and the organizing of the essential elements of what gradually became, for practical purposes, a dynamic new religion' (Frykenberg 1989: 34).

Processes of reification, selection and definition (also of reduction and 'impoverishment'; Gombrich 1992) surrounding the construction of 'Hinduism' and 'Hindu community' also characterize the efforts of numerous indigenous leaders and movements arising in the nineteenth century. Among the most salient are: Ram Mohan Roy (1772–1833) and the Brahmo Samaj, who produced a kind of Hindu catechism (an anthology of Upanishads and Smrtis) and sought 'Hindu' parity with Christianity; Dayananda Sarasvati (1824–83) and the Arya Samaj, emphasizing a unitary ancient 'Hindu' heritage based on the Vedas; Ramakrishna (1834–86) and Vivekananda (1863–1902), who both preached a non-sectarian, universalist 'Hinduism'.

The definitions of 'Hinduism' and 'Hindu community' which were promulgated by these figures and movements were appropriated by early regional and pan-Indian nationalists. This appropriation was undertaken since, in India, 'The need for postulating a Hindu community became a requirement for political mobilization in the nineteenth century when representation by religious community became a key to power and where such representation gave access to economic resources' (Thapar 1989: 229).

Sandria B. Freitag (1980, 1989) describes a parallel process stimulated in the competition for resources in colonial India. This entailed, among those eventually to define themselves as Hindus, a 'self-conscious development in opposition to a narrowly defined "Other"' (Freitag 1989: 146). In the 1880s, one important 'Other' was the Arya Samaj, whom many Brahmins and others saw as a threat to their own ritual traditions. The Sanatan Dharm Sabha movement arose in many parts of North India to counter the Arya Samaj's anti-Brahmin, anti-idol, exclusively Vedic doctrines with its own, selective, 'orthodox Hindu' doctrines (see Jones 1976). By the 1920s, Muslims were especially targeted as the 'Other' against which 'Hindus' collectively defined and mobilized themselves.

Throughout the colonial period and through to the present day, Indian religious traditions continue to exhibit the extensive regional, sectarian and caste-based diversity they always have. Yet the homogenizing notions of 'Hinduism' and 'Hindu community' created in rather recent history hold considerable sway throughout Indian society and politics. Hindu nationalism is the obvious result. 'This reifying religious system, combining ideological, institutional, and ritual structures into an "All-India" sense of "patriotism" (or better, "matriotism"), did not need to possess very deep structures', Frykenberg (1990: 35n) comments. 'Indeed,' he observes, 'its self-conscious manifestations within the emerging "public" of India did not even need to be common, or uniform, or held by more than a tiny but creatively influential minority for it to become powerful' (ibid.).

The Hindu nationalist movements which have perhaps had the most impact ideologically are the Hindu Mahasabha, founded in 1909, which claims to promote 'Loyalty to the unity and integrity of Hinduism' (Klostermaier 1989: 403); the Rashtriya Swayamsevak Sangh (RSS) which took shape in 1925 (largely in reaction to Hindu–Muslim riots) in order to work towards 'bridging the differences between different Hindu denominations in the interest of a united, politically strong Hinduism' (ibid.: 406); and, of particular importance in recent years, the Vishwa Hindu Parishad (VHP) – founded in 1964 as an offshoot of the RSS – which propounds a very broad definition of Hinduism that overrides differences of a doctrinal, organizational, or regional/local nature. The VHP attempts

11

to supply such a definition with 'a centralized form of ecclesiastical organization, matching a more subtle standardization of doctrines and ritual practices' (Jaffrelot 1992: 24; see van der Veer 1994; Jaffrelot 1996; Bhatt 1997).

In addition to these largely political features of nationalist movements, what are the characteristics of the modern concept of Hinduism in India? These are, of course, quite complex, and have been described by numerous social scientists. One widespread trait has been the adoption of the term – as a ready synonym for 'Hinduism' – 'Sanatan Dharm' (*sanatan* meaning 'eternal', *dharm* essentially meaning at once 'cosmic order, sacred duty, mode of being' – though in many quarters it has come to mean 'religion' in a Western sense). Among other characteristics are: a tendency towards rationalization of belief and practice (Bellah 1965); an incorporation of facets drawn from neo-Vedanta philosophy into popular (largely Purana-based) belief (Fitzgerald 1990); an insistence that Hinduism does not essentially differ in nature from Christianity or any other world religion (Bharati 1971); a diminution of beliefs and practices surrounding parochial or so-called 'little traditions' in favour of those of the Sanskritic or 'Great Tradition' (ibid.); and an emphasis on *bhakti* or loving devotion to God in any form, an orientation which 'inspires not so much sectarian and denominational formations as a diffuse emotion of brotherhood, which softens the rough edges of group differences' (Singer 1971: 158). And in keeping with a centralization of the 'Great Tradition' aspects together with *bhakti*, there seems to be a dominant drive towards Vaishnavism (devotion to Vishnu and his incarnations, particularly Rama and Krishna) as probably the single most prominent orientation in worship.

Further, the modern manifestation of 'Hinduism'

> seeks historicity for the incarnations of its deities, encourages the idea of a centrally sacred book, claims monotheism as significant to the worship of deity, acknowledges the authority of the ecclesiastical organization of certain sects as prevailing over all and has supported large-scale missionary work and conversion. These changes allow it to transcend caste identities and reach out to larger numbers.
>
> (Thapar 1989: 228)

In the conclusion to her significant article on the development of the concept, Thapar (ibid.: 231) suggests that modern formulations of

Hinduism amount to 'communal ideologies [which] may be rooted in the homeland but also find sustenance in the diaspora'. Indeed, all of the characteristics discussed above also serve to describe Hinduism as it is usually conceived of by believers outside the subcontinent. However, as in India the ideological formulations of Hinduism in a variety of diasporic locations have been, and continue to be, patterned by a host of unique contextual factors. The following sections explore the background and extent of the Hindu diaspora, some developments that have marked it as well as ways in which we may begin to account for how and why such developments have differed.

The Hindu diaspora: breadth and background

The newspaper *Hinduism Today* prides itself on a claim to being the voice of 'a billion-strong global religion'. Such a statement is probably rather hopeful. It is currently impossible to gain an accurate count of Hindus, or Indians for that matter, outside India (cf. Clarke *et al.* 1990a; Peach 1994; Jain 1989). Even in countries in which government censuses include ethnic or country of birth statistics, a census category for religion is usually absent. Intelligent guesses and broad estimates, based on national statistics (while recognizing problems often inherent in these), are the best we can gather to arrive at any kind of picture of the size and extent of the Hindu diaspora.

There is of course a vexed question as to 'who is a Hindu?' The permutations of possible make-up and extent of belief and practice obviously pose important problems of definition which bear on any attempted count of religious adherents (Sander 1997). Aside from a 'religious' meaning, depending on the context, 'Hindu' can refer to an 'ethnic', 'cultural', or even 'political' identity among individuals who do not particularly profess a faith or engage a tradition. The following numbers are derived from a variety of sources, and I am uncertain – indeed sometimes dubious – about the criteria probably used to estimate them. Often there are national guesses of Hindus relative to Muslims, with both numbers assumed to reflect the presumed proportions of these religions in the parts of India whence migrants came. None of the available data for any place can suggest to us 'how Hindu' people are, or indeed, 'how they are "Hindu"'. All the numbers below can really indicate are rough aggregates relating to people whose heritage – despite whether or how it is continued – falls within that broad category of traditions that have come to be constructed as 'Hinduism'.

13

Encyclopaedia Britannica Online suggests there are 761,689,000 Hindus spread across 144 countries. This amounts to 12.8 per cent of the world's total population of around 6 billion. Enumerating by world region, the *Encyclopaedia* lists 755,500,000 Hindus in Asia, 2,411,000 in Africa, 1,382,000 in Europe, 785,000 in Latin America and 345,000 in Oceania.

Table 1.1 gives some broad estimates for Hindu populations around the world (based on figures from the CIA World Factbook, *Encyclopaedia Britannica Online*, the Himalayan Academy, Barrett 1982, Thiara 1994, Prins 1994, Bilimoria 1997, Coward 1997, Baumann 1998, Rogers 1998a, Voigt-Graf 1998).

There are certainly some discrepancies between the estimates in Table 1.1 and those offered by *Encyclopaedia Britannica Online*, but, as broad estimates go, the numbers are not irreconcilable. As Table 1.1 indicates, outside of India there are around 48,646,000 Hindus among a larger Indian diaspora that includes Sikhs, Muslims and Christians (as well as Jains, who are counted as Hindus in some estimates).

Outside of South Asia (India, Pakistan, Bangladesh, Nepal, Sri Lanka, Bhutan), there are perhaps 12,316,000 Hindus. In Indonesia, where there are said to be 3.4 million Hindus (2.7 million in Bali alone), Hinduism has been an important part of the cultural context

Table 1.1 Estimated Hindu populations, mid-1990s

Country	Number	Country	Number
India	719,000,000	Kenya	140,000
Nepal	17,250,000	Canada	120,000
Bangladesh	14,000,000	Surinam	115,000
Indonesia	3,450,000	The Netherlands	71,000
Gulf States	3,000,000	Germany	65,000
Sri Lanka	2,750,000	France	60,000
Pakistan	1,950,000	Australia	47,000
Malaysia	1,350,000	Martinique	20,000
USA	930,000	Guadeloupe	16,000
South Africa	685,000	Reunion	14,000
Mauritius	530,000	Tanzania	10,000
UK	400,000	Nordic countries	9,000
Bhutan	380,000	Portugal	8,000
Myanmar	310,000	Hong Kong	4,000
Trinidad	275,000	Switzerland	2,000
Fiji	290,000		
Guyana	235,000		
Singapore	160,000	Total	767,646,000

since the fifth century AD. Therefore, in Indonesia Hinduism can be said to be more 'at home' than 'in diaspora'. The remaining number of Hindus around the world – almost 9 million – are located where they are mainly by way of some experience or history of migration. The massive population of Hindus in the Gulf States such as Oman, Bharain and Saudi Arabia (where numbers can only be guessed at due to extensive illegal migration) is largely made up of contract labourers who spent relatively short periods outside India, often replacing each other in succession. The rest of the diaspora numbers represent mainly settled communities.

The history of large-scale migration and settlement of South Asian peoples abroad can be divided into two major periods (Clarke *et al.* 1990a). The first involved migration under imperial auspices from India to other colonies in the nineteenth and early twentieth centuries. This witnessed Indian labour migration under contracts of indenture to Mauritius, Guyana, Surinam, Trinidad, Jamaica and other British and French West Indian islands, South Africa, East Africa and Fiji, and by other contract labour schemes to Burma and Malaysia (see Tinker 1974). During this period, too, Indian (mostly Gujarati) merchants substantially extended their enterprises in East and Central Africa, South Africa, Mauritius and Fiji, while British authorities sent Indian colonial administrators to Burma and East Africa. In each of these places, Indians have settled and – through the ensuing generations – have had major social, economic and political impact on these societies (see, *inter alia*, Jayawardena 1968; Tinker 1976; Brennan and Lal 1998).

The second period, primarily occurring in the post-World War II, post-independence era, mostly involved movement to industrialized Western countries. Early on, this included students and some businessmen, their main destination being Britain. Eventually, large numbers of skilled and semi-skilled labourers moved to Britain in the 1950s and early 1960s, while from the mid-1960s increasing numbers of Indian students and professionals transplanted themselves and their families to the United States, Canada and Australia. The 1970s saw the beginnings of much movement of skilled labour from South Asia to the Arab Gulf states. Over the past twenty years there has been a rise in the number of refugees (especially Sri Lankan Tamils) from South Asia, while there has also been substantial growth in the number of 'twice migrants' (cf. Bhachu 1985) – that is, those moving from one part of the diaspora to another. Such migrations include East African Asians to Britain, Surinamese Hindustani to The Netherlands, Indo-Guyanese to Canada, and Indo-Fijians to New

Zealand. What are the implications of such a variety of historical experiences and locations?

Comparing diasporic phenomena

Over time, social and cultural phenomena have come to differ among groups who share common origins but who now are located in different places. The following section provides examples of such differentiation in social and cultural phenomena surrounding diasporic Hindus in order to indicate not only variety, but methodological problems of comparison. How does one understand the ways in which this variation arose and the functions or meanings that historically modified socio-cultural institutions have in their present-day settings?

The following examples are reported developments among Hindu populations around the world. They provide some ideas as to the diverse ways that patterns of Hindu socio-religious organization and practice have developed in diaspora.

• In Mauritius (Hollup 1993), East Africa (Morris 1968; Nagar 1997), Malaysia (Ramanathan 1997) and Britain (Barot 1980; Michaelson 1979), certain caste, regional and sectarian groups have maintained distinct practices, associations and institutions while in many other countries such phenomena have almost totally fallen into desuetude (see Schwartz 1967a).

• Hindu temples in Guyana and Fiji have been said to differ in kind and function (Jayawardena 1968, 1980): in the former country, many have come to be of a generalized sort whereby any one 'dispenses the same rituals and doctrines' as any other, while in the latter context more tend to be 'specialized centers that confer unique benefits' (Jayawardena 1968: 444–5); in Malaysia temples have been shown both to unite local Hindus in a sense of *communitas* as well as to simultaneously reproduce social hierarchies (Mearns 1995); in the United States Hindu temples remain identified with four main types – Hare Krishna, sectarian (e.g. Swaminayaran or Sai Baba), broadly North Indian and South Indian (Bhardwaj and Rao 1990; Rayaprol 1997); and in Britain, temples have come to function in a variety of ways reflecting the regional backgrounds, settlement patterns and institutional strategies of their founders and users (see Chapter 6), and in Malaysia, the role of similar factors in effecting modes of temple use are compounded by varying degrees of conformity to scriptural standards (Aveling 1978).

- In some places, Hindu ritual procedures have become truncated (Hutheesing 1983), refashioned (Michaelson 1987), or eclectically performed (Bharati 1976); in others, much of the style or corpus of rites has been virtually 'invented' in conjunction with social change in the community (Vertovec 1991a, 1992b), and in still other places, basic rites have been mutually 'negotiated' so as to provide a kind of socio-religious bridge between migrants from regionally distinct traditions (Knott 1987; Nye 1995; Lessinger 1995); in most places, many rites have been embellished or popularized in order to appeal to young, diaspora-born Hindus even to the chagrin of conservative elders: in Malaysia, for instance, Hindu leaders have complained that the inclusion of India-produced music has wrought the 'disco-ization' of Hindu ritual (Willford 1998).
- The role of Brahman priests has differed around the diaspora as well, ranging from those who had total dominance over systems of belief and practice in the early years of settlement in the Caribbean (van der Veer and Vertovec 1991), to those virtually at the mercy of market forces and local Hindu associations in present-day Britain (Barot 1987a) and to those openly rejected by the progressive and well-educated Surinamese Hindu youth of The Netherlands (van der Burg 1993).
- Ethnographic studies of Hindu communities in places such as South Africa, Malaysia, Sweden, the United States and Britain highlight the changing status and role of women: this includes evidence of women's empowerment within the community (Diesel 1998), their maintenance of control over domestic religious practice (McDonald 1987; Mearns 1995), their activities as primary agents of religious nurture (Logan 1988), their emergent roles in public space through organizing temple practice (Rayaprol 1997) and therefore, in all these ways, their key positions as shapers of diasporic traditions (Hole 1996) and cultural reproduction (Wilkinson 1994).
- In Malaysia (Jain 1968), Trinidad (Vertovec 1992b) and Fiji (Kelly 1988) it has been suggested that entire paradigms of devotional orientation have developed in accordance with local structural and social environments; but also in Malaysia (Lee 1982; Mearns 1995) and Trinidad (Klass 1991), as well as Canada (Goa *et al.* 1984), Britain (Nye 1996), South Africa (Hofmeyr 1983) and Fiji (Kelly 1995), some observers point to the growing influence or conflict surrounding recently imported, Western-influenced 'neo-Hindu' movements such as ISKCON

and the Satya Sai Baba movement among Indian immigrants; also in South Africa (Diesel 1990), as well as in Singapore (Babb 1974) and the Caribbean (Vertovec 1993 and present volume, Chapter 2), there simultaneously appears to be a resurgence of ecstatic 'folk' traditions of Hinduism.

• And with regard to emergent patterns of group formation and institutionalization, trends in both Britain (Bowen 1987) and the United States (Bhardwaj and Rao 1990) indicate successive processes of community 'fusion' and 'fission' given the size and distribution of migrants drawn from distinct caste, regional and linguistic backgrounds (Williams 1992b); these processes can be seen to differ importantly from those historically evident in Mauritius (Hollup 1993) and the Caribbean (van der Veer and Vertovec 1991, present volume Chapter 2), where 'homogenized' cultural and religious forms emerged to facilitate social cohesion among immigrants.

• Virtually regardless of the above mentioned differences of development, however, in virtually every context outside India, Hinduism has emerged as a core feature of ethnic consciousness and community mobilization (even into political spheres) among Indian migrants and their descendants (see, for instance, van der Burg and van der Veer 1986; Burghart 1987a; Lee and Rajoo 1987; Vertovec 1992b; Nagar 1997; Willford 1998).

In many ways, of course, the disparate nature of these reported developments are attributable to the differing research paradigms, objectives and approaches of the researchers who described them (Vertovec 1991b). Nevertheless, very different things have come about among Hindus across the globe.

Towards a comparative method for the study of diasporas

To create a set of broad comparative features, as above, is not in and of itself very elucidating since such kinds of phenomena among Hindus outside of India – castes and sects, temples, rituals, priests, and so forth – though deriving from a broadly common heritage, cannot be treated as discrete traits having the same meaning or value across what are now very different contexts.

Instead of seeking to understand differential developments affecting variables of society, culture and practice among religious groups outside South Asia by way of merely describing these typologically across contexts, we might best follow J.D.Y. Peel (1991: 109) in recognizing that

> Between [such] variables there seems to be much 'free play': we are forced to conclude that the linkage of variables in particular cases often results less from their inherent properties than from *how they have come to be combined* through human action in a succession of contexts.
>
> (emphasis in original)

Hence Peel urges that anthropological comparison must ideally be a method for 'comparing histories or societies-in-change' so as to offer 'a clear path to the explanation of social phenomena without misrepresenting the general way in which they are brought about' (ibid.).

The first task in such an approach should be to gain a firm grasp of the succession of structural conditions encompassing the variables found in any historical situation under analysis or comparison. These are the 'contextual parameters', as J. Clyde Mitchell (1987) calls them – conditions which, though lying beyond the immediate influence of social actors, nonetheless affect and effect their social actions and relationships.

A historical perspective is not only necessary generally for comparative social analysis, but specifically for the study of transnational populations. This is because, as Robin Cohen (1995: 16) observes, 'Some diasporas appear to have mutated across several phases and assumed different forms, refurbishing themselves as they go along.' Hence, by way of approaching the study of diasporic peoples and phenomena, Roger Ballard (1994a) has emphasized the need to account for variable 'trajectories of adaptation', Paul Gilroy (1987, 1993a) has called for an appreciation of *'routes'* as well as 'roots', and James Clifford (1994: 319) has underscored the need for 'specific maps/histories'.

Previous studies accounting for patterns of change in the Hindu diaspora have examined – indeed, have focused upon – structural conditions obtaining for different Indian communities overseas (especially Jayawardena 1968; Patel 1976; Angrosino 1983). These studies have underscored such conditions to the extent of being deterministic and functionalist in their explanations of diversity and change. In these accounts, social, cultural and religious transformations outside India occur almost entirely due to 'external' structural conditions, especially demography and political economy.

19

Evaluating aspects of structure – and change among such aspects over time – is certainly a necessary step in 'comparing histories' of social formations like Hindus outside India; however, without additional levels of analysis, such structure-only analyses often result in portraying social groups as but passive recipients of change wrought by overwhelming 'forces', rather than as active agents initiating and participating in transformational processes of many kinds.

While bearing in mind structural matters – 'the constraints imposed upon these actors by the wider social order in which they are enmeshed' (Mitchell 1987: 9) – we must also bring into the equation '(a) social reality as constructed through actors' practical accomplishments and (b) the meaning of social phenomena as resulting from actors' construction and negotiation of their interpretations' (Holy 1987: 6).

By way of these latter, subjective features, Bhikhu Parekh (1994) offers a comparative overview of Hindu diasporic developments focusing on what he describes as core meanings, ideas and values surrounding certain Indian cultural phenomena (especially family, religious belief and practice, and facets of social structure). He provides an important approach and a useful, often overlooked, mode of appraisal. For instance, Parekh accounts for the centrality of the sacred text, the Ramayana, among numerous overseas Hindu communities. He does so by highlighting several themes, images, messages conveyed by the text, relating the ways these resonate with and appeal to the diasporic condition.

Clearly, diasporic phenomena need to be approached by way of both structure (historically situated socio-economic and political conditions) and agency (the meanings held, and practices conducted, by social actors). A social anthropological approach is perhaps best, therefore, given this discipline's combined view towards structure (or 'concern with interaction and process studied through the medium of detailed cases interpreted within the framework of the wider social, economic, and cultural contexts in which they occur' [Grillo 1985: 8]) as well as its interest with matters of agency (or the subjective dimension of 'models, definitions, orientations that actors consciously or unconsciously employ in their management of relations with one another' [ibid.]). With regard to the study of Hindu diasporic phenomena, for instance, this kind of approach is what van der Veer and I (1991: 153) had in mind when seeking to understand the emergence of Caribbean Hinduism 'by way of examining the creation of religious ideology and organization *vis-à-vis* broader, encompassing social configurations and cultural terrains'.

A framework for comparative study of South Asian diasporas

In order to account for meanings, actions, and 'contextual parameters' among Hindu people in a variety of geographical and historical locations, a broad range of factors must be accounted for in a systematic way. Clarke, Peach and I (1990a) have proposed a number of such factors, grouped under four general rubrics, appropriate for comparative analysis of overseas South Asian populations (cf. Jayawardena 1968; Knott 1986a; Hinnells 1997b). These are reiterated below:

1 Migration processes and factors of settlement

    (a) *type of migration* (such as contract-bound, economic or political refugee, entrepreneur or student; plus, whether for purposes of temporary work and the sending home of remittances – a situation including a 'myth of return' – or whether the move is deemed permanent);

    (b) *extent of ties with South Asia* (presence of social or economic networks spanning pre- and post-migration context; involvement with formal associations in homeland; ability to visit homeland for variety of purposes);

    (c) *economic activity in new context* (type of employment, extent and nature of capital owned, degree of economic specialisation, encapsulation and interaction *vis-à-vis* other ethnic groups);

    (d) *geographic features of settlement* (nature of areas of predominance – especially rural or urban; proximity to other ethnic groups – bearing in mind the socio-economic standing of all such groups in the society in question; location of important community centres and employment sources);

    (e) *infrastructure of 'host' society* (nature of governmental policies towards migrant/refugee groups; availability of housing, loans, grants; existence of governmental bodies to monitor race and ethnic relations or discrimination).

2 Cultural composition

    (a) *religion* (proportions of South Asian population comprised of main faiths – Hindu, Muslim, Sikh, Jain, Christian; presence of sects or movements within each of these; extent of institutionalization, including formal organizations and places of worship; presence of formally trained clergy);

(b) *language* (diversity of South Asian/Hindu population; extent to which these, or a South Asian *lingua franca*, are used in the new context; availability of literature in these languages);

(c) *region of origin* (proportion of South Asian/Hindu population comprised of groups of such diverse origin, having implications with regard to a host of cultural practices and values);

(d) *caste* (again, proportions of – correlated with regional, linguistic, and sectarian backgrounds – within migrant population; presence of distinct religious traditions associated with; degree of institutionalization, especially in terms of formal associations; or, conversely, nature and degree of attenuation of caste consciousness and caste interrelationships);

(e) *degree of 'cultural homogenization'* (degree and nature of mutually constructed, 'generalized' or non-regional/caste/linguistic based corpus of South Asian cultural practices and forms of social organization).

3 Social structure and political power

(a) *extent and nature of racial and ethnic pluralism* (proportions of different ethnic groups; period of arrival in relation to each other; existence of ethnically associated economic 'niches'; nature of ethnic 'boundary markers'; social 'stigmas' attached to different groups, and South Asians/Hindus in relation to these; history of discrimination in various sectors of society; history of racial or ethnic violence);

(b) *class composition* (whether South Asian/Hindu group spans a number of localized class groupings or is characterized largely by a single class make-up; nature or absence of solidarity with non-South Asian/Hindu members of same or similar class);

(c) *degree of 'institutionalized racism'* (patterns of discrimination by public authorities, including legislation against civic incorporation, bias in housing, civil service employment; nature of media stereotyping);

(d) *involvement in party politics* (nature of state constitution and franchise with respect to South Asians/Hindus and other ethnic groups; extent of membership or representation in prominent local and national political parties; existence of South Asian/Hindu-dominated parties; history of coalition or experience of government of such parties; weight of South Asian/Hindu vote in local and national elections).

4   Community development

   (a) *organizations* (political, union, religious, cultural, leisure; their history, objectives, effectiveness; existence and use of forms of media; history and patterns of factionalism);
   (b) *leadership* (nature of charisma and/or ideology; role as 'cultural brokers' with non-South Asians/Hindus; legacy of success, conflict or corruption);
   (c) *ethnic convergence or conflict* (trends towards intra-communal fragmentation or inter-ethnic/inter-religious co-operation).

A comprehensive examination of the development of any South Asian population outside South Asia should take account of most, if not all, of these factors. That is, both structural and agency-based perspectives should be combined. The scale of analysis – from small communities to national populations – undertaken in such exercises of contextualization will largely determine the nature of the relevant data.

Aspects of social organization

Contextual accounts tell us a good deal about constraints and opportunities facing social groups, but still other matters must be addressed in order to understand important dynamics of change among Hindu communities outside India. Shifts in social organization represent one area of inquiry where structural description alone is not sufficient for explanation. Instead, a host of pre-migration factors must be examined, such as the 'traditional' nature of certain social forms and institutions, as well as post-migration phenomena, including – in addition to the new contextual parameters – the acquisition of new values concerning lifestyle and behaviour, new definitions of situations and groups conceived by members or imposed by others, and new strategies among groups and individuals regarding appropriate courses of action in a variety of social, economic and political spheres.

There is hardly an identifiable social institution, system of relationships, or set of roles among overseas Hindus which has not altered significantly from what it had been in places whence the migrants had come (bearing in mind that these differ substantially, and change differentially, in various parts of the subcontinent, too). Important variations from place to place in the diaspora, and between these places and regions of origin in India, are to be found in each

23

of the following spheres of inquiry: social networks – their density, multiplicity, longevity and span of ties, whether in terms of village or neighbourhood, ritual activity, marriage, economic transaction, or patronage; kinship and domestic structures and roles (including women's roles and sibling duties); priests' roles and religious bureaucracies; voluntary associations; and political movements or factions. While various structural conditions impose constraints on these (for instance, by way of scale of group involved, resources at hand, ease of contact, and kinds of arena for social interaction), it is cultural patterns and individual dispositions or motivations which nonetheless temper the emergent forms of social organization.

But perhaps the sphere of social organization having the most wide-ranging consequences for Hindu communities abroad is that of caste. In India, the caste system (in all its variations) revolves around individual membership through birth in hierarchically ranked, mutual interdependent, endogamous corporate groups often associated with given occupations, ritual duties and roles, modes of economic and behavioural transaction, essential attributes surrounding degrees of purity/pollution, specific customs and traditions of worship. Outside of India, the complex systems of interaction which comprise the living stuff of caste are absent; caste identities are usually all that remain.

In Trinidad, for instance, in addition to originating in geographically distinct linguistic, religious and cultural traditions, Indian migrants had come as individuals from innumerable castes and sub-castes throughout the Gangetic plain. This basic fact itself largely precluded the re-formation of corporately ranked caste groups. Further, had any such groups formed, they would be in no position to exercise control over resources or interactions among other such groups, given the confines of the plantation system into which they migrated and the economic opportunities open to Indians after indenture.

Only Brahmans (who amalgamated their own diverse sub-caste origins into one caste category) successfully manipulated corporate status due to their ongoing control over the resource of ritual knowledge in Trinidad. Relatively few females migrated from India to the Caribbean, and they too represented a wide range of caste origins: hence preference for endogamous marriages had to be abandoned (only to remain, in some cases, on the level of *varna*, relating to the four broad categories into which all castes and sub-castes can be said to collapse). In Trinidad, only the highest (Brahman) and lowest (Chamar) retain any sort of group reputation or stigma – but even this only rarely comes into play in social relations. For all others, consciousness of caste identity has almost entirely dwindled into insignificance, and rarely if ever are special rights, privileges, roles or relationships ever claimed by way of caste (see Niehoff and Niehoff 1960; Klass 1961; Clarke 1986; Vertovec 1992b). Practically the same developments are evident in other places where indentured Indian labour was imported, including Guyana, Surinam, Fiji, Mauritius and South Africa (see Schwartz 1967a; also Rambiritch and van den Berghe 1961; Jayawardena 1971; Moore 1977).

Something else altogether developed among Hindus in East Africa, however. There, much of the Indian population was comprised of Gujarati traders originating largely from a set number of castes or sub-castes of Kathiawad and Cutch. In East Africa there was no complete cross-section of ranked castes from any region, however, and the systems of resource control and exchange obtaining in urban areas of Uganda, Kenya, Tanzania and elsewhere were so dissimilar to those obtaining in India that nothing like a traditional set of caste relationships emerged. Still, the Indians of East Africa desired to be closely linked to India through marriage and kinship, business, pilgrimage and other ties. This fact, plus their presence in sizeable communities, allowed for the continuance of corporate caste identities, statuses, endogamy and caste-related customs. With traditional systems of caste transactions gone – but with caste identities firmly maintained – corporate caste groups were perpetuated not by way of long-standing roles and relationships, but essentially 'by virtue of their differences' (Pocock 1957: 296). Moreover, in order to better liaise with government authorities and to provide all kinds of secular and religious facilities to their members, caste groups in East Africa increasingly 'crystallized' into formal associations (Morris 1968).

In Britain, the transformation of caste-related phenomena among Hindus has proceeded in ways paradoxically similar to both Trinidad and East Africa. The disparate caste origins of some migrants, and especially their inability to control resources on a corporate basis, have contributed significantly to the lack of a viable caste system in Britain. In some Punjabi or Punjabi/Gujarati mixed neighbourhoods, for instance, caste identity is of little matter to most daily affairs, and a more generalized sense of 'Hindu community' has been established (see Knott 1986b; Nye 1995). Yet particularly among Gujaratis from East Africa, caste consciousness is little abated due to the presence of caste associations and the continued importance of caste identity in matters surrounding family status, patronage, marriage, leadership and voluntary organizations (Michaelson 1979, 1983; Bowen 1987; Knott 1994).

What are the implications of these shifts in caste-related phenomena for Hindu community development outside India? Again, in Trinidad the almost total breakdown of caste relationships and identities allowed the creation of a single Hindu religious tradition, and facilitated commensality, congregational worship, and other patterns of consociation through which a sense of general Hindu communalism was fostered. In Britain, on the other hand, a fair amount of commensality (but usually only in public, rather than domestic, contexts), congregational worship, and other forms of communal activity among Hindus do, in places, exist. Yet in the extensive circles where they are continuously bolstered – that is, especially among East African Gujaratis – corporate caste identities provide substantial barriers to the co-operation of all Hindus and make it almost impossible for joint Hindu activity to be achieved other than on the most superficial levels. Where there are so-called umbrella groups which supposedly embrace all Hindus or all Gujaratis, their effectiveness is severely limited by the nature of leadership and recruitment to associations. Leaders tend to be recognized as such only by members of their own caste, and if any person does set himself up as a leader, people of other castes may vehemently deny that he has any following or power (Michaelson 1984).

In India, attention has been given to ways in which the caste system has changed under the impact of accelerating urbanization and 'modernization' (usually described as involving technical improvement and industrialization, Western-style education and science, increased occupational opportunity, participatory democracy): for decades, observers concluded that traditional caste interrelations and identities are highly threatened by these processes (for instance, Marriott 1965; Berreman 1967; Hardgrave 1970). Among Hindu communities overseas, we witness developments which may 'isolate and magnify' those trends in Indian society (Pocock 1957: 290). This is true not only of caste, but in other spheres of social organization. The variegated social effects of 'modernization' among Indians outside India have sometimes prefigured those under way in the subcontinent, including shifts towards nuclear families, greater independence of women, larger yet less multiplex social networks, increased occupational mobility, and more saliency of values surrounding egalitarianism and individualism. Moreover, such processes – in India and abroad – have had considerable impact on the construction of Hindu religious 'orthodoxy'.

'Official' and 'popular' religion

Modernization, in all of its variegated forms, has had far-reaching impact on the practices and social institutions – even basic belief structures – of Hinduism in contemporary India. Among these patterns of change, many of which began with responses to the intrusion of British thought and culture into the subcontinent, there has been both a new rationalization of Hindu belief (evident in a variety of so-called 'neo-Hindu' movements like the Brahmo Samaj, Arya Samaj and Ramakrishna Mission) and an increased prominency of certain broad, 'Great Tradition' beliefs, rites and values (Bellah 1965; Ashby 1974; Bharati 1971). Due in no small way to contemporary forms of social and cultural change throughout India, parochial Hindu traditions – long the mainstay of living Hinduism – give way to more homogeneous ones.

> Everywhere village deities traditionally associated with epidemics of diseases such as plague, smallpox, and cholera seem to be losing ground, while the prestigious Sanskritic deities are becoming more popular . . . The horizon of the peasant is widening . . . Films, radio, text-books, newspapers, journals, and paperback books are strengthening 'regional' and 'all-India' Hinduism, at the expense of strictly 'local' forms . . . Moreover, there has been a growth in secularization, egalitarianism, and rationalism.
>
> (Srinivas and Shah 1968: 365)

'The net result of these processes,' Milton Singer (1966: 66) observed, is 'an ecumenical sort of Hinduism that is blurring sect and caste lines.' Central to this emergent, modern, generalized Hinduism is the doctrine of *bhakti*, or direct, loving devotion to God (in any form, though most often as an incarnation of Vishnu). Through *bhakti*, individualism takes precedence over caste and class such that democratic and egalitarian ideals – which, some say, go hand-in-hand with modernization – are promulgated (Lannoy 1971; Ishwaran 1980).

Throughout the Hindu diaspora the same broad processes have been in evidence. In his survey conducted over three decades ago, Chandra Jayawardena (1968: 444) concluded that among overseas Indians, 'In general, trends have led from village and caste beliefs and practices to wider, more universalistic definitions of Hinduism that cut across local and caste differences.' Raymond Williams (1988) sees this kind of pattern among overseas Indians as producing an 'ecumenical Hinduism', which 'builds on the traditional Hindu tolerance by including in one religious fellowship the followers of many different regions, language groups, and sects'. Perhaps at the core of this tendency among Hindus throughout the worldwide diaspora, the importance of *bhakti* is paramount. This is especially the case where Vaishnavite (Vishnu/Rama/Krishna-focused) traditions are salient. However, Ninian Smart (1987) points out that neo-Vedantin accounts of Hinduism (highlighting spiritual/philosophical teachings following figures such as Vivekananda and Radhakrishnan) have been coming into prominence throughout the diaspora, particularly among the most westernized, well-educated Hindus.

One corollary of the trend has been the gradual separating, in ever more concise terms, of what might be called 'official' and 'popular' strains of Hinduism (described in Chapter 2). 'Official' religion can be taken to mean tenets, rites and values which have been formally institutionalized: usually this entails a formally trained clergy and some kind of lay/clerical organization which decides on matters of orthodoxy and legitimacy, which conducts a variety of public socio-religious activities, and which disseminates information or proselytizes by means of various modes of communication. 'Popular' religion here refers to beliefs and practices maintained by lay persons outside of 'official' auspices: these may include community or domestic phenomena recognized as officially orthodox, as well as unorthodox magico-religious and charismatic phenomena (healing rites, spirit possession, pursuit of miracles, combating evil forces) and 'cult' phenomena (collective activity directed towards some usually unorthodox focus). The trend towards generalized or 'ecumenical' Hinduism overseas – and, one might argue, in India itself – usually involves a conscious separation of 'official' and 'popular' elements, with many of the latter often being increasingly relegated (by advocates of the former) to a rather disdained or peripheral status. Peter van der Veer (1991) has described the resultant dichotomy between such official–orthodox and popular–unorthodox practices in Surinam and The Netherlands as that between 'frontstage' and 'backstage' (or 'hidden') Hinduism.

In Trinidad, the trend towards a homogeneous, lowest common denominator Hinduism emerged early under Brahmanic direction. The form it took was that of *bhakti*-focused Vaishanivism, replete with Sanskritic rituals and frequent recitation of the popular sacred texts of this orientation, especially Tulsidas' Ramayana and the Bhagavata Purana. This remained a rather loosely and locally practised corpus of belief and practice until the 1920s and 1930s, when confrontation with Arya Samaji missionaries from India provided the catalyst for its reactionary institutionalization as an official, orthodox religion deemed Sanatan Dharm (a process paralleled throughout the Hindu diaspora; see Jayawardena 1968; Bharati 1976; Bilimoria 1985; Naidoo 1992; Nye 1995; in Fiji and Mauritius, however, are two contexts where the doctrines and rituals of Sanatanists and Arya Samajis were largely merged without causing splits among Hindus; Kelly 1991; Hollup 1993).

While a national Sanatan Dharm organization has long maintained sway over most Hindu activity in Trinidad, a variety of unorthodox 'popular' practices have continued on another level (including blood sacrifice to lesser deities, *ojha* or sorcery, exorcism and spiritual healing). These kinds of popular practice are not usually talked about openly among ordinary Hindus, and are often even publicly castigated by representatives of the orthodox national body. Other official Hindu bodies exist in Trinidad, too – most joined in a National Council of Hindu Organizations. All are self-conscious of overtly demonstrating a 'respectable' tradition in the face of an overwhelmingly Christian society. However, the success of these official organizations is currently in question as well-educated and thoroughly 'westernized' young Hindus in Trinidad claim these formal bodies seriously fail to relate to them (see Chapter 3).

In some parts of Britain, ecumenical forms of Hinduism are continuously being 'negotiated' among regionally distinct groups (Knott 1986b; Nye 1995). Elsewhere, regional, caste or sect (*sampradaya*) based groups monitor their own forms of orthodoxy or tradition. In large part because of this as yet developing and fairly fragmented setting, congregational Hinduism in Britain (which evolved to be perhaps the foremost expression of the religion in places like Trinidad) has yet to take prominence over the domestic sphere, where the bulk of Hindu religious practice – including spiritual healing, magico-religious activity, and 'cultic', as well as various mainstream, observances – is still to be found (Michaelson 1987; McDonald 1987). Hence no clear separation of 'official' and 'popular' strains of Hinduism has emerged, largely due, perhaps, to the nascent character of all-encompassing Hindu organizations and to the continued centrality (as in India) of domestic, rather than communal, worship.

But there is certainly no shortage of Hindu associations in Britain (see Chapter 4). However, most of these associations appear to be rather small, regional/linguistic- or caste-dominated bodies of widely varying activity and effectiveness. But while fragmentation appears to be the order of the day, there are appearing some early signs of communal amalgamation and 'Hindu ecumenism'. Important examples include the National Council of Hindu Temples (UK) (which coordinates sporadic activities and produces occasional information sheets) and the 'Virat Hindu Sammelan' or 'great gathering' of Hindus in 1989 sponsored by the international Vishwa Hindu Parishad (VHP). This trend (following the VHP's own thrust) rests on the development of an 'officially' orthodox, Vaishnavite *bhakti* orientation. Among Hindu migrants and their offspring in Britain, the popularity of religious events and publications of the International Society for Krishna Consciousness (ISKCON, often called 'the Hare Krishnas') represents another important example of such a trend through which a rationalized, 'official' *bhakti* tradition (albeit originally tailored for Westerners) is bringing together Hindus of diverse regional, linguistic, caste and sectarian backgrounds (Carey 1987; Nye 1996; cf. Williams 1988).

It also seems that Hindu desires for more adequate religious nurture for their children, as well as national strategies for multi-faith religious education, may encourage Hindus to organize themselves and to promote a universal style of Hinduism by way of creating and distributing their own educational materials for use throughout Britain (Kanitkar 1979; Jackson 1985; and Chapter 4).

Attempts to define creeds and establish 'orthodoxy' have perpetually existed in Hinduism's long history. Van der Veer (1991: 43–44) emphasizes:

> Basically, there have always been Brahmanical formulations of Hinduism which made a distinction between *shastrik* (scriptural, unchanging, higher) and *laukik* ('folk', changing, lower) beliefs and practices . . . On the other hand there have never been unequivocal, absolute standards to decide for each and every Hindu what should be considered higher and lower.

What is perhaps new – especially as observed in the diaspora – is the tendency towards all-embracing forms and (nominally, at least) democratic associations to oversee and promote them. In some cases, overseas Hindus have been practically forced to develop these. During the 1920s in Singapore, for example, the government imposed a largely European-run body to co-ordinate the management of Hindu temples. Further, the development of a universal Hinduism need not oust other variants of the religion. Both in Singapore and in Malaysia, the homogenizing process has occurred alongside a continuance of regional/linguistic, caste and sect traditions. Temples dedicated to these parochial traditions are maintained especially in rural areas while there are also 'large urban temples dedicated to universal deities. In these places the unity of the Hindu congregation is brought about, and contributes to emphasizing emotionally the Indian identity and separateness' (Arasaratnam 1979: 167). It should also be noted that, since in these territories it is South Indian communities which predominate, the 'universal' style of Hinduism to emerge is one marked by Shaivism and 'agamization', rather than Vaishnavism and 'sanskritization' (Aveling 1978; Lee and Rajoo 1987).

Among Hindus in whichever context outside India we consider, such evidence indicates a growing self-awareness *vis-à-vis* other communities (cf. Thomas 1993). Alongside this, there is often a trend towards greater self-definition (including a greater rationalization) as to what they consider fundamental or orthodox in terms of doctrine and ritual practice. Again, to provide a further important example from Malaysia: with the rapid development of Hindu associations that took place there in the 1930s, there was an accompanying reform movement to 'cleanse' Hinduism of 'archaic folk traditions'. The movement held that it was necessary not only to keep pace with the modernization movement in Hinduism in India, but also to bring Malayan Hindus onto a status level with the other prominent ethnic and religious communities in Malaya – a characteristic which Sinnappah Arasaratnam (1979: 172–3) describes as a 'constant concern with the image of the Indian in the eyes of other Malayan ethnic groups'. Such a pattern or characteristic appears in other fields and processes as well.

Religion/culture

David Pocock (1976) has noted that in many circles the goal of 'emulating the Jews' has been advocated for Hindus in Britain. This goal is said to entail preserving distinct religious ideas and customs while achieving a highly successful level of socio-economic integration with the encompassing society. He observes that in one branch (the Bochasanwasi Shri Akshar Purushottam Sanstha) of the Swaminarayan movement, whose members long resided in East Africa before settling in Britain, there has emerged a tendency to consider certain aspects of Gujarati culture (including family structure, language, diet, marriage networks, and the position of women) as quasi-religious phenomena – that is, as behavioural and ideological facets contributing to the fulfilment of *dharma*. However, by co-equating religion and culture:

> The Sanstha is faced with a dilemma: to the extent that Gujarati culture becomes *the* culture of religion and succeeds in establishing this conception in the minds of its youngest adherents, it can ensure its own continuity and emerge not unsimilar to the Jewish orthodox and conservative congregations in Great Britain. But the parallel with the Jews would break down to the extent that such an assimilation of 'culture' to 'religion' could heighten the isolation of the Sanstha member, and thus frustrate the second part of the advice, 'Emulate the Jews' which urges not only the preservation of religion but also the maximum degree of integration compatible with that.
>
> (Pocock 1976: 362)

The problem Pocock discerns for the Sanstha is that of 'disembedding a set of beliefs and practices – a "religion", from a "culture" which would then be defined as "secular"' (ibid.). This is a critical yet common dilemma for Hindus throughout the diaspora (and, some observe, in India itself; see Bellah 1965; Streng 1979; Tambs-Lyche 1990). It entails moves towards a self-conscious 'rationalization of the distinction religion/culture' (Pocock 1976: 357) despite the everywhere-asserted dictum that 'Hinduism is a way of life.' With regard to this conundrum throughout the Hindu diaspora, Raymond Williams (1984: 191) comments:

> The critical assumption here is that there are some aspects associated with past religious practice that are fundamental and essential to the continuation of the religion and others that are cultural accoutrements that are not so fundamental. Thus, the process of searching for an adaptive strategy becomes the attempt to distinguish what is essential in the religion and what is not.

Processes of self-consciously distinguishing elements of religion/culture are bound to have differing results in various domains (in temples, in religious or cultural associations, in homes, in the workplace). In each case among Hindus in diaspora, such processes inherently involve both some kind of adaptation to religiously and culturally plural environments and the generation or heightening of distinct 'ethnic' sentiments.

In Trinidad, the distinction of religion/culture was largely produced inadvertently by way of the early formation of a homogenized Hindu tradition that brought together migrants from a wide range of cultural backgrounds (see Chapter 2). What had been forged was a universal set of beliefs and practices which any Hindu – regardless of regional, linguistic, caste or sectarian background – could adopt as his or her own: hence, in this way, religion and specific culture of origin were unconnected. Without affecting the ideas and practices of the emergent Hinduism, any cultural predilections (of style, cuisine, mannerism, custom) owing to these separate origins could nonetheless be exercised in the household or among fellow migrants of like origin. However, most of these diverse cultural traits were themselves eventually amalgamated into a generalized 'Trinidad Hindu' cultural corpus (a set of values, material items and art forms, lifestyle preferences and behavioural characteristics, that is, which were identifiably those of most Trinidad Hindus without being deemed essential for the maintenance of their religion: thus religion/culture remained distinct).

With the rise of a common religion, and subsequently, a common set of cultural attributes, a shared sense of Hindu ethnicity was formed, finding collective expression through the turn of the century and crystallizing into formal associations and public campaigns during the 1920s and 1930s. Awareness of their own distinctiveness was constantly underlined by way of contrast to the many other distinct religious-*cum*-ethnic groups in the island (including Indian Muslims and Indian Presbyterians, African Catholics and African Anglicans, members of Afro-Catholic syncretic religions, Chinese and Portuguese Catholics, and more). By the 1950s, Trinidad Hindu ethnicity had been honed to the point whereby a Hindu political party formed and became one of two primary contenders for power. Today, conditions in Trinidad have changed considerably such that no wholly Hindu party exists; still, Hindu ethnicity is very strong – continuing to have considerable impact on politics (Tewarie 1988), and there is a growing movement to ensure basic rights for, and promote a range of values among, ethnic Trinidad Hindus (see Chapter 3).

In Britain, as described by Pocock (1976) and others, the process of disjoining religion/culture, among certain groups, has been under way for some time. In other associations and temples, there is at present little cause to undertake such a process; gatherings and practices of all sorts are successfully conducted wholly in a specific regional, linguistic, caste or sectarian manner. For this reason there have been deep feelings of alienation, in relation to these associations or temples, among some smaller groups of Hindu migrants who feel unable to participate (see Chapter 6). Hence the continuing regional, linguistic, caste and sectarian fragmentation among Hindus noted in the above sections.

Further, Kim Knott (1986b: 46) points to another important dimension of the trend towards separating religion/culture, one akin to what sociologists of religion deem 'secularization':

> For some people [Hinduism] has the status of a 'compartment', or one of a number of aspects of life . . . Many Hindus in Leeds are only too aware that their religion is one amongst others. Not only are there indigenous faiths, generally grouped together by Hindus as 'Christian', but there are also other South Asian faiths . . . In this country Hinduism is just one minority faith amongst others. An awareness of religious pluralism has affected the way Hindus think about themselves and their faith. Some are beginning to think of Hinduism as many people do Christianity, something to be remembered [only] during large festivals and at births, marriages and deaths.

This conceptualization of Hinduism as yet another religion among others tends to support the creation of a general category of 'British Hindu'. (The inclusion of a religious question in the 2001 census, which is scheduled to have a single 'Hindu' box, will further propagate this categorization.) Similarly, both Raymond Williams (1988) and Diana Eck (1996) describe the emergence of an identifiable 'American Hinduism'.

Ideology

Such 'sharpening of awareness' seems to be a prominent development, in one form or another, throughout many Hindu communities overseas. It is a trend common to diasporas, since it is fostered by the kind of self-reflection stimulated among minorities in contexts of ethnic and religious pluralism. Hence Ninian Smart (1987) suggests that the condition of diaspora stimulates the members of a faith to formulate, usually under some general principles, a universal account of the particular religion and its teaching. Such confrontation with, and reaction to, cultural and religious otherness can be seen especially to engender what Bruce Kapferer (1988: 210) calls 'processes of reification common in religious action': 'These are processes whereby modes of understanding reality are systematically removed from their embeddedness in the flow of daily life, fashioned into symbolic things, and placed in a stable, dominant, and determinate relation to action.' Elsewhere, Kapferer (1983: 19) has similarly referred to a kind of active formulation of 'ideology' out of an undifferentiated field of 'culture'.

With regard to the Hindu diaspora, then, it is possible to say that the process of 'reifying religion' or extracting 'ideology' from 'practice' is akin to – indeed, part of – the above described processes of differentiating 'official' and 'popular' strains of the religion and distinguishing facets of religion/culture. Each of these developments entails Hindus' reflexive viewing of – in relation to the changing contexts in which they find themselves – their complex, once taken-for-granted traditions; subsequently certain features are conceptually isolated and held up, as it were, through public statements and symbols, so as to provide explicit guidance for daily action among individuals and for political action among the (itself, newly- or re-defined) group.

In Trinidad, the history of Hindu ideology formation occurred in successive stages. By the 1920s, a number of local Hindu associations had been formed throughout the island so as to better sponsor a range of collective celebrations. Such moves were among the first for institutionalizing certain, what were perceived as key, doctrines, rites and other practices. The Arya Samaj debates of the 1930s sparked the next major phase, when opponents to this reformist movement took explicit steps towards establishing Hindu ('Sanatanist', after Sanatan Dharm) orthodoxy. Such steps ultimately resulted in the founding of a single national organization which elaborated and directed the constructed orthodoxy by affiliating almost all temples in the island, building an impressive number of Hindu schools, and publishing materials of many kinds. This body, in turn, became indistinguishable from the Hindu political party which arose in the 1950s, thus marking yet another significant phase of Hindu ideology formation. Today, self-conscious re-examination of beliefs, practices and values mostly occurs among young Hindus who not only question their place in Trinidad society, but who especially see themselves as wholly different, in terms of experience and interests, from their parents and forebears. Therefore they are undertaking a fresh phase of Hindu ethnic ideology formation through new associations, publications, and activities.

In Britain, correlated with the more variegated patterns of official–popular tradition and religion–culture distinction, processes of Hindu ideology formation are much less established. The most common locus of such processes to date is probably that of voluntary Hindu associations. Since the early 1960s – and even more so, since the arrival of the organizationally well-experienced East Africans – local Hindu associations have proliferated throughout the country. In each, speeches and sermons, written constitutions, and news-sheets or occasional publications set forth explicit summaries of ritual and doctrine while proposing strategies for development in the future. As discussed in the above sections, however, many if not most of these associations function on behalf of specific caste, sectarian or linguistic/regional groups, rather than for a greater 'ethnic Hindu' community. This may end up being their strength. In a comparative study of broadly defined 'Sanatanist' and sectarian temples, Johanna H. Dwyer (1988) found the latter far more effective in appealing to young British Hindus. This was not least because 'The young people at the Sanatan Mandir, although having a strong feeling of being Hindu, seem largely lost in the amorphous nature of Hinduism' (ibid.: 268).

The two examples of emergent universal Hinduism mentioned earlier – the National Council of Hindu Temples (UK) and the Virat Hindu Sammelan – have given evidence of a process of ideology formation with all British Hindus as its target. The National Council sponsors religious events and youth workshops considered to be of value to Hindus of all backgrounds. Among the publications it has produced, there is a booklet describing itself as 'the authoritative statement on the tenets of the Hindu religion'. At the Virat Hindu Sammelan, which took place over two days at the Milton Keynes Bowl in August 1989, there were a series of public addresses and, in the Souvenir Booklet, dozens of small articles setting forth what were meant to be definitive, universal statements concerning the nature of Hinduism (almost all of a Vaishnavite *bhakti* and neo-Vedantin character). Signs of an 'ethnic Hindu' communalism were present too, especially in statements suggesting that

'Hindu' is the name of a group of human beings who enter the world polity as one unity distinct from all others . . . Our political and cultural interests on the international plane

36

are common, our friends are common and our foes are common. We enter the world scene as one group.

(Sharma 1989: 94)

Whether, and in what way, such a singular 'ideologized' universal Hindu identity might take hold of the, as yet, somewhat fragmented Hindu population in Britain still remains to be seen.

An alternative model of 'ecumenical', rather than homogeneously defined, Hinduism may still predominate. Such a model is represented by *Hinduism Today*, a magazine published by the monastic Himalayan Academy in Hawaii. Recognizing the tremendous diversity of Hindu belief and practices both in India and the diaspora, *Hinduism Today* portrays itself as providing a global public service to 'the family of Hindu faiths' (http:// www. hinduismtoday.kauai.hi.us/ashram/htoday.html). Such an all-embracing perspective allows considerable flexibility-yet-connection for a diaspora comprising often divergent community trajectories.

Yet another possible course of development facing Hindu communities overseas, of course, is a diminishing of Hindu attachment altogether, or one in which 'Hindu' remains largely a symbolic ethnicity (cf. Gans 1999). Chandra Jayawardena, who was one of the few anthropologists to have conducted research among overseas Indians in many parts of the world, foresaw such a path several decades ago. Jayawardena noted that, in many parts of the world, while many aspects of cultural tradition had been discarded, the selective retention of some aspects often remained 'as media for maintaining and expressing the solidarity of the Indian community *vis-à-vis* other ethnic groups' (1963: 25). Again, context remains paramount.

In broad terms, the situation among Hindus in America that Raymond Williams (1988: 54) describes also serves well to depict diasporic conditions generally:

> The strength and growth of sectarian and regional forms of Hinduism and the secularization of the Asian-Indian community are threats from opposite sides . . . What results from the tension will be a redefinition of what 'Hindu' means in the United States and the redefinition of boundaries through the manipulation of symbols and the expansion of their cultural contextualization so as to include as many Asian Indians as possible under a single religious identity.

37

The following chapters describe some of the different ways in which the meanings of 'Hinduism' and 'Hindu identity' have been redefined through such processes of symbol manipulation and contextualization outside India. As we shall see, sometimes rather discrepant definitions seem to have emerged even in the same diasporic location.

2

'OFFICIAL' AND 'POPULAR' HINDUISM

Historical and contemporary trends in Surinam, Trinidad and Guyana

The religious traditions of Hindus in the Caribbean are the products of over one hundred and forty years of inadvertent permutation, deliberate alteration or innovation, and structurally necessary modification. Caribbean Hindu traditions are also currently in process of transformation, and will doubtless continue to undergo changes for a host of reasons or purposes. Mutability is one of the hallmark characteristics of many concepts, rites, social forms and other phenomena generally subsumed under the rubric of 'Hinduism'. As discussed in Chapter 1, in India the range of such phenomena is so large, varied, and variable that many scholars are dubious of any single notion or category 'Hinduism'. In the Caribbean, historical courses of change have been such that a generally unitary Hindu religion has indeed arisen. Yet although a standardized and institutionalized orthodoxy has come to dominate the religious life of Hindus in each of the major communities in the Caribbean, more variegated beliefs and practices nonetheless occur on local levels. Such interrelated levels or sites of socio-religious activity perhaps parallel those traditionally present in India; yet local settings have conditioned their development in particular ways.

Hinduism, descriptive categories, and the diaspora

Since the 1950s, some anthropologists have found heuristic value in the notions of 'Little Tradition' and 'Great Tradition' for addressing the diversity within, and relation between, local and India-wide Hindu religious phenomena (see, for instance, Marriott 1955; Weightman 1978). 'Little Tradition' has generally referred to highly parochial, non-Brahmanic/non-Sanskritic beliefs and practices. These tend to invoke minor or potentially malevolent deities and super-naturals, often towards pragmatic ends. The 'Great Tradition' of Hinduism, on the other hand, has been said to include mainly the beliefs and practices found in Sanskrit texts and maintained by Brahmanic authority across the entire subcontinent. These invoke the highest or most widely-known pantheon of deities, and also promote transcendent or philosophical ideals.

There is much literature describing the dialectic relations between these two categories (sometimes doing so in terms such as 'classical vs folk' or 'textual vs practical' religion; see Leach 1968). Many scholars have come to agree that such categories can often obscure the continuity of types or levels of religious phenomena – as well as their co-existence in any village or town – by reifying an artificial polarity. Instead, perhaps, such terms should represent Weberian ideal types placed on the ends of a kind of descriptive continuum. Depending on what is being undertaken, the activities of Hindus in India could then be represented at one point or another on the continuum (Weightman 1997). In such a model, for example, Hindu belief and practice might be described as being towards the 'Little Tradition' or pragmatic end when a person employs a low-caste specialist to invoke a blood-demanding deity during an exorcism, and towards the 'Great Tradition' or transcendent end when the same person makes a pilgrimage to a major Vaishnavite site; subsequently, other concepts and activities (elements of domestic worship; acts or obeisance to holy men; participation in certain oblatory rites, and so on) may be placed in-between according to their means and ends as conceived by the worshipper. The most important thing to recognize is that such categories or models are merely abstractions pertaining to phenomena which are inextricably linked in believers' minds and in their social relations (Pocock 1973: xiv).

With reference to the Hindus who now reside in a wide variety of contexts outside India, the categories of 'Little' and 'Great' Tradition have even more limited value. For numerous reasons and in different ways, the range of religious phenomena so long associated with the Hindu 'Little Tradition' has been narrowed or displaced alto-gether among migrants and their descendants. Anthropologists have described this trend in similar ways. Regarding Hinduism in East Africa, Agehananda Bharati (1970) observed the occurrence of a complete fusion of 'big' and 'little' tradition elements; regarding South Africa, Hilda Kuper (1957) suggested that migrants' beliefs and practices have evolved into a 'regional Hinduism' in their own right; regarding Trinidad, I have described how Hindu phenomena characteristic of different analytical 'levels' and drawn from various regions of India have been historically 'homogenized' in the new context (Vertovec 1989, 1992b); and, regarding Surinam, Cors van der Burg and Peter van der Veer (1986) discuss how rituals and ceremonies peculiar to specific castes disappeared altogether – indeed, as did the division between a perceived brahmanical religion of the higher castes and a folk religion of the lower castes.

In Western countries like Britain and the United States, Indian migrants have often retained many sectarian, caste-based or regionally-specific Hindu traditions. Reasons for this include: migration and settlement in large group numbers (as opposed to indentured migrants' transplantation as individuals), allowing for the continued use of regional language (whereas these had been blended or attenuated in places like the Caribbean) and for the greater maintenance of caste identities (which have largely disappeared among the post-indenture descendants). Also, recent migrants have importantly been able to retain many kinds of social and economic links with India, facilitated in recent years by advances in telecommunications.

Especially due to the relatively small size and socially isolated status of their communities, a single corpus of belief and practice has usually come to be pervasive among Hindus in each post-colonial context outside India (that is, in places like the Caribbean, Mauritius, and Fiji). Thus to continue to describe the variety of Hindu beliefs and practices among overseas Hindus in terms of 'Little' and 'Great' Traditions – even by way of an ideal-type continuum – would be for the most part an irrelevant exercise. Instead, it is suggested here that the notions 'official' and 'popular' religion may be more useful in describing strands or levels of Hinduism in places like these.

'Official' religion can be taken to mean a set of tenets, rites, proscriptions and prescriptions which are promulgated through some institutionalized framework: this usually entails a formal network of priests (often hierarchically structured) and/or a lay organization which determines orthodoxy and orthopraxy, arranges and administers a variety of socio-religious activities, usually controls some sort of communication network (such as publications or pronouncements dispensed through subordinate bodies – especially temples), and is often directly involved in religious education through schools and other programmes.

'Popular' religion can be understood basically as beliefs and practices undertaken or maintained by lay believers: these include orthodox practices undertaken outside 'official' auspices (especially domestic worship, but also including local festivals which celebrate mainstream deities or saints), so-called superstitious (magic-religious) and/or charismatic phenomena (such as healing rites, spirit-possession and exorcism, pursuits of miraculous ends, or steps taken to ward off evil forces), and 'cult' phenomena (collective religious activity directed towards some specific but usually unorthodox focus, such as an extraordinary person, sacred place or item, or supernatural being propitiated by a relative minority).

'Official' and 'popular' features are found in every world religion today, although in Hinduism (in India or abroad) certain dimensions reflect a rather unique newness. Largely because it is without a single founding prophet, single sacred text, single geographical focal point or unitary institutionalized priesthood, the sizeable cluster of traditions which has come to be deemed 'Hinduism' has, until relatively recently in its long history, been without a single 'official' dimension. The resultant heterogeneity of belief and practice is Hinduism's leading characteristic, and has been cause for the anthropologists' conundrum of 'Great/Little Tradition'.

However, especially since the British imposition on India and the subsequent 'Hindu renaissance' of the early nineteenth century, there has been an increasing rationalization and institutionalization of Hindu beliefs and practices (Bellah 1965). Consequently, a variety of organizations have arisen in India to provide Hinduism with new 'syndicated', 'corporate', or other 'official' forms. These range, for example, from the Brahmo Samaj and Arya Samaj (both of which advocate largely doctrinal and social reforms) through the Sanatana Dharma Raksini Sabha and Bharata Dharma Mahamandala (which arose, it might be said, as counter-reformist bodies seeking to standardize 'Great Tradition' tenets) to the Hindu Mahasabha and Shiv Sena (which have advocated staunch Hindu political activism). Still, their impact on Hindu religious traditions in India itself has been variable and sporadic (especially regarding village-level phenomena), and their membership or activity has been undercut by caste and class considerations. Outside of India in places like the Caribbean, on the other hand, such organizations have come to play a dominant role.

In order to trace adequately the development of 'official' Hinduism in the Caribbean, it is first necessary to examine migrants' religious backgrounds and early social conditions in the colonies. This chapter concentrates on the largest Hindu communities in the region, those in Surinam, Trinidad and Guyana, where 1997 estimates suggest that Hindus respectively comprised 27 per cent of the total population of 424,560 in Surinam, 24 per cent of 1,130,337 in Trinidad and 33 per cent of 706,116 in Guyana.

The arrival of Hinduism

The first Indians to arrive in the Caribbean were brought to British Guiana (today's Guyana) in 1838 as part of the global transplantation of Indian indentured labourers to European tropical colonies after the abolition of formal slavery. Indian indentured labourers were introduced to Trinidad in 1845, Jamaica and the French West Indies in 1854, Dutch Guiana (Surinam) in 1873, and other, smaller Caribbean colonies such as Grenada and St Vincent intermittently. For decades, colonial planters were keen to obtain additional Indian indentured labourers. Despite the costs of recruitment and transport, Indians were regarded as a cheaper and more controllable source of labour than free wage-earners, which the ex-slaves of African descent had by then become. When the indenture system was finally halted in 1917, well over half a million Indians had been brought to the Caribbean.

Most Indian immigration to the Caribbean – as to Mauritius, Fiji and South Africa – was governed by a system of indenture contracts. Though the details of these contracts varied over the years and from colony to colony, their common features included: recruitment by indigenous agents who ranged over vast areas of northeast and southeast India; inducement to enter into a contract lasting at least five years to work on a plantation, usually cultivating sugar; transport to the port of embarkation (Calcutta or Madras) and thence abroad; receipt of basic pay (often on a task basis), rudimentary housing, rations and medical attention during the course of the contract; and a partly or fully paid return passage to India after the end of the contract (often after a further five years' labour in the colony). Although the system appeared to provide an outlet for poverty-stricken people in economically devastated and famine-struck areas, indentured labour proved a harsh alternative, being often associated with poverty, disease, malnutrition and social oppression.

Yet despite the dire conditions, around 80 per cent of Indian immigrants in the three largest Caribbean colonies opted to stay on once their period of indenture was complete. Not only was it expensive to return (especially in the later period when free return passages were no longer on offer), but opportunities to acquire land and achieve some degree of social mobility often seemed greater in the Caribbean than back in India. Former indentured labourers were quick to acquire land: well before the end of the century numerous settlements had sprung up throughout the cane- and rice-growing areas of Trinidad, as well as in the coastal areas of British and Dutch Guiana. Subsequently Indians came to make up, as they still do, the backbone of the agricultural sector in each of these countries.

Throughout the period which witnessed the large-scale migration of Indians into the Caribbean under schemes of indentured labour, a total of 238,909 Indians arrived between 1838 and 1917 in what was then British Guiana, 143,939 in Trinidad during 1845–1917, and 34,304 in Surinam between 1873 and 1916. Subsequent to the return of a number of migrants (32 per cent, 22 per cent and 34 per cent, respectively) following the expiration of their five-year terms of indenture, this amounted to net immigration figures of 153,362 in British Guiana, 110,645 in Trinidad, and 22,745 in Surinam (Lawrence 1971). Hindus formed the overwhelming majority of these transplanted populations (around 85 per cent in each case).

Most migrants came as individuals, recruited piecemeal from vast areas of north-east and south-west India. Depending on their original region, district and village, migrants would have experienced substantial differences in culture (including language and dialect, dress, cuisine, caste composition and structure, architecture and village layout) and economy (including the nature of agricultural production and labour relations, taxation and patronage, land distribution, local and distant markets). Their religious backgrounds, too, were highly idiosyncratic, reflecting parochial traditions of worship, pilgrimage, and festival observance as well as incorporating locally recognized sacred landscapes, varying influences of Islam or particular Hindu sects, and differing roles of castes within particular religious activities.

The first major, geographically derived differences in socio-religious heritage can be inferred between migrant groups predominantly from North India (passing through the port of Calcutta) and South India (passing through Madras). Between 1845–62 some 48,729 South Indian migrants came to British Guiana, while between 1845–60 Trinidad received 22,616 South Indians (Geoghegan 1873). Migration from Madras was sporadic due to restrictions imposed following particularly high mortality rates affecting South Indian migrants at sea and abroad. The scheme for indentured migration from Madras to the Caribbean was terminated in 1862, long before the commencement of Indian migration to Surinam (however, over 3,000 South Indians were again shipped to Trinidad during 1905, 1910 and 1911, and a further 376 to British Guiana in 1913–14; Government of Madras, *Annual Reports* 1899–1916). Reasons for termination included: strong competition from Mauritius in recruiting workers, lack of both a suitable depot and an active recruitment service in Madras, and colonial planters' dissatisfaction with the working and other habits of the so-called 'Madrassis' (generally attributed to the contemporary notion that these migrants were originally city dwellers, as opposed to the rurally derived 'Calcuttans'; though this may have been true in some cases, some historians now suggest that many of the South Indian migrants were originally coastal fishermen, an occupation which many indeed took up in Guiana following their indentureship).

Thus in the early years of indentured immigration, relative to North Indians there was a sizeable South Indian presence in the two main receiving colonies. Drawn from a number of Tamil districts (including Trichinopoly, Ramnad, Tanjore and Salem) and Telegu districts (as far apart as Nellore, Ganjam and Vizagapatam), the South Indian Hindu migrants would tend to exhibit general religious characteristics of Shaivism (involving ascetic practices and rites directed towards Shiva), and to a lesser extent, Shaktism (involving ecstatic behaviour associated with cosmic power and healing derived from various goddesses). Regional variations in belief and practice were doubtless present among the South Indians, as they were among the far more numerous North Indian migrants.

The places of origin of North Indian migrants to the Caribbean were widespread and varied considerably over the years. For instance, migration from Bihar to all colonies was high in the 1880s, but dropped substantially by the turn of the century; conversely, migration from the Native States (and therefore, of tribals or *janglis*) and from Central India rose considerably after the turn of the century, especially to Trinidad. Variation over the years is attributable to many factors such as droughts and famines, recruitment strategies or government restrictions.

Based on figures from the annual reports of the contemporary Protector of Emigrants in Calcutta, the proportion of migrants from different parts of North India to the three Caribbean colonies was remarkably similar. This is despite the fact that different numbers were requisitioned by planters in each territory, and that British Guiana (also known as 'Demerara'), Trinidad and Surinam had separate recruiting agencies and depots based in Calcutta. Between 1874–1917, around 14 per cent of indentured Indian migrants to all three Caribbean colonies came from Bihar, between 24–28 per cent came from Oudh (today's eastern Uttar Pradesh), and between 48–52 per cent came from what was then called the 'Northwest Provinces' (also part of today's Uttar Pradesh). The areas of origin of the remaining proportion were places as far afield as East Bengal (now Bangladesh), Central India and the Punjab.

Of the North Indian areas of origin, Bengal, Bihar and Orissa have long been dominated by Shaktism (though Vaishnavism, or devotion to Vishnu and his incarnations, has had some influence particularly from the Chaitanya sect in Bengal), while eastern and western Uttar Pradesh and the Punjab are mainly Vaishnavite. Regardless of the regional religious patterns, however, each area is dotted with important, age-old centres of pilgrimage devoted to particular deities, which hold great sway over the religious orientation of surrounding vicinities. According to contemporary nineteenth-century colonial Gazetteers, these included Shaivite, Vaishnavite and Goddess-focused sites in West Bengal (Bishnupur, Kenduli, and Amta), Bihar (Sonpur, Gaya), eastern U.P. (Varanasi, Ayodhya), western U.P. (Garmukhtesar, Soron, Deoband) and Orissa (Bhubaneswar, Puri). In addition to propitiating the 'higher' Sanskritic gods, other deities are regionally popular as well, such as Gaininath, Naika, and Dharha in Bihar (Grierson 1885: 403–7) and Bhumiya, Sitala, Joginya and Panch Pir in Uttar Pradesh (Planalp 1956: 159–61).

Though the bulk of Hindu migrants were drawn from three provinces, they came from a great number of districts within each, among them Kanpur, Ghazipur, Basti and Azimgarh in the 'Northwest Provinces', Shahabad, Patna, Darbhanga and Gaya in Bihar, and Lucknow, Faizabad and Gonda in Oudh. Each district – and further, each village – recognized an array of supernatural beings and had various traditions associated with them. Such beings would locally include a protective village deity (*gramadevata*, often called a *dih*), saints or martyrs, ghosts, demons, witches as well as sacred or malevolent trees, river banks, wells, stones and animals. In one village in Uttar Pradesh, McKim Marriott (1955: 175) observed, religious activity is 'fragmented to an extreme point. There is no temple of the whole village, no one cremation ground, no sacred tank or well. Instead, dozens of different trees and stones and tiny shrines are made objects of worship separately by members of the many caste and lineage groups.'

A widely heterogeneous caste composition among Hindu immigrants also had religious consequences, since certain beliefs and practices were specific to these as well. Further, not only did certain castes have special deities and rites, but these varied from locale to locale. Thus one contemporary observer wrote that 'the manners and customs of the various castes vary from one end of the Province ['Northwest Provinces'] to the other . . . A custom or mode of worship prevailing among a caste in Saharanpur or Ballia may or may not extend as far as Aligarb [sic] on the one side or Allahabad on the other' (Crooke 1886: vol. 1, p. vi).

For instance, again according to the Gazetteers, among some of the castes which came in large numbers from Uttar Pradesh to the Caribbean, Ahirs (cowherders) traditionally worshipped Bittiya and Vinhyabasini Devi in many places, but also Bimath in Mirsipur district and Bangaru Bai in south Bhandara: Kurmis (cultivators) generally worshipped Thakurji, but also Surdhir in Gorakhpur and Baba Pir in Basti; and among Chamars (leatherworkers), a host of deities were worshipped from place to place, including Jagiswar, Nagarsen, Kuanwala, Sairi Devi and Parmeshwari. Finally, each lineage or clan within a caste had rites and other practices centring on a deity special to themselves (*kuldevata*).

Therefore, in sum, the Hinduism that came to the Caribbean was comprised of a complicated array of religious traditions determined by the heterogeneity of the Hindu migrants themselves. Out of such profusion, however, common forms were forged.

Early Hinduism in the Caribbean

Patterns of Hindu worship during the early years of Indian presence in the Caribbean seem to have been diffuse, by all available accounts. Perhaps the first written account of Hindu religious activity in the Caribbean was a goat sacrifice – reflecting presumably non-Brahmanic activity – observed in Trinidad in 1849 and again in 1855, when a goat 'wearing garlands of red flowers and surrounded by pans of washed rice and bottles of molasses and rum . . . was beheaded to the sound of drums' (in Wood 1968: 150). In 1865, a Christian missionary in Trinidad visited

> a place where the Hindus sacrifice. There was a pole with a small flag flying, a small altar of mud, and near it two stakes . . . a sort of yoke into which the neck of the goat to be sacrificed is placed and its head severed at one blow. The blood is burned on the altar and the body made a feast of.
> (Morton 1916: 23)

The same missionary explained that at this time, Hindu rites were bound to occur anywhere since 'They had no temples. Gatherings for worship were conducted at any selected spot by their Brahmans or priests': moreover, 'each priest had his own disciples' (ibid.: 52).

Unco-ordinated and perhaps random rites and practices at that time would be quite expected, given the basic fact that early migrants on colonial estates were so linguistically unrelated due to their diverse areas of origin. Bengali, Hindi, Maithili, Magdhi, Punjabi, Telugu, Tamil, tribal languages and others were spoken by the immigrants, as were dialects such as Kanauji, Avadhi, Bhojpuri, Brajbhasa and Tondai Nadu. A missionary in British Guiana pointed out that 'nearly all these languages spoken in India are in free and constant use among them in the Colony, and only a very small portion among our immigrants can understand more than one language' (Bronkhurst 1883: 226). He explained, 'The proprietors or managers of sugar estates purposely choose men speaking three or four separate and distinct languages not understood by each other, in order to prevent combination in cases of disturbances among them' (ibid.). 'When these [Indian] people meet in Trinidad,' one contemporary Englishman wrote, 'it strikes one as somewhat strange that they may have to point to water and rice, and ask each other what they call it in their language' (Gamble 1866: 34). Gradually through the years, a common, creolized Indian tongue or 'plantation Hindustani' (Tinker 1974: 208) developed in each Caribbean context (based largely on Bhojpuri and Avadhi, and blended with non-Indian languages especially in the case of Sarnami in Surinam). Until that time, however, collective religious activity was doubtless hindered by lack of effective communication among the transplanted Hindus.

Religious activities among the indentured Indians were quite tolerated – even in some cases facilitated – by plantation managers as long as these activities did not conflict with economic production (Ramnarine 1977). Yet, given the breadth of religious traditions characterizing the migrants' backgrounds, consensus on devotional focus and procedure was most probably hard to achieve at first. In British Guiana, for instance, Bronkhurst suggested that Vaishnavites and Shaivites were 'strenuously contending for the supremacy of the chief object of their worship, and the consequent inferiority of the other' (Bronkhurst 1888: 17). It is perhaps more plausible that Bronkhurst actually discerned some division between North Indians, mainly comprising followers of the former broad orientation, and South Indians, generally equated with the latter, because among North Indians alone such contention between Vaishnavites and Shaivites would be less likely since they have co-evolved for centuries in that part of the subcontinent. There was no major distinction between Vaishnavites and Shaivites in Surinam, basically because the colony never received shipments of South Indians (Arya 1968).

Some Hindus in the Caribbean may have tried to continue adhering to traditions directed towards regional, village, caste or kin group gods. However, the basic fact that they were an amalgam of individual Indians, thrust together on plantations far from India, militated against any such successful continuity. The absence of shrines, legend-filled landscapes, and co-worshippers would spell the rapid relinquishment of parochial traditions. Certain sects or orders were more successful in maintaining their ways, however, since these were roughly institutionalized prior to migration. Examples here include Ramanandis, Kabir panthis, Aghor panthis, and Shivnarayanis, whose presence in Trinidad was noted by D.W.D. Comins in 1893.

Eventually, more durable, collective modes of Hindu worship were established in the colonies. This was evident particularly in the creation of temples. In many estates and nascent villages, small shrines (in the form of raised platforms with clay images) persisted through the nineteenth century. Yet very gradually, more elaborate structures were constructed, often with the help and encouragement of the estate management (who, Robert James Moore [1970: 369–70] suggests, saw this as a way to keep the Indian workers socio-culturally isolated and therefore more easily manipulated). Edward Bean Underhill (1862) visited one of the earliest temples in Trinidad, while the novelist Charles Kingsley (1905: 300) provided the first detailed description of such structures observed in 1871:

> Their mark is, generally, a long bamboo with a pennon atop, outside a low dark hut, with a broad flat veranda, or rather shed, outside the door. Under the latter, opposite each door . . . is a stone or small stump, on which offerings are made of red dust and flowers. From it the worshippers can see the images within.
>
> . . . Sometimes these have been carved in the island. Sometimes the poor folk have taken the trouble to bring them all the way from India on board ship. Hung beside them on the walls are little pictures, often very well executed in the miniature-like Hindoo style by native artists in the island. Large brass pots, which have some sacred meaning, stand about, and with them a curious trident-shaped stand, about four feet high, on the horns of which garlands of flowers are hung as offerings. The visitor is told that the male figures are Mahadeva, and the female Kali.

Bronkhurst (1883: 255) likewise gave us a good account of Hindu temples in Guiana:

> A Hindu temple is not constructed like a Christian sanctuary . . . It is not intended to accommodate a crowd of worshippers within its walls. Its worshippers stand outside in an area opposite the door which is the only entrance belonging to the building. The priest, the representative of the people, is the only person who enters the temple through that door in order to perform the duties of his office in the presence of the idol, which stands at the lower end of the door, and so placed that the worshippers from outside might have a full view of, and fall down before it. There is no window to a Hindu temple to let in light or admit air. The room, including the small space which is called the residence of the idol (*Swami stalam*), before which burns a small oil lamp, and the space sufficiently spacious for the temple utensils, the offerings, and the officiating priest to stir or move about, is always dark and awe-inspiring . . . These hut-temples are considered so sacred by the coolies, on account of the visible presence of the deity – the idol – they worship, that no unclean person can enter any of them without the preparatory ablutions being performed.

These small *shivalas* and *kutis* (or *kutiyas*), also described in Trinidad by James A. Froude (1888: 75–6), appear to have closely resembled those normally found in villages of Bihar and Uttar Pradesh. In British Guiana, only two small temples were observed by a Royal Commission in the 1860s; by the onset of the 1890s, at least thirty-three Hindu temples were to be found, funded through individual donation or group subscription. By the early twentieth century, such structures were commonplace in most estates and Indian villages (MacNeill and Lal 1914: 73).

The celebration of Hindu festivals, too, grew in number and importance by the early part of this century. Lengthy and elaborate plays such as the Ram Lila, depicting epic stories of the gods, were already performed in estates and villages in the nineteenth century. Diwali and Phagwa (Holi) were the most popular annual events celebrated by Hindus in the colonies by the turn of the century. And whereas Comins (1893), based on a visit of a mere ten days, believed there were few Indian festivals celebrated in Surinam,

Pieter Emmer (1984) suggests that no less than thirty-two Hindu festivals were annually recognized on Surinamese colonial estates. Some of the earliest Hindu activities became notorious, however, which led to their suppression. One was a practice in which a devotee would impale various points of his flesh with hooks and subsequently swing by them from a pole. During the nineteenth century this was widespread both in Bengal (where it was known as *chrakpuja*, a penitential rite directed to Shiva) and in South India (called *soodaloo* or *chedul*, a self-sacrificial rite to a goddess; see Oddie 1987). This proved too 'barbaric' for white colonists, and hook-swinging was banned in British Guiana in 1853 (Mangru 1987). Another extraordinary Hindu activity was fire-walking, a practice which – though carried out in Bihar and the tribal states as well as in South India (O'Malley 1935) – became wholly associated with the immigrant 'Madrassis'. In Trinidad, one colonial observer reported that fire-walking 'is not observed by Hindus of Northern India, but, on the contrary, is repudiated by them' (Collens 1888: 235). Though publicly suppressed, fire-walking continued in 'Madrassi' circles in both Trinidad and British Guiana until at least the mid-twentieth century. Animal sacrifice was abhorred by colonists as well, and was looked down upon especially by Brahmans; however, this still continues in the Caribbean as part of non-orthodox observances.

Apart from occasional celebrations or temple-based activity, it was the ordinary, daily practices which formed what could be considered the core of Hindu religiosity in the early years of Caribbean settlement. Sacred plants, vessels and implements used in worship, and images of deities were brought from India (Poynting 1985), Hindu scriptures were imported and sold, and wandering Brahmans and *sadhus* (world-renouncers) gathered together Hindus, told tales and recited the Ramayana and other popular religious texts. All these elements contributed to the construction of a religiously affirmative environment.

The domestic sphere was perhaps of greatest importance, since it was where the most common beliefs and modes of worship were perpetuated by the migrants and taught to their offspring. Household shrines, personal prayers and small acts performed by various family members constitute the essential ingredients of Hinduism in any of its forms or traditions, and these were carried out in the colonies among plantation barracks and homes in the early villages. Invoking images of village life in North India itself, Kingsley published a print of a Hindu performing morning oblation outside a thatched house in Trinidad, while in British Guiana Bronkhurst observed:

Before a Coolie eats, he places a small quantity of the prepared food before the idol or god of the house to propitiate his favour . . . Rising at dawn, the Hindu goes to the trench, or takes the water into his own yard, and there, with religious care, he cleanses his teeth, performs his sacred ablutions, imprints the emblems of his faith upon his forehead, arm, and breast, visits the idol of the house, or faces the rising sun, before which he falls down.

(1883: 257–8)

However normal such basic religious practices became in the nineteenth-century Caribbean, though, the fact remained that Hinduism was a minority religion – considered 'heathen' and even demonic by members of the ruling community – within highly pluralistic societies. This situation had the effect of stimulating self-consciousness about religious belief and practices, subsequently entailing perhaps deeper reflections on choice in religious belief and practice, more attempts to justify ideas and activities, and more sharpened skills at defending religious tenets than would have been the case in villages of India. Exacerbating these circumstances were missionary activities directed primarily at Hindus, especially by Methodists and Anglicans in British Guiana, Moravians in Surinam, and Presbyterians in Trinidad (Samaroo 1982). While these missions were not without considerable success – some 10 per cent of Indians in British Guiana and Trinidad were Christian by 1911 (Singaravelou 1987, vol. 3: 69) – many Brahman pundits became quite adept at verbal combat with Christians and, through such channels, Hinduism came to be portrayed more and more as a unitary religion like any other in the colonies. In time, formal Hindu organizations were established with the expressed goal of standardizing and promulgating such an opinion.

The growth of 'official' Hinduism in the Caribbean

Probably the most significant socio-religious change that occurred among Hindus in the Caribbean, and one which was a prerequisite for the rise of an institutionalized and all-embracing Hindu orthodoxy, was the attenuation of the caste system. Space does not permit a full treatment of this process as it occurred in the Caribbean (see Vertovec 1992b). In sum, specific caste *identities* were often retained through the years (particularly in terms of *varna* and, to a much more limited extent, of *jat*, and only effectively called into play in the arrangement of marriages or sometimes with regard to claims of public status). Yet caste could never be transplanted as a *system* (as it was in India, simultaneously being a hierarchy and social relationships, a network of economic interdependence, an order of reciprocal ritual duties, and a conceptual continuum of ontological states according to notions of purity and pollution). This incapacity for reconstruction occurred because the caste system is a highly localized phenomenon in villages of India; it had no chance of being maintained through historical conditions in which individual members of diverse caste groups (many unheard of from one region to another) were plucked out of local hierarchies throughout North and South India and placed together in contexts where their proximity and commensality, economic activities, and social relationships were managed by non-Indians on estates and, after indenture, altered by wholly alien socio-economic circumstances.

Still, Brahmans retained a special religious role, albeit different from that in India. 'As pandits', van der Burg and van der Veer (1986: 517) point out, 'they monopolized the sacred knowledge of rituals and Sanskrit texts, so that ritual knowledge replaced purity as the legitimation of the Brahman's status.' In the new context of the Caribbean, Brahmans gained clients for their ritual services by offering to all – regardless of caste background – the beliefs and practices previously within their own exclusive preserve. The 'Brahmanization' of Hinduism thus occurred in the Caribbean, whereby throughout each Hindu community, there came into ascendency a core of Brahmanic ritual directed towards Sanskritic gods (van der Veer and Vertovec 1991).

These Brahman-dominated practices, which became the routine features of Hinduism in all three Caribbean territories, included: the performance of formal *puja*, involving Sanskrit formulae governing sixteen offerings, or *shodasopachara*, made to various deities (though Hanuman *puja* was by far the most popular in all three contexts under consideration); *samskaras* or rites of passage marking key life-stages; *kathas* involving routinized recitals of sacred lore (particularly a text devoted to Satyanarayan); weddings (though only the climactic formal rites were overseen by Brahmans); funerals involving a host of ceremonies over a period of at least ten days; *bhagwats* or *yagnas* which are remarkable socio-religious activities centred on the reading of a sacred text (usually the Bhagavata Purana) spanning seven, nine, or fourteen days and involving a variety of rites; massive communal meals (indicative of caste's demise), and much social interaction among possibly hundreds of participants.

These have continued through to the present, often in vibrant and uniquely modified forms.

Organizational development of this 'Brahmanized' Hinduism was marginal for some time before undergoing a rapid acceleration. In Trinidad, for instance, a Sanatan Dharma Association was said to have existed since 1881 (Kirpalani *et al.* 1945), though it is not known for having accomplished much in terms of influence or activity. By the 1920s, other small, Brahman-led groups were in existence (such as the Prabartakh Sabha of Debe and the San Fernando Hindu Sabha), but their endeavours were modest and essentially of local scope.

During the early decades of the century, a loose kind of pundits' *parishad* or council was said to have existed between Brahman priests in Trinidad, Surinam and British Guiana, such that their communication – though more through an informal network than through official channels – did much to standardize practices within the region. Such communication, including trips to perform rites, was most frequent between pundits in British Guiana and Surinam, owing to their common border. It was even common for individuals from one country to have a Brahman 'godfather' or *guru* in the other.

In all three Caribbean contexts, the primary catalyst for the national organization of a unitary, standardized Brahmanic Hinduism was the introduction of the Arya Samaj. The Arya Samaj, a reformist movement calling for a Vedic purification of Hindu belief and practice, was established in the Punjab by Swami Dayanand Saraswati in 1875. This radical movement had tremendous impact across North India, where it forced many Hindus to reflect on and articulate what it was they themselves believed. The result was a conservative backlash, part of which involved the creation of formal bodies to promote a formulated, 'official' orthodoxy deemed 'Sanatana Dharma' ('the eternal duty or order'). The Arya Samaj sent well-trained missionaries from India to Hindu communities throughout the diaspora, where they had the same effects.

A succession of Arya Samaji missionaries undertook prolonged visits to three Caribbean colonies. The first arrived in British Guiana in 1910, travelling that same year to Trinidad. Surinam received its first representative from the Samaj in 1912. Visits turned into sustained presence by the 1930s, highlighted by the charismatic personalities of Mehta Jaimani and Ayodhya Prasad. The Arya Samajis caused much consternation within Hindu communities through their staunch and knowledgeable advocacy of fundamental reforms in doctrine (especially by way of promoting their exclusive,

Vedic-centred monotheism and rejection of idols) and in social structure (including efforts to upgrade the status of women and to criticize the Brahmans' self-ascribed authority). In each country, great debates were waged between Arya Samaji and 'Sanatanist' camps, some even ending in violent clashes (Speckman 1965). The Arya Samaj made significant inroads into the Caribbean Hindu population. In Surinam, for example, by 1931 about 16 per cent of Hindus adhered to the Arya Samaj (Ramsoedh and Bloemberg 1995).

Just as in India, the forces of Brahmanism came together in each Caribbean country to create a sustained front against the Arya Samaj and to quell the doubts that the reformists had sent rippling through the Hindu population. This involved moves to tighten and structure their own ranks through organizational effort. In 1927, a Pundits' Council was formed in British Guiana to act as the sole authority concerning matters of doctrine and ritual, along with the Sanatan Dharma Sabha, created to act as a national representative body for Hindus in British Guiana. In Surinam, the Sanatan Dharma (sic) was founded in 1929 to fulfil a similar role. In Trinidad, the dormant Sanatan Dharma Association was revitalized and incorporated in 1932, the same year a rival Brahmanic body was formed, the Sanatan Dharma Board of Control. And in 1934, the Sanatan Dharma Maha Sabha was established as the most prominent Hindu organization in British Guiana. (Meanwhile, the Arya Samajis had followed suit by instituting formal bodies, too: the Arya Dewaker in Surinam in 1930 and the Arya Samaj Association – later called the Arya Pritinidhi Sabha – in Trinidad in 1934.) Most of these Caribbean Hindu organizations forged links with kindred associations in India, thereby declaring further legitimation for the 'official' forms of Hinduism which they propagated.

The unitary and Brahmanic thrust of these is exemplified by Trinidad's Sanatan Dharma Board of Control, which stated:

> The registration of this society is regarded by the Hindu community as being an important step in the direction of the unification of Hindu interests . . . and it is laid down as a definite policy that the Board of Control shall always be predominantly composed of orthodox, practising pundits.
>
> (quoted in Forbes 1984: 60)

These 'Sanatanist' organizations consolidated much support, especially from rural Hindus who preferred conservative modes of worship. They thereby far eclipsed the Arya Samaj, whose supporters tended to be well-educated, middle-class Hindus. In each country, the 'Sanatanist' groups achieved other important gains during the 1930s and 1940s when – after years of difficult campaigning – they succeeded in obtaining, from the respective colonial governments, legal recognition of Hindu marriages and permission to perform cremations. But perhaps the most effective organizational developments were those of Trinidad's Sanatan Dharma Maha Sabha, the body created in 1952 by Bhadase Sagan Maraj after he united the country's two previously rival Sanatanist organizations. In addition to obtaining the affiliation of dozens of temple congregations throughout the island (co-ordinated by the Maha Sabha's Pundits' *parishad*), Maraj oversaw the construction of no less than thirty-one Hindu schools between 1952 and 1956.

With such schools, temples, publications, collective celebrations, and the participation of almost every Brahman pundit, these highly centralized Hindu bodies culminated the long processes of standardizing and routinizing Hindu belief and practice in Trinidad, Surinam and British Guiana. In each context, the national organizations dominated Hinduism in ways akin to those which Raymond T. Smith (1962: 1233–4) described regarding the Sanatan Dharma Maha Sabha in British Guiana during the 1950s and early 1960s:

> This form of Hinduism [promulgated by the Maha Sabha] has gradually replaced all the lower-caste cults and special practices which used to exist among the immigrants, and it claims the affiliation of practically all the temples in the country. With its sister organisation, the British Guiana Pundits' Council, it may be said to control orthodox Hinduism (or the nearest Guianese equivalent to it) in British Guiana, and has come to constitute a 'church' in the technical sense.

The 'official' Hindu bodies became so predominant, in fact, that they became major political forces. The Brahman leaders of Sanatan Dhann in Surinam established their own, short-lived Surinamese Hindoe Partij in the late 1940s. They later merged with other Indian parties to form the Verenigde Hindostaanse Partij, but continued to play a central part in this party's endeavours (see Dew 1978). In Trinidad, under the strong-arm tactics of Bhadase Maraj, the leadership and support of the People's Democratic Party (later becoming the Democratic Labour Party) was virtually indistinguishable from that of the Maha Sabha (Ryan 1972). And in British

Guiana, though the Indian-backed party was Cheddi Jagan's explicitly Marxist People's Progressive Party, it, too, was comprised of many Maha Sabha leaders (Vasil 1984). Thus Hinduism had not only been 'Brahmanized' and 'officially' standardized, it had now become 'politicized'. This was particularly the case in the years immediately preceding each nation's independence (Trinidad 1962, Guyana 1966, Surinam 1975), when there were fears of political repression under Creole-backed parties – fears which were subsequently justified.

Though the central 'Sanatanist' bodies have continued to hold much financial and organizational power, their popularity with many Hindus has dwindled. This is especially so in Trinidad and Guyana. Many Hindus cite the two Maha Sabhas' lack of assistance to affiliated schools and temples, along with the arrogance of associated pundits, as reasons for this. But perhaps most damage was done in Guyana in the late 1960s and early 1970s, when the ruling, Creole-backed People's National Congress successfully gained sway over the Maha Sabha leadership, an intolerable occurrence in the eyes of the average Hindu. Similarly, Trinidad's Maha Sabha suffered a crisis in leadership following the death of Maraj in 1971. Much of the Hindu community grew dismayed with the Maha Sabha due to the ensuing political infighting and allegations of misconduct and corruption – made worse by its eventual leader's public support for the Creole-backed government of the People's National Movement.

Instead, new, alternative Hindu organizations have been created. While still advocating the same type of essentially Brahmanic, Sanskritic Hinduism, these have become more popular by demonstrating more grassroots activity and, importantly, more attention to the interests of young people, than the centralized organizations. These include the Nav Yuvak Sabha in Surinam, the Gandhi Youth Organisation in Guyana, the Hindu Seva Sangh in Trinidad (see Chapter 3), and a number of other groups operating locally through mutually supportive networks.

Today a great deal of Hindu socio-religious activity in Surinam, Trinidad and Guyana takes place under the formal direction of the national bodies and the alternative groups. Yet much occurs outside of these auspices as well. The current range of all types of practice can be described with reference to their degree of institutionalization (that is, very basically, the extent to which activities are arranged and managed by certain individuals performing specific roles). Institutionalized Hinduism can be characterized on a kind of continuum from most 'official' to most 'popular' modes of religion.

Contemporary Caribbean Hinduism

The following list provides a classification of the most common contemporary Hindu practices in Surinam, Trinidad and Guyana. The sequence of listed items is according to the degree of ordered, collective activity (or, again, extent of institutionalization) undertaken in each type of practice.

Official forms

This rubric concerns those activities directly undertaken by the central, national organization (Maha Sabha) in each country. These include: weekly rites and *Kathas* held at temples; large-scale celebrations of annual holy days (particularly Divali, Phagua, Ramnaumi, Shivratri, and Krishna Janashtami – though affiliated temples also celebrate, on local levels, Navratri, Ganesh jayanti, Katik Nahan, and Vasant *panchami*); publications (including prayer books) and radio programmes; religious curricula in affiliated schools; contests (for Hindi language skills, debating, devotional singing and other arts); and, importantly, the pundits' *parishad* whereby doctrine and procedure is monitored.

Alternative official forms

Concerning most of the same activities listed above, these are undertaken by organizations other than the Maha Sabhas, including practices in non-Maha Sabha-affiliated temples. Small-scale committees or groups (*goles* and *mandals*) also exist in villages for the specific purpose of holding *yagnas* and Ramayan *satsangs* (local meetings in which Tulsidas' sacred epic is recited). Such alternative bodies have also creatively established practices aimed at Hindu youth, such as summer camps, marches, fund-raising bazaars, sports clubs and theatre groups.

A wholly different set of 'alternative official' Hindu phenomena is that centred on Kali worship (generally known as Kali Mai Puja), which has been gaining support in Guyana from a wide segment of the Hindu community – and even among some Creoles – for many years (Phillips 1960; Khan 1977; Bassier 1987). More recently it has been re-instituted in Trinidad (Vertovec 1993). The tradition has developed from practices observed among the so-called 'Madrassis' in Guyana since the middle of the nineteenth century. These routinely involved animal sacrifice, possession (altered states of consciousness), and the worship of deities characteristic of South Indian Hinduism (such as Katheri, Munishwaran, Madraviran and Mariamma – the latter often identified with Kali). Such non-Brahmanic practices have long been castigated by pundits and others advocating a Sanskritic, 'Sanatanist' Hindu religion in the colonies. In Surinam, the tradition never really existed since the colony lacked South Indian practitioners. In Trinidad, it remained only in isolated pockets where 'Madrassis' had settled in number. But in Guyana, Kali Mai Puja became an active religious tradition (particularly in an area known as Demerara, which is home to a large proportion of South Indian descendants). Its mode of worship became increasingly standardized in the 1920s and 1930s under the direction of Kistima Naidoo, apparently waned in attendance during the 1940s and 1950s and has undergone a prominent renewal under James Naidoo since the 1960s. There are now estimated to be some one-hundred Kali 'churches' (*koeloos*) throughout Guyana, exhibiting numerous variations from the core set of rites long associated with the tradition. There are presently formal bodies representing this form of Hinduism, such as the Guyana Maha Kali Religious Organization.

There are also other formally organized Hindu traditions, regarded as 'non-Sanatanist', which are present in the Caribbean, including those of Kabir Panthis, Arya Samajis, devotees of Satya Sai Baba, 'Hare Krishnas' (members of the International Society for Krishna Consciousness) and followers of various Hindu-derived yoga and meditation groups. These are quite small in membership, and moreover, their members quite often participate in 'Sanatanist' activities with little contrariety.

Collective forms

These are religious activities self-organized by groups of people (especially networks of extended kin and/or co-villagers). They include annual festivals marking important periods of the Hindu calendar, such as celebrations for Divali (religious plays, Lakshmi Puja, and the building of elaborate lighting displays) and Phagua (devotional singing, the construction and burning of a special bonfire, and traditional forms of playing with red dye), the staging of Ram Lila or Krishna Lila plays, and the co-operative management of *yagnas* and *satsangs* sponsored by individuals. Weddings and funerals are usually fairly large events organized *ad hoc* by groups of family and friends who systematically undertake a considerable number of chores in order to perform successfully the elaborate complex of accompanying rites. Also considered under this heading are the last vestiges of caste-specific rites: namely, sacrifices of hogs to the goddess Parmeshwari, still performed privately only by a few Chamar families.

Domestic forms

Religious activities conducted in the home by members of Hindu families include: *puja* (sponsored annually or for special occasions – such as birthdays or anniversaries – in which a pundit is hired to perform the necessary Sanskritic rites; this is ideally undertaken over a weekend period, with Fridays reserved for Hanuman Puja, Saturday for Satyanarayan Katha, and Sunday for Suruj Narayan Puja); *samskara* (naturally held at the appropriate times of children's lives – though presently, perhaps only three to five of the prescribed sixteen rites are actually performed); and daily rites, usually performed by children or grandparents, involving prayers and the lighting of incense and lamps at an indoor shrine and/or outside in a little sanctum at the base of the house's *jhandi*, or coloured flags erected on the occasion of *pujas* (see Vertovec 1992b). The use of *jhandi* demonstrates one important source of difference between Hindu practices in the three countries: whereas only red (for Hanuman) and, less frequently, white (for Satyanarayan) flags tend to be erected following 'Sanatanist' *pujas* in Surinam and Guyana, a range of coloured flags are displayed by 'Sanatanist' Hindus in Trinidad (including pink for Lakshmi, dark blue for Shiva, yellow for Durga, orange for Ganesha, and more). There are also infrequent pilgrimages to rivers or the sea – representative of the Ganges in all three countries – or to special sites such as in Trinidad, where one small temple has an allegedly growing stone regarded as a Shiva *linga* and a Catholic church has a reportedly miraculous statue of the Virgin Mary regarded by many Hindus as a manifestation of the one great Goddess (Vertovec 1993).

Individual forms

It is harder to list religious phenomena in this category, since they are by definition idiosyncratic. These features generally involve a person's *ishtadevata*, or form of god chosen for personal worship (such as Hanuman, Krishna, Durga or Shiva), and individual mode of worship (such as paying devotion to special images or symbols, reciting certain prayers at particular times, fasting on specific days of the week or periods of the year, making votive offerings and fulfilling promises to the god in specified manners, and so on). Also of an essentially individual nature is the mantra (Sanskrit sound or prayer) imparted to a person by their Brahman 'godfather' on occasion of *gurumukh*, the 'christening' *samskara*.

'Amorphous' or peripheral forms

Because a considerable set of beliefs and practices fall far outside the 'official' forms of Hinduism, as these have come to be constructed in the Caribbean contexts, they have often been maintained in a rather clandestine and unformulated, often quite vague, manner by a decreasing minority. These are usually directed towards therapeutic or protective ends, and include: beliefs and precautions regarding the evil eye, *jharay* and *phukay* (the use of specific *mantras* and motions to cure various afflictions), *tabij* (talismans) and *totka* (specific acts to undo the work of malevolent forces or omens), *ojha* (black magic, often blended with Creole forms, called *obeah*), exorcism of ill-meaning spirits, and offerings to minor deities (especially Dih, originally a guardian village godling, and 'the seven sisters' – which, though few can actually name them – are conceived to be manifestations of the Goddess).

Conclusion: ongoing trends and debates

The transformation of Hinduism in Surinam, Trinidad and Guyana is by no means complete. The long process of 'Brahmanization' and standardization, which culminated in domination by centralized organizations, has begun to unravel. A kind of fragmentation has begun – yet not one which necessarily divides Hindus, but rather, one in which Hindus are again recognizing the viability of a diversity of devotional orientations and modes of worship. Thus a more 'ecumenical', rather than unitary, type of Hinduism may be developing.

The beliefs and practices of 'Sanatan Dharma' are still by far the most pervasive – particularly among older Hindus, but also among a considerable number of youths. Yet especially among the well-educated young people in each of these countries, interest is building in more philosophical and less sacerdotal forms of Hinduism (such as the teachings of Vivekananda and Aurobindo). This trend is fostered by some of the 'alternative' Hindu associations. Whatever the variety of approach taken by various groups and individuals, however, they are all being justified under the banner of *bhakti* (devotion to God).

But the trend towards acceptable heterogeneity is not proving smooth, and several issues are presently being debated. These include: the questions as to whether only Brahmans can serve as priests, the place of Hindi and Sanskrit in Hinduism – which is a key part of the general conundrum of Caribbean Hindus' relation to India (cf. Chapter 5), the role of women in Hinduism, and the problem of whether certain practices should be deemed 'low' and therefore undesirable.

A number of new, transnational dynamics are likely to have a pervasive impact on the nature and content of religious practices among Hindus in the Caribbean as well. These include: increased Internet access (through which Hindus in the Caribbean can interact virtually with co-religionists in India or anywhere else in the diaspora), increased media access (by way of which, for instance, religious materials and popular films increasingly reach the Caribbean), increased connections with Hindu organizations in India (including the Vishwa Hindu Parishad and Rashtriya Swayamsevak Sangh) and elsewhere in the diaspora (represented by and facilitated through cheap communications and travel), and intensified inter-diasporic feedback (involving many kinds of information exchange between Indo-Caribbean communities in The Netherlands and Surinam, New York, Toronto or London and Trinidad or Guyana; in each of these places, too, there is exchange between Indo-Caribbeans and Hindus from India and elsewhere, the result of which also can get channelled back to the Caribbean).

Contradicting the statements of pessimistic observers during the 1960s who predicted its final demise in the Caribbean, Hinduism is thriving in Surinam, Trinidad and Guyana. The beliefs and practices which were drawn from throughout the subcontinent, merged and modified in new contexts, formulated and formally managed by purpose-made authoritative bodies, nevertheless continue to be maintained in a variety of ways, on a number of 'levels', in cities and villages of each nation.

3

RELIGION AND ETHNIC IDEOLOGY

The Hindu youth movement in Trinidad

Religious concepts, practices and symbols are central to the identities, interests and intents of numerous ethnic diasporas throughout the world today. Indians are no exception. One way to explore the significance of religion among ethnic movements is to isolate its role in what can be termed the 'ethnic ideology' of a group. The following chapter (a) suggests some working definitions for 'ethnic ideology'; (b) underscores implications which the inclusion of religious phenomena, within an ethnic ideology, may have for ethnic movements; and (c) explores these issues by way of what can be seen as an exemplary case involving the interplay of religion, ideology and ethnic mobilization.

On ethnicity, ideology and religious movements

Here, the notion of an 'ethnic ideology' is based on the premise that at certain historical junctures, various processes may occur through which ethnic collectivities – groups with distinct linguistic and cultural traits determining marked social boundaries with others, often, further, with a distinct structural position within a given socio-politico-economic system – are stimulated to reflect on the features and effects of their distinctiveness. Greater self-consciousness among groups may be stimulated by migration, economic shifts affecting traditional livelihoods, political change wrought by decolonization, rapid governmental swings to the right or left, or by other conditions perceived by members to be somehow unstable, unfair, or threatening. The subsequent reflections (promulgated by leaders, formulated by organizations and represented by symbols) tend to centre around a set of observations, specially produced and/or assembled in the light of the given context, concerning the group's past, present, and future plight (observations which, as numerous scholars have pointed out, may include the 'invention' of tradition and of the notion of the 'community' itself). This set of observations provides the rationale behind programmatic calls for action, of one sort or another, among group members. The sum total is an identifiable, though not necessarily concise, ethnic ideology. While it is recognized that individuals in modern societies possess a range of collective identities, ethnic ideologies propound and sanction group consciousness and group action based on rather particular criteria.

Prior to processes of 'ideologization', it is important to recognize (following Bentley 1987, himself interpreting Bourdieu 1977) that much of what can be considered 'ethnic' among members of a community lies in largely non-conscious phenomena. Such phenomena are comprised of unarticulated, though shared, rules for behaviour, experiences, values, sentiments, dispositions, aesthetics, rhythms: in short, as 'culture' habituated and inculcated through 'practice'. Consequently, cultural differences may divide members of a society without necessarily involving a high degree of self-consciousness regarding group membership or communal interest. '[E]ven where ethnic divisions are salient,' Malcolm Cross (1978: 38) observes, 'it does not follow that the members of ethnic groups necessarily *perceive* their ethnicity as a critical allegiance' (emphasis in original). In response to various conditions or types of social change, however, groups marked by distinct characteristics undertake forms of mobilization 'entailing the identification of group members with these characteristics' (ibid.: 39), usually towards some goal involving proposed collective interests. The formation of an ideology is often the key to the process of ethnic mobilization.

In this kind of approach, 'culture', as practice, is contraposed with 'ideology', as conceptualization. Thus, Bruce Kapferer (1983: 19) refers to 'culture' as

> an ensemble of beliefs, ideas and instituted practices which constitute the common-sense, taken-for-granted and, usually, not consciously reflected upon aspects of routine daily action. Ideology, by way of contrast is a creation of reflective consciousness and is typically manifested in the problematic and non-routine dimensions of social life. People do not proselytize their culture, but they do proselytize ideology. In the overt and observable ideological process, ideas are held consciously and openly before action, guiding but not determining the organization of action.

Drawing upon Gramsci, Kapferer emphasizes:

> Ideology is a particular organized selection of ideas and practices *within* a cultural ensemble or wider cultural terrain . . . which is made a matter of conscious reflection. This selection takes shape in a social and political process and incorporates the structured interests of the ideological producers and their audience.
>
> (ibid., emphasis in original)

With regard to ethnicity, the formation of ideology articulates a conceptual order by means of establishing (formulating, institutionalizing, symbolizing) a set of references according to which members of a now-specifically defined group place themselves *vis-à-vis* other groups, economic structures, the state, or other facets of their environment.

When religion is part or the core of an ethnic ideology, the selected sets of reference may have an especially pervasive intellectual and affective power since they are believed to 'carry and bestow authority because they seem to emanate from a transcendent source' (Thompson 1986: 45). Among members of an ethnic group, religious sets of reference define in an ultimate sense who the group is in the world and in history, what the criteria of membership are, and what the proper courses of individual and collective action should be: in short (to readapt Geertz's [1973] well-known phrase), they provide the 'models of and for' the group's social reality. Ethnic ideologies are thereby legitimated in virtually uncontestable terms because they are often deemed to be directly handed down through the ages after some critical revelation or encounter between god(s) and certain believed 'ancestors' of the group.

Yet religious components of ethnic ideology, though in essence considered by believers to be 'ahistorical', are by no means necessarily frozen or fixed in form. These, like secular features, are part of a wider milieu, and may undergo modification in response to contextual changes. Thus Stuart Hall (1985: 272–3) underscores the fact that religious ideology may be subject to

> a constant process of formation and re-formation through which emphases are shifted, elements borrowed, abandoned or transformed, rituals reinterpreted and reshaped, doctrines elided, symbols fused, so as to constitute new systems of meaning out of old ones, new religious logics and practices

through which new social forces and new historical realities can be 'spoken'.

Furthermore, Hall stresses the potential these subsequently have for initiating social and political transformation:

> Religious ideologies, however 'other worldly' they appear, inform social practices and have a mobilising 'practical' impact on society. They organise men and women into action, win 'hearts and minds' . . . Religious ideologies are *both* the medium in which collective ideological social solidarities are constructed *and* the means through which ideological conflict and difference is pursued.
>
> (ibid.: 273; emphasis in original)

When collectivities, ethnic and/or religious, undertake self-conscious attempts to change institutions or to create a new social order, they are often said by sociologists to constitute social movements. Social movements, especially among culturally distinct peoples in situations of unequal status or power, are more likely to come to the fore during periods of political and economic uncertainty and change, or in other situations of strain or crisis in social relations (Banks 1972). American anthropologists have long described such developments among indigenous peoples in terms of 'relative deprivation theory' (Aberle 1962) and 'revitalization movements' (Wallace 1956); other social scientists have pointed to such developments in terms of ethnic allegiance and mobilization in contexts of decolonization (in the West Indies, for example, see Cross 1978; Hintzen 1989). Under such conditions, ideology formation is likely to occur. Or, in other such periods when instability and change arise, ideologies previously formed may be adjusted to take advantage of new opportunities, or honed to contest specific issues. In the study of social movements and the rise of ideologies, it is essential to examine historical antecedents, as well as current contexts, in order to 'unpack' the rhetoric, symbols and activities which embody the ideologies of ethnically and/or religiously motivated collectivities.

By way of example, then, the following is an account of the formation and development of ethnic ideology among Hindus in Trinidad, with particular reference to the contemporary Hindu youth movement and its role in fostering what those involved call their own 'Hindu renaissance'.

Hinduism in Trinidad: historical developments

Since the 1980s in Trinidad and Tobago where Asian (or 'East') Indians account for just under half of the country's 1997 population of 1,130,337, Hindus are experiencing a vibrant revival in sentiment and social action. Comprising some 24 per cent of the total population (about 60 per cent of all Indians) today, the Hindu community has generally been at the bottom of the society's ethnically-determined status hierarchy since the original immigrants arrived as indentured labourers between 1845 and 1917. Their contemporary 'renaissance' or revival has included the invention or modification of certain rites and activities, and the embellishment of others (Vertovec 1991a, 1992b). It has also involved the creation or reorganization of numerous groups and associations, both locally and nationally.

Along with the revitalization of devotional orientations and socio-cultural institutions among Trinidad Hindus, there has been a marked stimulation or intensification of ethnic sentiments – among some persons and groups, virtually to the point of militancy. This is especially the case among young, often well-educated Hindus. Yet this contemporary state of affairs is a historical product of the community's development, over 140 years, with a changing context of ethnic pluralism and unequal access to power. At various stages of this historical discourse, different elements of Hindu ethnic ideology were formed.

As described in the previous chapter, since their initial introduction to the island in the nineteenth century, Hindus in Trinidad have been both inadvertently and intentionally modifying their beliefs and practices to fit the gradually changing local conditions. This has included an initial 'homogenization' of Hindu phenomena drawn from a diverse range of parochial traditions of north India. The result in Trinidad, eventually, was an essentially unitary, congregational *bhakti* (devotion)-centred Vaishnavism focused on popular scriptures, especially the Bhagavad Purana and Tulsidas' Ramayana (Vertovec 1989). Such a trend arose through necessity: 'lowest common denominator' Hindu rites and tenets had to be found, by priests and their disciples, in order to provide for worship among the migrants who had come from such differing backgrounds and been thrust together in an alien environment. In Trinidad, the virtual absence of caste as a social regulator has allowed an egalitarianism, or access to and institutionalization of socio-religious activity, impossible in the Indian subcontinent. Still, Brahman priests have

long maintained a monopoly over matters of orthodoxy and orthopraxy (doctrinally legitimated and formalized ritual practice).

Among members of practically all other ethnic segments and
classes in colonial Trinidad, Hindus were regarded with disdain not
only for being the lowest of workers – indentured plantation 'coolies'
– but for being 'heathen idolators' as well. By the 1870s, public
outrage, represented in contemporary newspapers, led to the restric-
tion of Hindu practices, such as those involving hook-swinging
and fire-walking (Jha 1989). Both practices were derived from
traditions of the comparatively few Bengali and South Indian Hindu
immigrants, and were quite peripheral to those of the majority
of Hindus in Trinidad, who came from what is now Bihar and
Uttar Pradesh; most non-Indians, however, were quite ignorant
of intra-communal Indian distinctions, and their repugnance was
consequently directed towards all Hindu activity, and especially
towards rites involving blood sacrifice. Thus, from an early stage
of their presence in Trinidad, Hindus were perhaps most negatively
differentiated from and by others, of both African and European
descent (Brereton 1979). To be fair, it must be said that Muslims,
too, suffered from many prejudices directed against Indians in
general, although in many ways Muslims were granted more respect
as non-idolators. Professional opportunity or social mobility among
Hindus, most notoriously in the field of education, quite often
relied on conversion to Christianity. Over the years, the pressure
of external ethnic-religious discrimination (non-Hindus looked
down upon a variety of Hindu cultural practices, not just those
associated with religion), coupled with the need for unity or, at
least, commonality of interests and of practice, within their own
community, led to a gradual process of 'ideologization' among
Trinidad Hindus.

Initial moves towards the creation of what may be called a Hindu
ethnic ideology occurred even in the earliest phases of post-indenture
settlement. Brahman priests and *sadhus* wandered throughout the
island in the nineteenth century, and their sermons and services –
structured so as to be of interest and importance to Hindus from
a number of pre-migration local traditions, and conducted in the
creolized Bhojpuri tongue which functioned as an Indian *lingua
franca* – doubtless acted to bring the immigrant Hindus into common
cause.

By the 1920s, the trend towards a unitary Hinduism was virtually
complete: beliefs and practices associated with local or caste-based
traditions in India had largely given way to the homogenized, essen-

tially Brahmanic tradition forged in the island to provide common socio-religious forms. Subsequently, Hindu organizational activity became more effective (following secular organizations like the East Indian National Association, founded at the turn of the century by middle-class Indian businessmen). Local Hindu *sabhas*, or associations, organized and oversaw activities at temples and festivals. These loosely formalized groups, together with *ad hoc* committees of villagers, successfully managed to sustain the vitality of Hindu practices in the face of society-wide prejudice. However, prior to World War II, the greatest steps towards self-conscious Hindu ideologization and institutionalization were stimulated, not by reactions to extra-communal discrimination, but (as described in Chapter 2) by the intra-communal strife wrought by the Arya Samaj–Sanatan Dharma conflicts.

The first Arya Samaji missionary to Trinidad arrived in 1910, followed by others in 1914, 1917, 1928 and 1933. The earliest ones established a sustained presence (though no great following), while the latter two (Pundits Mehta Jaimani and Ayodhia Prasad) were renowned for their sophistication and scholarship. Of widening significance in the late 1920s and early 1930s, the Arya Samajis held popular public forums on the greatness of Indian civilization, the importance of the Vedas, the futility of idol worship, the equality of women, the merits of education, and more. Even those who were not motivated to convert to their brand of Hinduism were moved to reflect upon, and take pride in, the grand heritage of India. Yet Brahman priests (whom Arya Samajis derided and embarrassed in public debates), the leaders of local *sabhas*, and other more conservative followers of Sanatan Dharma by no means appreciated the sect's intrusion into the Hindu community.

These controversies over Hindu belief and practice provided a kind of catalyst for Trinidad Hindu ideologization and institutionalization. Just as it did across north India, 'Introduction of the Arya Samaj into many towns polarized Hindus, forcing them to define and identify just what it was that they regarded as their community' (Freitag 1980: 603). Everywhere in Trinidad the Arya Samaji missionaries went, Hindu religious leaders – Arya Samaji or 'Sanatanist' – responded by organizing themselves to provide more concise, or at least formulated, statements about their ethnic-religious community.

In 1932, the long dormant Sanatan Dharma Association was re-ordered and incorporated by act of legislature. The Association listed as its objectives:

To propagate Hinduism, teach the tenets of Hindu Dharma and establish branches in various centres in the colony; To establish Mardassars [sic] (schools); To teach morality and temperance, to promote harmony and goodwill and to take an interest in the social welfare of the people; To settle disputes among Hindus; To seek religious rights from the Government, and To raise funds to enable the Association to carry out its aims and objectives.

(in Kirpalani et al. 1945: 61)

The Association's effectiveness was undercut by personality clashes and intra-communal politics, such that in the same year of 1932, a rival Hindu body was established, calling itself the Sanatan Dharma Board of Control. Within a few years, and in order to gain, over its rival, more orthodox legitimacy, the Board affiliated itself with the Sanatan Dharma Pratinidhi Sabha, a conservative organization based in Lahore, India, which soon sent its own missionary to Trinidad. By the end of the decade, the Board had branches in thirty-two towns and villages throughout the island.

Within each Hindu camp, priests consulted each other on matters of orthodoxy and orthopraxy, formal statements were made and circulated to the Hindu and non-Hindu public, and numerous trends were set in course by which Hinduism in Trinidad took on westernized, even Christian-like, forms which may be interpreted as a drive to achieve greater 'respectability' in the eyes of the society's non-Hindu majority. In the late 1930s and early 1940s, both Sanatanist organizations played major roles in lobbying the colonial government for communal gains (cf. Jha 1982). Largely due to these bodies, Hindu marriages were legally recognized, cremations permitted, and, through combined efforts with secular organizations, Indians were given full franchise (after a prolonged battle against those who sought to bar Indians from the vote by means of a language clause; see Brereton 1981). Their successes notwithstanding, the two main Hindu organizations probably did more to fragment and stifle the Hindu community than to consolidate and advance it. Their intense rivalry fuelled stereotypes of chaos in the Hindu community, and undermined the effectiveness of emergent aspects of ethnic ideology.

Indians fared remarkably well in the first elections under universal adult suffrage in 1946. At that time, there was no fixed pattern of ethnic voting. The 1950 elections, too, witnessed few signs of ethnically polarized politics. Yet ethnicity gradually took on overtly political meanings with the development of national elections and the run-up to decolonization and independence. Knowing this, prominent Hindus undertook the task of more explicit ideologization. The early 1950s began a new era in Trinidad politics, when the Hindu community itself undertook a radical new trajectory.

The independence of India stimulated a heightened sense of identity and a flourishing of cultural activity among Hindus in Trinidad throughout the late 1940s and early 1950s. Riding the crest of this wave of sentiment, Bhadase Sagan Maraj, a self-made millionaire and the sugar workers' union leader, united the Sanatan Dharma Association and the Sanatan Dharma Board of Control in 1950. In 1952, he incorporated these as a single, national Hindu body, the Sanatan Dharma Maha Sabha. Maraj's domineering personality and, some say, strong-arm tactics, kept infighting to a minimum. The Maha Sabha's *parishad*, or council of pundits, worked towards complete co-ordination of temple activities and standardization of ritual procedures in all parts of the island. Yet foremost on the Maha Sabha's agenda was education, which members saw as the key to promoting Hindu unity, promulgating the faith among youth, and providing Hindus with greater opportunity for social mobility. Between 1952 and 1956, the Maha Sabha built no less than thirty-one Hindu schools throughout Trinidad. Maha Sabha religious publications became basic texts in these schools, as well as in practically all Sanatanist temples which became affiliated to the national organization. Thus, Trinidad Hindus were institutionally consolidated as never before.

Not coincidentally, in 1953 Maraj launched the People's Democratic Party (PDP), which functioned essentially as a Hindu political organ. By 1956, the PDP pitted itself against the African-dominated People's National Movement (PNM), led by Dr Eric Williams, a well-known scholar of slavery and imperialism. Trinidad's now notorious legacy of racial politics had begun. Williams helped to rouse communal sentiments by playing upon Africans' and other communities' fears of Indian numerical 'swamping' and political domination (Indians had long maintained the highest fertility rate in the country). Furthermore, Williams suggested that the PDP 'was nothing more than the political voice of the Maha Sabha' (Ryan 1972: 141). Pointing to the PDP's Brahmanic control and Hindu clientelism, Williams not only gained the support of non-Indians, particularly urban Africans, but also managed to win the support of many Christian and Muslim Indians as well (Vasil 1984). The PDP and the Maha Sabha were, in fact, practically inextricable in leadership and organization. This was Maraj's strength.

The PDP in fact had never really functioned as an autonomous political party with a constitution and a grass-roots organization. It felt no real need to organize since the branches of the Maha Sabha and the priesthood were easily convertible into political instrumentalities. There is considerable evidence to support the charge that many religious meetings in temples and in homes became political meetings, and that Hindus were enjoined to support their religion by ensuring that Hindus were elected to public bodies. It is said of that time that pundits made individual Hindus swear on the *lotah* (a holy Hindu vessel) to support candidates, and would threaten religious sanctions for broken pledges (Ryan 1972: 141).

The PDP was narrowly defeated in the national elections of 1956, after which Maraj reorganized the party and changed its name to the Democratic Labour Party (DLP). Maraj and other Hindu leaders rallied their community, claiming that the sacred texts like the Ramayana – and Sanatan Dharma itself – were in imminent danger should the party fail. At the time, Hindu hopes rose high, even though they were still socially relegated to the very bottom of the country's complex status hierarchy (Crowley 1957). Still acknowledged as the Hindu political wing, the DLP won a stunning victory in the 1958 election for Trinidad's seats in the first Parliament of the West Indies. The political backlash was fierce, and racial tensions increased. Williams' PNM soundly defeated the DLP in the national election of 1961, leading the nation into independence in 1962. This took much of the wind from the DLP's sails, and the party progressively collapsed through the course of the 1960s (see Malik 1966).

By the beginning of the 1970s, Trinidad Hindus were generally dejected as a group. Some suggest Hindu religiosity had declined: one anthropologist observed 'infrequent and selective commitment to Sanatanist beliefs and practices' among Hindu laity and priests alike (Schwartz 1967b: 245). Evangelical Christian missions from the United States were perceived as making numerous Hindu converts. Hindu political force certainly dwindled: the DLP boycotted the 1970 general election, while Maraj, campaigning with a new party, failed to hold even his own constituency. Together with many Muslim Indians, Hindus were economically the poorest Trinidadians (being largely agricultural labourers), discriminated against occupationally, and seriously under-represented in the civil service and other public sectors (see Cross and Schwartzbaum 1969; Malik 1971; Harewood 1971). During the Black Power uprisings in Trinidad in 1970, rural Hindus reacted with considerable anxiety.

The strong ideological and institutional tide that swept the Hindu community of Trinidad in the 1950s certainly ebbed by the turn of the 1970s. The Maha Sabha came under allegations of corruption and mismanagement, and letters appeared in national newspapers claiming that most Hindus no longer supported the organization mainly because of Maraj's leadership. Chaos in the national body was fully realized following the death of Bhadase Maraj in 1971. Factionalism, squabbling and mudslinging between numerous potential leaders ensued. Nearly two years passed and still no new chief emerged from the organization's ranks. Maha Sabha elections in 1973 and 1974 were condemned by many branch members as being rigged via false delegates and disallowed votes. While it cannot be claimed that religious devotion among average Hindus had declined, it can be said that ethnic-religious vivacity, as represented by a strongly committed and organized front with a discernible ideology, certainly had.

Hindu resurgence and contemporary Hindu youth

All Trinidad society was radically affected by economic events in the early and mid-1970s, when world oil prices rocketed (see Vertovec 1990b, 1992b). Trinidad had been a modest producer of oil practically since the turn of the century, but the sector had never contributed very substantially to the national income. After the quadrupling of the price of oil in 1973–74, the government levied new taxes on the foreign companies which drew Trinidad's oil. This created a quite sudden, and very substantial, cash injection into the country's coffers. Around the same time, world sugar prices leapt as well, adding more wealth, especially to the Indian-dominated rural areas. Through national and local government work schemes, new heavy industries, and spin-off sectors like construction and transport, large amounts of cash quickly percolated through all levels of the small nation's economy (that is, mostly throughout Trinidad; residents of Tobago claim that they were in many ways neglected during the oil boom).

Ethnic tensions were by no means assuaged by the influx of cash, however. The African-dominated PNM government used much of the nation's new riches, by way of work schemes, housing projects, and development plans, to bolster its system of party patronage (see Hintzen 1989). Rural Indians perceived themselves as purposefully excluded by the government from the benefits of the boom. Instead, the Indians, who still greatly profited during the period, indicated that much of their new-found wealth derived from the use of their own social networks and from individual initiative (both arising from values which, they would say, are integral to Indian culture).

Towards the end of the 1970s and early 1980s much of Indians' boom money went towards business investment, new houses and consumer goods. Yet Hindus also tended to pour money, as never before, into ritual activity. New, or at least newly embellished, rites and ceremonial events rapidly proliferated throughout the island. These included *satsangs* (readings and songs concerning the Ramayana: relatively simple domestic rites which became affordable to even the least well-to-do families), *pujas* (ritual offerings to gods: once rather special rites ideally held annually by Hindu families, which became common celebrations held on numerous minor occasions throughout the year), and *yagnas* (elaborate and expensive seven- to fourteen-day sets of rites, readings, songs and sermons: once relatively rare and usually, collectively managed events, which became rather frequent and family-sponsored).

At first, these activities may well have been undertaken by Hindu *nouveau riche* for ostentatious display and status acquisition. Regardless of initial motivation, the upsurge in ritual activity among all Hindus – facilitated by the oil boom – played a central part in fostering a resurgence or revitalization of Hindu collective sentiments. Increasingly at *satsangs*, *pujas* and *yagnas* during the late 1970s and 1980s, a message was propagated regarding how Hindus should act individually and as a community (to which the answer was given: proudly), what their history in the island was (exploited), what their place in contemporary Trinidad society was (discriminated against), and how they should pursue their rightful future (actively in full control).

The collapse of the oil boom, and the advent of a deep recession beginning around 1982, meant a gradual end to the period of ritual exuberance among Trinidad Hindu families (though many activities, like *yagnas*, subsequently became collective undertakings once more albeit retaining the newly embellished forms). By that time, however, a well-educated new generation had been habituated to, and stimulated by, a general context of vibrant, communal Hindu activity. As the economic downturn spelt a decline in domestic ritual activity (as well as other deleterious effects on families), highly motivated Hindu youth stepped up their own collective undertakings. It has been largely among them that a highly discernible ethnic ideology has been forged.

Around the mid-1970s, the Hindu Jewaan Sangha, or Hindu Youth Organization, was established in Trinidad. Officially this was the youth wing of the Sanatan Dharma Maha Sabha, but its original leaders attest that the parent organization actually had little to do with the activities of the Jewaan Sangha. Among its twenty-two aims and ideals which the organization listed were:

> To improve the physical, moral, intellectual, social and economic status of Hindu Youths [sic] and the community as a whole. To unite all Hindu Youths in Trinidad and Tobago, the Caribbean and the World. To strive to promote the understanding and appreciation of Indian Culture in Trinidad and Tobago and the Caribbean. To make, do and cause to be done all such acts and things that may be necessary to improve the standard and status of Hindus generally.

Ideals of promoting understanding and fraternity among peoples of all nationalities, creeds and races were also listed. One of their first activities was to organize a *yagna* that functioned as a charity fundraiser. This was a highly successful event which raised TT$50,000 towards clothes and food for the poorest members of the Hindu community in Trinidad. The Sangha's young, university-educated leaders quickly gained reputations as devoted, selfless community workers (as opposed to many Maha Sabha leaders, whom many average Hindus regarded as mostly self-serving).

Though endeavouring for the good of Hindus as a whole, the Jewaan Sangha focused most attention on problems confronting young Hindus. They assessed the condition of Hindu youth as one plagued by confusion, loss of identity and lack of direction. This, they observed, was due to a set of factors, including rapid 'westernization' through greater materialism and media 'bombardment' (as the oil boom developed, TVs, video recorders and stereos became common items throughout Trinidad, through which American and British 'pop culture' became increasingly dominant). They also pointed to a society-wide neglect, or disdain, of any attempt to include Indian cultural features in the promotion of a 'national culture' (which had evolved into one characterized almost wholly by cricket, calypso and carnival, all with an Afro-Caribbean face). It was also recognized that young Hindus experienced a growing generation gap with older Hindus; the young were far better educated, more westernized, and stood better chances of socio-economic mobility than their parents.

Throughout the 1970s, at the same time as Hindu communal activity began to flourish, Hindu youth consciously felt estranged from their religious culture. Many felt it was overly ritualistic and lacking in contemporary meaning (largely because rites, and sometimes sermons, were conducted in Sanskrit or Trinidad Hindi, which most under the age of around thirty-five could not fully understand; many young people also criticized Hindu priests, who could not adequately provide satisfactory instruction to the sophisticated new generation). At a Youth Seminar in 1977, one young Hindu leader delivered a paper entitled 'The Crisis of Relevance', in which he pointed out that within Hinduism, 'there has been a great gap between the rapid changes and requirements of our environment and our ability to adapt and to meet the demands of these changes'.

In 1978 the Jewaan Sangha called a regional Hindu Conference, on the theme of 'The Caribbean Challenge to Sanatan Dharma'. Its purpose was to discuss perceived problems and to initiate plans for action. The letter of invitation explained:

> Over one hundred and forty years ago our forefathers were uprooted from Bharat Desha and transplanted in an alien environment to supply labour for the sugar plantations in the West Indies. They brought with them their religion, their culture, their songs, music, dances, their food, their dress – in fact, they brought a way of life, the Hindu way of life! Today this way of life is being threatened, its values are being questioned, its forms of expression are being frowned upon and pronounced irrelevant to the society in which we live.
>
> Let us never forget one thing. WE HINDUS HAVE NEVER FAILED HINDUISM IN A CRISIS!
>
> We Hindus must wake up and commence our march for unity, peace and progress. For too long we have been living in isolation. 'We have been committing religious and cultural suicide.' We must unite the scattered, disorganised and demoralized Hindus throughout the Caribbean. We must mobilise ALL HINDUS in the Caribbean and instil in them pride and dignity in our priceless cultural heritage. Then and only then can we proclaim the glory of Shri Sanatan Dharma.
>
> (emphasis in original)

One highly effective strategy that emerged was to take their mobilization efforts directly into local communities. Jewaan Sangha members travelled throughout the country organizing film shows, speeches, debates and other public forums for the promulgation of an ethnic-religious message.

Around the same time, a related body, calling itself the 'Indian Revival and Reform Association' (IRRA), had begun large-scale efforts to promote annual celebrations of Indian Arrival Day (30 May), marking the immigration of the first Indians to Trinidad. These events were couched with notions of how Indians, though terribly exploited and abused throughout the island's history, simultaneously saved the economic well-being of the nation and managed to retain their (Hindu) cultural ways and values. On stage amid programmes of speeches and songs, elderly Indians were encouraged to detail severities associated with their experiences on colonial planta-tions; the lives of important historical leaders like Bhadase Maraj were highlighted; and the evolution of discriminatory attitudes by non-Indians – all in the light of the society's debt to Indians – were espoused. Thus, a firm ideology was well in the making, with the Jewaan Sangha taking the lead in describing the current problems affecting Hinduism in the country, and with the IRRA propounding an emotive view of the community's past.

By 1980, the leader of the Jewaan Sangha finally fell out with the Maha Sabha, taking with him a core of supporters and the vital force behind the organization. Yet by that time, local associations of Hindu youth had been formed to take up where the Jewaan Sangha had left off. In one rural village, the leaders of the local Hindu Youth Group, all college or university-educated males and females, described their initial motives to establish themselves in 1977. At first, they emphasized that especially among young Hindus, there was great disaffection with the Maha Sabha and all it represented: 'De youths grow up', one said, 'knowin' de Maha Sabha is not a reputable organization – it doesn't serve dem.' Moreover, they strongly disliked the way the Maha Sabha continued to be Brahman dominated, adding to their perception of a Hindu 'crisis of relevance'. Especially within the context of an upsurge in religious activity in homes and communities, they simply wished to have a greater under-standing of their own religious traditions; however, the priests tended to alienate young people. As one of the Group noted, 'mos' a' de Brahmans: dey livelihood depend on knowin' somet'in' dat you don' know'. A core group of about ten young Hindus in the village, therefore, took matters into their own hands and began their own organizational efforts. They considered the Jewaan Sangha to be their parent body (though refusing to recognize any Maha Sabha connec-tion), trying to emulate it in every fashion. They conducted numerous fundraising events, stage-managed highly popular public celebrations on important holy days, gave money and labour to local temples and disaster-struck families, and held religious education classes for children. For a period, they even took over control of the Management Committee in one local temple and of the entire Village Council.

This kind of activism, which the Jewaan Sangha originally stimulated and which local youth groups carried through, soon found even stronger expression. In 1983, ex-leaders of the Jewaan Sangha and IRRA co-founded the Hindu Seva Sangh (Hindu Service Organization). They were joined by two well-versed and articulate Trinidad Indian graduates of Benares Hindu University in India (where, it is said, they had close contact with the youth wing of the fundamentalist All India Mahasabha). The Seva Sangh embarked on a programme of action that has became one of the most dynamic forces in Trinidad Hinduism.

One of the Seva Sangh's basic premises is that, due to prejudice exhibited against Hindus in schools, the media, and throughout daily life in Trinidad, Hinduism has been put 'on the defensive'. Hindus, the Seva Sangh emphasize, have been made to feel embarrassed or ashamed of their beliefs and practices. The President of the organization described, for example, how devastated he once was when he heard a Hindu girl say 'I wish I was a Negro'. The Seva Sangh has formulated a strategy to promote a positive self-image among young Hindus by means of establishing an 'aggressive Hinduism'. The goal is that Hindu youth should be made into a mobilized force for the elevation of Indians (namely, Hindus) and the transformation of a discriminatory society. In their publications and meetings, they are fond of quoting Vivekananda:

> When a man has begun to be ashamed of his ancestors, the end has come. Here am I, one of the least of the Hindu race, yet proud of my race, proud of my ancestors . . . Learn everything that is good from others, but bring it in, and in your own way absorb it; do not become others. Do not be dragged away out of this Hindu way of life.

One vehicle for propagating their ethnic ideology has been a periodical publication called *Jagriti* (which can be translated as 'Revival'). It is published by the Hindu Education Trust, which draws its editorial board and main authors from Seva Sangh leaders. Its editorials and articles argue that Hindus are under a constant and deliberate cultural attack. For example:

78

We accept that Hindus are in a crisis today. It is as though we are in a siege – I get the feeling that we are being ambushed. The guns that are trained at us are the television, newspapers – the media – and also policies. We are under ambush. We are under siege.

(*Jagriti*, 1 June 1985, p. 4)

Letters attributed to Hindu children and teenagers complain of feeling ashamed or being ridiculed at school, to which there are replies such as:

you are not just an individual, alone. You are an important part of our great Hindu race and Hindu culture in this country. So when your friends make fun of you they do so because they: (a) are ignorant of the meaning of your name, your religion and your culture. (b) are jealous – for they have no such culture as such. They have to imitate the culture of the 'white-man,' while you have your own. (c) they are prejudiced and want all things to be their way.

So do not feel ashamed! You have to first understand your problem and that of those other people who make fun of you. You have to start saying to yourself: I AM A HINDU.

(ibid.: 13)

Not only is a positive self-image promoted, but a radical shift in the position of Indians in society is called for:

rather than bow to a so called 'Master race' to do these things for us, we must take control of our socio-political destiny. We must not only think of spiritual salvation, but also of our socio-political salvation on earth, which are two sides of the same coin . . . We must turn our yagnas, crusades, festivals and social gatherings into 'factories of socio-political consciousness'.

(ibid.: 18)

Within this view, Hindus are regarded as a 'distinct ethnic group' (cf. Tewarie 1988), and are also considered to be 'a racial grouping as well, for the Hindus are all or most, of Caucasian stock coming from the Indian subcontinent. The Moslems are mixed, as we have both Moslems of Caucasian stock as well as negroid stock' (*Jagriti*, 2 July 1985, p. 25). As well as being culturally and racially distinct,

Hindus are considered as upholding virtuous ways, as opposed to 'the African contribution to our national culture . . . the revelry of carnival or the smut of calypso or the general atmosphere of licentiousness that accompanies carnival and the steelband activities' (ibid.). Moreover, in their promotion of Indian culture, the stress is that '*Indian culture is the culture of the Hindus*' (ibid.: 28, emphasis in original). This of course amounts to a dissocation of, and slight against, Muslim Indians. Finally, the publication adds a more contemporary edge to historical views of anti-Hindu discrimination:

> Then came the oil boom of the 70's and many Hindus graduated upwards the scale [*sic*] of vertical mobility. By virtue of hard work and sacrifice they made their small businesses flourish . . . Thus it was that upward mobility of the Hindus in our heterogeneous society created a fear and was seen as a threat by the non-Hindus . . . This further added to inter-group hostility.
>
> (ibid.: 32)

By way of promoting this ideology, the Seva Sangh organizes a variety of public events, often working with local Hindu groups and regularly drawing crowds of many thousands. These events include Nagar Sankirtan (day-long chanting processions between various towns, where speeches and other programmes are conducted) and Indian Arrival Day ceremonies (which they naturally inherited from the IRRA). In 1985, the 150th anniversary of Indian immigration, the Indian Arrival Day ceremonies sparked a national controversy when one Hindu leader vehemently criticized the Trinidad media for disregarding equal treatment of Indians (*Trinidad Express* 31/5/85). Yet, the Seva Sangh's greatest influence on young people comes through their numerous camps, held throughout the year to promote an 'aggressive Hinduism'.

The highly popular Seva Sangh camps accommodate up to 250 boys and girls between the ages of about seven and eighteen. From 4.30 a.m. to 10.00 p.m. each day for a week, they engage in a full schedule of lectures, discussions, creativity workshops and 'Indian' games. Messages like those in *Jagriti*, especially ones advocating a strong identity and willingness to stick up for oneself, dominate the proceedings. *Naras* (slogans, like 'Hindustani zindabad' or 'long-live India') and special songs are constantly sounded. One song in particular, 'Jaago Hindu Veer', is widely sung or hummed by individuals, and may be considered as a kind of theme song for the Seva Sangh and the Hindu youth movement as a whole. Below, the words are given with two varying translations, both appearing in Seva Sangh publications.

Jaago Hindu Veer Shatru Ne
Phir Lalkara Hai
Sankat Mein Hai Pada Aaj Priya
Dharma Hamara Hai
Hamto Shanti Marg Par Chalte Jag Mein Sab Ko Bandhu
    Samaihte Durbal Ko Par Kahbi Ne Deta Jagat Sahara
    Hai
Jan Jan Mein Kabhi Rishi Na Kam The Jag Mein Sab Se
    Bardh Kar Ham The Yug Yug
Se Santapt Manuj Mein Yahin Nihara Hain
Hindu Yuvakon Kamar Bandh Lo Shatru Vinashak
    Shatra Sadha Lo Veer Tapasvin
Bhagwa Dhawaj Ne Humein pukara Hain
Nas Nas Mein Hain Rakt Ram Ka Kita Ka Upadesh
    Shyam Ka Apna Apna Pran 5th an
Se Dharm Hi Pyara Hain
Is Par Aanch Na Aane Payein Chahe Praan Bhale Hi
    Jaayein Tan Man Dekar Use
Bachana Dharam Hamara Hain

Translation 1
Hindu Youths [sic] Now Awake! Beware! There's too
    much at stake Dharma's in a
crucial state Rise up now, It's not too late
shanti [Peace] we chant from age to age
For man is one, told our saint
and sage. History has taught us
though, my Friend The world won't
won't ever the weak defend
Amongst the Hindu masses once
No dearth of saint nor dearth of
sage. Of all mankind we were
esconded. Foremost on the world's
vast stage
The Saffron Flag of Dharma calls
Man! Woman! One and all
Dharma's flag shall ne'er fall
While we live! Not at all!

In our veins course [sic] the blood
of Ram. In our minds resound
the song of Shyam. Higher than
Dharma nought is there
Higher than self is Dharma Dear
For Dharma's sake this life may go
Dharma for weal Dharma for woe
In Dharma's cause to give we Yearn
This body, this mind, and what
e'r we earn.

Translation 2
Wake up Hindu Heroes, the enemy
has challenged us again.
Today our beloved Dharma is
in trouble!! in crisis.
We Hindus walk the part of peace.
In this world everybody (each one)
consider friends But the world does
NOT GIVE refuge to the weak.
Amongst our people SAINTS and SAGES
were never less. In the world of all
peoples, we are progressive.
From us the most excellence.
Oh Hindu youth get alert!!
Learn to use the weapon aginst the
enemy. Heroes of Excellence. yellow flag is calling out
to us.
The blood of Ram flows in every pore As Krishna said in
the Gita Whatever the
situation out here More Dharma is (needed) Belove [sic]
I would not let any fire come and burn Even if my life
should go.
I would give my body and mind to save My DHARMA.
THIS IS MY DHARMA!!

In both translations, there are clear notions of Hindus comprising
a spiritually infused ethnic community (linked by 'the blood of Ram'
– an incarnation of God, a community among which saints and
sages have been many), the current threat posed by outsiders ('a
crucial state' wrought by 'the enemy'), and the necessity of active
resistance.

Furthermore, the concept of *dharma* here is most significant. As in India, the term has at least two meanings: the transcendent order or way, according to which nature and human society are, and should continue to be, structured; and the individual performance of action throughout life in particular accordance with the transcendent order. Within the context of the song, and within the Trinidad Hindu youth movement as a whole, the concept draws on the traditional meanings, but more specifically, portrays *dharma* as the way of an ethnic community (not the cosmos as a whole), and individual duty, as that of a person born into the community (not as a human in general). Yet, like the original meaning, *dharma* here refers to a way and a duty created and monitored by God.

In addition to the spiritual underpinning of the movement, the more secular message – of a legacy of Hindu pride and activism in the face of racial and cultural oppression – has become pervasive among Hindu youth. In one Seva Sangh seminar, participants were asked to write a spontaneous poem about Hinduism. Three teenagers worked together to produce the following poem, entitled 'Not Again, Not at All':

> For too long, the Hindus has [*sic*] been trampled upon
> these days has past and gone
> We Hindus have worked and toiled to make Trinidad a
> productive soil
> With blood and sweat they worked til death
>
> they have shown us the light to brighten our path
> and brought with them their culture and art
> For we the Hindu youths of today should work towards a
> better way
> Not again, not at all for we the Hindu youths would
> never fall
> This is our call
> This is our call

Classes organized by the Seva Sangh not only promote a more positive identity and relentless attitude, but also educate young people about drug abuse, familiarize them with facets of Indian music and dance, teach Hindi language skills, and provide philosophical insights into Hindu traditions. Local, village-based Hindu Youth Groups liaise with the Seva Sangh and utilize their techniques, slogans and songs. Energetic leaders, together with plenty of fun and games, ensure the continued popularity of the Seva Sangh's activities among Trinidad Hindu youth.

The Hindu revitalization movement, which was ushered in during the oil boom, bolstered by local groups, who were themselves inspired by the Jewaan Sangha and currently maintained by the Seva Sangh, has undoubtedly led to more affirmatively felt and assertively vocalized ethnic sentiments. This is evident, for example, in the successful sales of one newspaper called *Sandesh* ('News'), which is devoted to the promotion of Indian (mainly, Hindu) culture. Often citing the Seva Sangh, the paper covers Trinidad Indian cultural events and Hindu religious activities, profiles leading figures in the community, underscores values (such as sobriety and the importance of the family), depicts fashions acceptable to Hindu modesty, and generally espouses views such as: 'Indian culture is the spring board for the promotion of moral and spiritual values in a decaying society' (II 8/86: 1). The movement, some could argue, has contributed towards chauvinism, racism and intolerance; members insist that it has fostered a constructive sense of multiculturalism.

Significantly, the heightening of Hindu ethnic consciousness and the calls for socio-political change in Trinidad eventually found expression (see Tewarie 1988). In the national elections of 1986 the long-seated, African-dominated PNM was soundly ousted by a bi-racial, multi-party coalition called the National Alliance for Reconstruction (NAR), of which one of the two leaders, Basdeo Panday, was a prominent Hindu. Panday's own United National Congress (UNC) won the national election in 1995, when he became the country's first Indian Prime Minister.

Conclusion

Through recapping some of the general concepts set out earlier, we can see that the Hindu youth movement in Trinidad represents an exemplary case of ethnic-religious ideology formation.

First, given certain changes in their social-political-economic context, Hindus have been stimulated towards increasing self-reflection regarding their past, present and future plights. The most prominent instances of this occurred due to quite different circumstances: the sectarian controversies stirred in the 1920s and 1930s by the Arya Samaj, which led to greater institutionalization of Hinduism; the growth of electoral politics and the process of decolonization throughout the 1950s, which led to a centralized Hindu organization/political party and the beginnings of a system of racially polarized politics; and the very rapid socio-economic dynamics accompanying the oil boom and recession of the 1970s and 1980s, which brought about, among other things, Hindu demands for parity with other segments of society in terms of social status and place in the 'national culture'.

Second, through such self-reflection, as evidenced by the Hindu youth movement, many usually taken-for-granted aspects of culture became highlighted and proselytized elements of ideology. Not only did examinations of contemporary ethnic/race relations bring this about, but the increasing cultural and educational gap between young Hindus and their elders also highlighted the previously 'not consciously reflected upon aspects of routine daily action' (Kapferer 1983: 19). The movement has provided a renewed appreciation not only for religious rationalization and ritual practices, but also for what are consciously identified as 'Hindu' ideals of domestic life, cuisine, music, styles of dress, leisure activities and more. Rather than rejecting their heritage altogether – what some anthropologists predicted young Hindus would do with higher levels of education, greater occupational opportunities, increased exposure to western culture and more wealth (for instance, Schwartz 1967b; Nevadomsky 1983) – Hindu youth plunged further into it.

Third, religion has not furnished the criteria or focus for ethnic awareness and collective consciousness in a kind of utilitarian way, solely to promote communal interests in terms of equity in status and resource control. Much of the ideology espoused by a group like the Seva Sangh not only emphasizes collective attributes, action and goals, but underscores very personal religious sentiments, day-to-day values, family ideals and individual behaviour. A modified meaning of the notion of *dharma* has linked individual action and communal identity in a particularly powerful way. Similarly, *bhakti*, or devotion to God (demonstrated in singularly Hindu ways, such as chanting and making offerings to images), is a very real part of Hinduism in present-day Trinidad, fostered and emphasized by the Hindu youth movement. Essential Hindu beliefs and practices, as components of ethnic ideology, have been reformulated and reinterpreted as deemed necessary: for the current Hindu youth movement, this has been done in an attempt to overcome what has been perceived as the modern 'crisis of relevance' facing Trinidad Hinduism.

This brief history of the Hindu youth movement in Trinidad provides examples of 'new religious logics and practices through which new social forces and new historical realities can be "spoken"' (Hall 1985: 273). Religion is fundamental to the ways in which people often identify themselves not only in relation to others and to historical circumstances, but also in relation to some deeply believed transcendent reality, ordained code of conduct, and sacred symbols. This-worldly and other-worldly points of reference, as it were, are interposed. In the field of ethnic diaspora studies, therefore, greater recognition must be given to religion as a vibrant force which imbues – and, through ideology, may consciously order – the outlooks, aspirations, motivations and activities of individuals and communities.

4

REPRODUCTION AND REPRESENTATION

The growth of Hinduism in Britain

The large-scale, post-World War II migration of South Asians profoundly changed the religious (as well as ethnic and racial) landscape of Britain. Limitations of space do not allow for a full discussion here regarding patterns of immigration, settlement, and some of their general implications for British society and Indian culture (see, for instance, Robinson 1986; Clarke *et al*. 1990b; Ballard 1994b). Instead, I will focus, in this section, on features of migration and settlement as they have affected the composition of the population segment generally identifiable as Hindu. The following sections, respectively, look at various social institutions and how, within them, Indian traditions have been reproduced or transformed, as well as how settlement and institutional change in Britain has fostered and reified notions of 'Hinduism' and 'Hindu community' as *ethnic* phenomena.

Background, composition, differentiation

The migration of South Asians in the 1950s and early 1960s came about essentially to fill a gap in expanding British industry by providing cheap labour in the least desired jobs. This migration was one almost wholly undertaken by men (most of whom were in their twenties to forties). Systems of recruitment and patterns of 'chain migration' led to the establishment, in various locations throughout Britain, of pockets of men largely from the same kinship groups, villages, districts or regions of India. Parts of Gujarat and the Punjab – both regions with long-standing traditions of migration to destinations around the world – quickly became the prime source locations for migration to Britain. The main strategy of most migrants was to work and save money for a few years before returning home to the subcontinent. However, with increasingly restrictive (and racially politicized) immigration legislation during the 1960s, numbers of immigrants were curtailed and the original intentions of many were changed to a long-term orientation. By the late 1960s and early 1970s, wives and dependants of the men migrated. Contrasting ecological and cultural variables among certain regional and religious groups, however, have led to different patterns and periods of South Asian family reunion in Britain (Ballard 1990).

At the same time as this latter stage of transplantation from the subcontinent, there was an increasing movement of South Asians from territories in East Africa (Kenya, Uganda, Tanzania, Zambia, and Malawi). Though South Asians had conducted trade along the East African coast for centuries, it was in the nineteenth century that large, settled communities of South Asians were established there. These were comprised largely of entrepreneurs from parts of what is now the state of Gujarat, plus some ex-indentured labourers from Punjab (brought especially to build the Mombasa to Lake Victoria railway) and artisans from both regions of India. As the 1960s progressed, East African governments promoted various 'Africanization' policies (calling for the commercial and professional sectors of each state to be solely in the hands of indigenous black Africans) making things increasingly unpleasant for the 'East African Asians'. Therefore, holding British passports, great numbers came to Britain in the late 1960s, especially from Kenya where the effects of Africanization were more anticipated. In 1972, the sudden, wholesale expulsion of Asians from Uganda saw tens of thousands arriving *en masse* in Britain.

An estimated breakdown of the British Asian population by area of origin and religion in 1991 (largely following the reasoning of Knott and Toon 1982; Peach *et al.* 1988; Knott 1991) within Great Britain's total population of almost 55 million in 1991 is provided.

According to this 1991 estimate there are 1.48 million Asians in Britain, of which 840,000 are Indians. Approximately 48 per cent (= 403,200) of Indians in Britain are Hindu. Some 70 per cent of this 1991 Hindu estimate are Gujarati-speaking, of which 63 per cent are East African Gujarati and 37 per cent are Indian Gujarati. Of this 1991 Hindu estimate, 15 per cent are Punjabi-speaking, of which 20 per cent are East African Punjabi and 80 per cent are Indian Punjabi. Other Indians account for 15 per cent of the Hindu total.

It is important to underscore the geographical variance of British Hindu origins, for provenance has played a fundamental role in determining patterns of post-migration settlement, social institutions, religious practices, and identity formation. And with regard to such developments, distinctions of provenance are by no means limited to general regions (Punjab, Gujarat, 'East Africa'), but extend to particular provinces and districts, even towns and villages therein. This is so because each 'level' of provenance can be associated with salient differences of language and dialect, socio-economic bases, caste composition, kinship and domestic structures, and – as stressed earlier – specific religious traditions. Accordingly, in a context of diaspora, 'levels' of provenance may become the central reference points for the establishment of segmentary identities and social networks (cf. Crissman 1967). Below, some general features of provenance-associated difference are noted before a discussion of certain important, specifically religious ones.

On perhaps the most obvious, broad level, distinctions between Punjabis and Gujaratis are marked. In addition to major language differences (the former speaking Punjabi, Hindi and some Urdu, the latter, Gujarati, Kutchi and Hindi), a host of overt and subtle social and cultural differences abound, linked to human geographies and political and economic histories. In East Africa, Agehananda Bharati (1972: 268) observed that despite both being broadly defined as 'Hindus', the two did not have much to do with each other: 'There is very little actual religious participation between the Gujarati and Panjabi [*sic*] Hindus in East Africa . . . The most obvious fact is that Gujarati Hindus do not take Panjabi Hinduism seriously.' In Britain differences between the two groups are characterized in stereotypes that Punjabis and Gujaratis each have of themselves and each other (such as, that Punjabis are more prone to drinking and smoking openly in pubs, eating meat, having less regard for certain religious observance, Gujaratis being associated with the opposite of these behaviours; see Knott 1986b; Nesbitt 1987). It is likely that such differences and stereotypes partly account for Sims's (1981: 128–30) Birmingham residential findings of 'strong association between Punjabi Hindus and Sikhs, and high levels of spatial separation between Gujarati Hindus and Punjabi Hindus'.

While most British Punjabis are from the adjacent areas of Jullunder and Ludhiana – thereby sharing much in terms of geographic, economic, socio-cultural and political heritage – their composition includes various caste groups (including Jats, Khatris, Brahmins, Chuhras and Chamars). However, the overall salience of caste distinctions among Punjabis in Britain, and in India itself, is arguably less marked than those associated with other regional social structures (Sharma 1969).

Among British Gujaratis, in contrast, there are many significant levels or spheres of differentiation. 'It is almost impossible to talk about the "Gujaratis" in Britain as an undifferentiated category', Maureen Michaelson (1984: 2) writes, 'since there are several points of cleavage which divide different groups of Gujaratis and which make co-operation between them minimal or difficult to achieve.' Most generally, distinct regions of origin within the modern state of Gujarat are associated in Britain with distinct cultural characteristics and, thereby, with separate social groups. British Gujaratis hail from parts of Surat and Charotar (Kaira) on the mainland, and from Saurashtra (Kathiawad) and Kutch further west. Linked to a large extent with linguistic traits (given over twenty varieties of Gujarati language), there is often considerable social differentiation among Gujaratis, such as that between Kathiawadis and Surtis (Knott 1994) and between Kutchis and mainland Gujaratis (Logan 1988). Kutchis, for example, purposefully utilize their language 'to distinguish themselves as a category apart from other Gujarati groups' (Barot 1980: 124).

Also among British Gujaratis, there exist important characteristics and developments with regard to 'East Africans' v. 'Indians'. One consequential source of difference arose through the migration process itself. As mentioned, the original 'Indian' migrants to Britain came as individuals, usually young males who only at a later stage were joined by their wives and children. The 'East Africans', who were essentially refugees, arrived as complete multi-generational family units. Not only has this meant that the age structure of the two groups varies considerably, but 'The presence of elders and an accepted authority structure among the "Africans" has led to greater cohesion in the latter population and a greater acceptance of traditional Indian values' (Michaelson 1983: 31). Furthermore, with extensive implications for social organization in the British context:

> 'Indian' chain migration meant that immigration was on a more individualistic basis, and that while there are ties of kinship, village of origin, and caste between the 'Indians', they do not have the pre-existing strong and multiplex historical, kinship, political and economic links such as exist within the 'African' population.
>
> (ibid.)

With regard to these social identities, too, stereotypes among and between the groups persist. 'East Africans' are usually associated with higher educational and occupational backgrounds than Indians (Modood *et al.* 1997). This trait has been subsequently equated with greater status and wealth. The East African Asians' supposed longer and deeper acquaintance with the English language and with urban, middle-class 'European' (albeit colonial) lifestyles has connoted a better preparation for successful living in Britain. Though it would be difficult to prove the validity of all such traits, they remain common stereotypes that determine much by way of attitudes and social formations.

Yet 'East African' can be quite a misnomer when one considers the fact that large numbers of Gujaratis migrated to Kenya, Uganda and elsewhere in the region only after World War II. Thus their 'Indian' roots are as strong as those of the ones who came to Britain directly, yet they share experiences with those who were settled in East Africa for generations (Eriksen 1984). The same must be recognized for Punjabis as well (Ballard 1986). Moreover, a number of those born and raised in East Africa – regardless of actual place of birth or upbringing – maintained many pervasive ties of religion, kinship, caste and economy with India. The nineteenth-century and post-World War II migrations to East Africa, however, were largely by persons from different areas of Gujarat (the former mainly from Saurasthra and Kutch, the latter from Churottar and Surat), which had an important bearing on their linguistic and caste make-up, cultural practices and social institutions both in East Africa and, now, in Britain.

Within East Africa, there were important differences among Gujaratis too (see Pocock 1957; Bharati 1972). For instance, Carmen Voigt-Graf (1998) and Richa Nagar (1997) each point out the caste and class complexities of Hindu group differentiation in the relatively small population of Gujarati Hindus in Tanzania. Social differentiation among Gujaratis prevailed even among the same caste group. Due to a number of socio-geographic distinctions (including localized status hierarchies and different levels of education and urbanization), different 'kinds' of Patels or Patidars migrated from the end of the nineteenth century to Kenya and Uganda. Their self- and other-attributed characteristics, especially surrounding status, were perpetuated for generations following discrete marriage circles back to their villages of origin in Gujarat. 'Therefore,' conclude Pravin Patel and Mario Rutten (1999: 953):

> most of those who came from Kenya to the UK were relatively better-off and higher status Patels than many of

those who came from Uganda. Moreover, the Patels of big villages who had migrated earlier to Kenya also had a stronger tradition of retaining linkages back home than those who came later and settled in Uganda due to various socio-historical reasons. This different tradition of maintaining linkages back home in India seems to be reflected in these two groups even in the UK.

Gujarat is well known in the subcontinent for the number, complexity and distinctiveness of caste and sub-caste groups, and the same can be said for Gujarati caste phenomena in Britain. Michaelson (1983) notes the presence of at least thirty distinct Gujarati castes in Britain, each with a specific provenance in India. These prominently include Patidars from Surat and Charottar, Lohanas and Visa Halari Oshwals from Kathiawad, Bhattias and Leva Kanbi Patels from Kutch (cf. Pocock 1976; Barot 1980). Although in East Africa and in Britain – as throughout the South Asian diaspora (and described in Chapter 1) – a caste *system* could no longer govern social, economic, ritual, or other relationships, caste *identities* among Gujaratis have continued to be of considerable importance with regard to status, marriage, social networks and formal institutions. Caste has also played a major role in differentially reproducing and transforming socio-religious phenomena in Britain.

Disparate religious traditions among British Hindus derive from diverse regional, caste and sectarian origins. Differences of religious heritage between regions in India reflect varying histories involving the presence of certain *sampradays* or sects, revivalist or reformist movements, contact with Islam and with other major religious traditions (including Buddhism, Jainism, Sikhism). Within a given region, sacred geographies and pilgrimage sites devoted to specific, sometimes parochial, deities make for further variance in popular religious orientations and traditions. This is compounded, in addition, by the local or provincial prevalence of certain castes and sub-castes, sometimes holding their own unique beliefs, practices, or sectarian attachments. Such diversity is reproduced in several ways within Britain.

Although most persons in Britain who regard themselves as Hindu recognize many of the same special days in an 'All-Hindu calendar', several festivals, periods of fasting, and other times of religious significance are additionally prescribed given one's place of origin (see Nesbitt 1987; McDonald 1987; Logan 1988; and Chapter 6). Modes of celebrating such holy days or periods vary by region and district of origin, even given an event mutually recognized (such as Diwali, Navratri, Janashtami).

Further, the regional and caste-based differences exist not only with regard to annual religious observances (particularly celebrated by caste associations) but also to the number, form, and importance of certain rites of passage and other domestic religious practices.

The presence of identifiable doctrinal or devotional traditions (again, many of which have regional and caste-based affiliations) further complicates the British Hindu make-up. These include three rival divisions of the Swaminarayani *sampradaya*, along with Arya Samajis, Radhasoamis, Pushtimargis (Vallabhacharyas), and people with special devotion towards the Mother Goddess, Sathya Sai Baba, Shirdi Sai Baba, Santoshi Ma, Baba Balak Nath, or Jalaram Bapa. What are sometimes called 'neo-Hindu' movements are also prevalent in Britain, having both South Asian and indigenous British membership; these include the Ramakrishna Mission, Brahma Kumaris, Brahmo Samaj, various yoga and meditation associations, and, importantly, the International Society for Krishna Consciousness (ISKCON) often known as 'Hare Krishnas'.

There are also what might be called regional-minority communities – including Bengalis, Tamils and Telugus, Indo-Caribbeans, Indo-Mauritians and Indo-Fijians – with their own styles and focuses of worship (see Chapters 5 and 6). Further, in Britain, there are South Asian religious communities or local populations which 'blur the boundaries' (Nesbitt 1987: 4) between what are often commonly thought to be discrete traditions, particularly between Jains and Hindus (Michaelson 1984) and between Sikhs and Hindus (notably represented by Valmikis and Ravidasis; Nesbitt 1989). And even though generally both Punjabi and Gujarati religious cultures at large are steeped in Vaishnavism, one can witness a greater emphasis on Rama and the Ramayana as a core text in the former, and on Krishna and the Bhagavata Purana in the latter. It is the presence of such varied religious traditions and orientations that gives rise to questions regarding reproduction and representation.

Facets of reproduction

Here, I use 'reproduction' to refer to two identifiable, but not necessarily unconnected, cultural processes among migrant or diaspora communities. The first is that of cultural transmission between generations, whereby, through 'messages sent and received at different levels of consciousness' (Nesbitt 1987: 8), children and young people learn and gain competence in manifold kinds of group-specific knowledge, action, and 'disposition'. After Pierre Bourdieu (1977: 214):

> The word *disposition* seems particularly suited to express what is covered by the habitus (defined as a system of dispositions). It expresses first the *result of an organizing action*, with a meaning close to that of words such as structure; it also designates a *way of being, a habitual state* (especially of the body) and, in particular, a *predisposition, tendency, propensity*, or *inclination*.
>
> (italics in original)

The second sense of reproduction invoked here is that of institutionalization, or the organization and routinization of certain roles, relationships, meanings and symbols stemming from a desire to ensure their continuity (from context-to-context – here, pre- and post-migration, but also from generation-to-generation and from day-to-day). This notion is employed in its Weberian sense, which S.N. Eisenstadt (1968: xxxix) summarizes, in part, as 'the capacity to create and crystallize . . . broader symbolic orientations and norms, to articulate various goals, to establish organizational frameworks, and to mobilize the resources necessary for all these purposes'.

It might be said that the foremost environment for cultural transmission in any social group is the domestic sphere, and this is no different concerning 'religious nurture' among British Hindus (Jackson 1985; Nesbitt 1987). Much of what is observed to be domestic Hinduism in India and Britain involves the beliefs and practices of women in the household (McDonald 1987). Indeed, Sandra M. Wilkinson (1994: 63) found, 'British Hindu women are unmistakably the sustaining and dynamic force behind the perpetuation and transmission of traditional religious practices in the home.' Penny Logan (1988: 122) describes some of the many ways this is achieved:

> The child's mother is the most significant figure in this process, but other women, such as the paternal grandmother or aunt, may also be important, especially if they live in the household or nearby. It is they who show the children how to perform *puja* or let them learn by participating; teach them prayers; explain what to eat and how to fast; tell

or read them stories of the deities and show them how to celebrate festivals. It also tends to be women who answer children's questions and decide that they should attend *satsangs* [religious gatherings], discourses, cultural performances and the temple.

Furthermore, since the domestic sphere is where the greater part of the religious activity occurs among Hindus in Britain, Logan (ibid.: 8) observes that 'most children gain the bulk of their knowledge of Hinduism at home, from women, particularly through observation of and participation in ritual' (see also Jackson and Nesbitt 1993). This accounts for her findings regarding the religious knowledge of British Hindu children:

> The first, and most important, point to make is that it centres on practice, rather than on belief. The children are very good at describing what they do or what is done, particularly when it comes to their familiar household rituals . . . The children's knowledge of myths, the reasons for celebrating particular festivals and theological concepts is weaker than their command of ritual practice. Certainly these represent gaps in their knowledge, but then it is probably the case that the same could be said of many Hindu adults. Moreover, their greater knowledge of practice merely reflects the nature of much of popular Hinduism.
>
> (Logan 1988: 123–4)

The traditions associated with provenance, sect, and social group or caste are those which largely condition these popular, domestic forms of practice. Therefore, at present, Hindu reproduction by way of cultural transmission or religious nurture in Britain is dominated by widely varying features reflecting the diverse social and geographic origins of the South Asians.

Regarding reproduction by institutionalization, a more complicated pattern is emerging (which, as described in the next section, has much to do with processes of representation as well). Bowen (1987) has outlined three phases of institutional development among British Hindus which, although initially intended to describe the evolution of the Gujarati population in Bradford, may serve to characterize processes on the national scale. 'Taken together, the phases entail a dialectic between homogeneity and heterogeneity, unity and diversity' (ibid.: 15; cf. Dahya 1974).

The first phase pertains especially to the period in which the British Asian population was comprised predominantly of young male migrants. Since the number of migrants was relatively few, living and working conditions dire, and racism and discrimination unabated, most migrants desired a routinization of mutual networks for moral support and sociality along with some collective 'cultural' activity, no matter how artificial or 'watered down'. Hence in the late 1950s and early 1960s, some loosely-knit associations or committees were formed locally in various cities around Britain, particularly functioning to organize for all – regardless of area, sect or social group/caste of origin – modest celebrations of important 'All-India Hindu' holy days (Diwali, Navratri, etc.)

The second phase witnessed the growth of diverse regional-linguistic, sectarian, and caste associations. Towards the end of the 1960s, coinciding with the reunion of husbands with their wives and children, there had been a marked growth in the number of persons from distinct regions, sects and castes in each locale around Britain. This growth in numbers was also marked by much 'secondary migration' within Britain, leading to geographically self-segregated groups within the British Asian populations, particularly regional ones (see Jackson and Smith 1981; Robinson 1986). The growth of regional, sectarian and caste communities in given locales combined importantly with individuals' concerns about social, cultural, and religious provisions for – that is, reproduction among – their newly established families (who now especially developed views on their children's future in an alien environment). These factors led directly to the establishment of numerous, group-specific associations and institutions. Also, many people arriving from East Africa in the late 1960s and early 1970s had gained considerable experience there in organizing and maintaining caste, sectarian, and other communal organizations (see Morris 1968); such experience was quickly utilized to create or expand similar associations after settlement in Britain. This phase of particularistic institutionalization has continued with momentum to the present day: from but a handful of Hindu associations dotting the map of Britain in the early 1960s, according to the Religious Resource and Research Centre of the University of Derby, there are now some 737 Hindu organizations of many kinds spread over at least 146 British towns and cities and boroughs of Greater London.

Many associations were set up with a view to providing or co-ordinating religious activity – ideally and ultimately, to raise funds towards, to establish, and to manage a temple or centre which could also function as a place of worship. Initially, specific devotional groups met in private homes, 'serving in a sense as congregations without temples' (Burghart 1987a: 9). A temple in Coventry, founded by Hindus from Kenya in 1967, is reputed to be Britain's first formal place of Hindu worship (Tambs-Lyche 1975). Currently the Religious Resource and Research Centre lists 303 places of Hindu worship across the country.

The establishment of temples in Britain has been a major source of social, cultural and religious reproduction, yet it has also entailed many significant kinds of change as well. This has included fundamental changes in the role and status of priests (Barot 1987a), and in the frequency and procedure of key rituals – especially in temples which have arisen through 'negotiation' among people from different regional origins (Knott 1986b, 1987; Nye 1991, 1995). Temples in Britain are valued by their users not only for providing a source for the accumulation of spiritual merit (*punya*) through devotional worship and service (*puja*, *seva*), but they also may be the arenas for enacting more secular aspects of communal compliance and status acquisition, the latter particularly by way of publicly presented donations (cf. Barot 1973, 1987a). Temples are also significant contexts for the reproduction of religious practices, especially as this is where children learn many basic ritual acts and modes of behaviour (Dwyer 1988). Although a number of 'generalized Hindu' temples and associations exist, the great majority are characterized by regional and sectarian/devotional orientations.

Major regional orientations (by way of distinctions concerning both language and specific traditions surrounding a focus of worship) are reflected in the names of organizations such as: the Bharata Mandal – Gujarati Samaj, Surrey Gujarati Hindu Society, Punjabi Hindu Society, Panduranga Hindu Temple, and Ram Nivas – Gujat Vaishnav Mandal (and similarly for the non-Gujarati/Punjabi, 'regional minority' populations; for example, the Maharashtra Mandal, London Tamil Society, Caribbean Hindu Society, and Fiji Sanatan Dharam Ramayan Mandli Leeds). Other regional orientations are not so clear, although the names may suggest such: for example, one may associate names like Shree Vishwa Hindu Mandir and Shri Ram Mandir as reflecting a largely Punjabi membership, and Radha-Krishna Temple, Shri Krishna Mandir, and Shri Gita Bhavan Mandir to be largely Gujarati.

Sampradayas and other devotional traditions are evident in names like: Sri Sathya Sai Centre, Shri Nathji Temple, Vedic Mission Arya Samaj, Jalaram Prathna Mandal, and Balmiki Adi Bir Vir Mahasabha (further, region and *sampradaya* may even be combined such as with the Shree Kutch Satsan Swaminarayan Temple).

In addition to the large number of associations organized for specifically religious purposes, the number of caste associations has proliferated dramatically since the 1960s. It was particularly in East Africa where, for a number of reasons, a process of 'communal crystallisation' (Morris 1968: 34) took place through which mainly Gujarati caste groups created and elaborated formal caste associations to oversee collective social and political, as well as religious, interests. It is especially such East African Gujarati-derived caste associations that currently abound in Britain (see Michaelson 1979, 1983). Of the 737 existing associations among British Hindus mentioned above, no less than 90 have specifically caste-based names (and doubtless more are assumed under other, more general 'Hindu' or 'Gujarati' appellation. Caste associations in Britain are organized on both a local and national scale in order to hold regular or annual gatherings, to celebrate religious festivals, and to produce detailed directories of members. Further, the workings of caste associations assist in the arrangement of marriage and act to maintain links of many kinds with villages and regions in the subcontinent.

Local caste associations have names such as: the Shri Gurjar Kshatriya Gnati Mandal, the Charotar Patidar Samaj, Chovis Gam Patidar Samaj, Shree Lohana Mohajan. Some examples of UK-wide bodies linking such local associations are: the National Council of Banik Associations, the National Association of Patidar Samaj, the Shree Sorathia Prajapati Community, the Saree Limbachia Hittechhu Mandal, the Leuva [*sic*] Patidar Samaj (S.N.B) of UK, and the Federation of Anavil Samajes (UK).

The third phase characterizing institutional development is that marked by the formation of 'umbrella' organizations. So far few actually exist, on either national or local levels, which operate very effectively to undertake or to co-ordinate Hindu activities, or to express and to safeguard common interests, across the board of regional, sectarian and caste groups. The National Council of Hindu Temples (UK) is one body created in an attempt to provide these services. Some ninety temples and societies are directly affiliated to the Council. Among its endeavours, the Council has been known to use its network to raise funds in one city so as to help found a temple in another (Barot 1987a). It also publishes a quarterly newsletter and sponsors large-scale weekend 'Hindu Youth Festivals' (involving sport and games, dance, music and drama, lectures and discussions), drawing young people from around the country. Despite its broad network, however, some Punjabis complain that the Council appears Gujarati-dominated, that it seems to favour Gujarati temples and organizations, and that, therefore, its name should be changed to reflect a regional bias.

Such problems are found locally as well. David Bowen (1981: 45–7) observes that within Bradford's Hindu Cultural Society, the office-bearers hail from all over India; moreover, it 'does not set out to cater exclusively for any particular section of Bradford's Hindu community' and therefore 'has articulated its own view of itself as an "umbrella association" for all the Hindus in the area'. Nevertheless,

> the Hindu Cultural Society of Bradford does not draw regular substantial support from the Gujarati community – because of differences of language, Bradford's own urban geography, the settlement patterns of the South Asian migration to Bradford, and subtle regional characteristics. There does not appear to have been any policy of deliberate exclusion on the one side or of deliberate disassociation on the other, but those potent cultural and social factors have taken their toll.

These examples demonstrate different dimensions of how, when the scope of Hindu reproduction becomes broader, serious questions of representation arise.

A final facet of reproduction also throws up important, related issues regarding the representation of 'Hinduism' in Britain: that of religious education, both in the sense of 'formal religious nurture' provided by supplementary classes on offer from various organizations, and in the sense of Religious Education (RE) as offered in British state schools. These are described in the following section, along with other sources, arenas, and subsequent formulations involving processes of representation.

Facets of representation

In Britain there are a host of individual and institutional agents, both within and outside the South Asian community, who – although involved in varying discourses – assume or propound certain unitary representations of Hinduism. Each of these operate in different ways, but all have effects on the nature and content of identity in relation to symbolic boundary formation, social interaction, 'community' relations, and resource allocation. This section looks at some of these kinds and implications of representation.

Broad-based organizations

Formal organizations promulgate the most clearly defined representations of 'Hinduism' in Britain. The National Council of Hindu Temples (UK), in virtually everything it does, assumes or declares Hindu commonality. Suggesting that 'all Hindus' believe, understand, and do the same things, the Council has produced a pamphlet entitled 'Hinduism: An Introduction to the World's Oldest Living Religion'. The pamphlet is portrayed as 'the authoritative statement on the tenets of the Hindu religion, confident that you will gain from it a true and clear understanding of the oldest religious tradition in the world'. Though well meaning, and containing many statements which few believers would dispute, the booklet propounds a wholly Krishnaite orientation (cf. Burghart 1987b).

The Vishwa Hindu Parishad (VHP) – which has emerged as a prominent force of 'Hindu communalism' in India – is now well established in Britain with at least fifteen reported branches (see Knott 1986a; Jackson and Nesbitt 1993; Bhatt 1997). One of its most prominent manifestations came by way of sponsoring the 'Virat Hindu Sammelan' ('Great Hindu Gathering') attended by tens of thousands at the Milton Keynes Bowl in 1989. This event, together with its large souvenir booklet, promoted the kind of understanding of 'Hinduism' and 'Hindu community' one would associate with the VHP. In one article in the booklet we read of 'the Hindu race', and that

> In fact the word Hindu ought to be understood in the context of the nationhood sense and not in the limited religious sense
> . . . 'Hindu' is the name of a group of human beings who enter the world polity as one unity distinct from all others
> . . . Our political and cultural interests on the international plane are common, our friends are common and our foes are also common.
>
> (Sharma 1989: 94)

In 1985, a comparable event called the 'Cultural Festival of India' was held over the course of one month at the Alexandra Palace in north London. It was organized by the Bochasanwasi Shree Akshar Purushottam Sanstha, a branch of the Swaminarayan *sampradaya*.

According to the Festival Guide, 'The objective was, [first], to present the glory of India in its pristine purity to the new generation of Asians and to the British People'; it was, secondly, an attempt to create cultural understanding and harmony' (Brear 1986: 23). The 'general motive, however, was crystallized into the particular one of showing how the religion of Lord Swaminarayan (who was "the Supreme God Himself") inherits this ancient richness and focuses it' (ibid.: 24). Similarly, Logan (1988: 74) concluded that 'the exhibition had a distinct bias towards Gujarati Vaishnavism'.

The International Society for Krishna Consciousness (ISKCON) has assumed an exceptional place among British Hindus, particularly the majority East African Gujaratis (Carey 1987). Although the prime movers of ISKCON are white converts, British Asians usually show great respect for the strength of ISKCON members' devotion, their knowledge of Sanskrit, their strict vegetarianism, and their elaborate, detailed rituals (this view is paralleled among Hindus in the United States; see Williams 1988; Zaidman 1997). ISKCON's magazine *Back to Godhead* is widely read by Indians. Its *Bhagavad-gita As It Is* – a translation and commentary of this key Krishnaite text written by ISKCON's founder, Bhaktivedanta Swami Prabhupada – is perhaps the most common translation of the Bhagavad-gita found in Britain (it is, in fact, the version quoted in the National Council of Hindu Temples' pamphlet on 'Hinduism'). Malory Nye (1996) has suggested that ISKCON had become so involved with influencing the transformational course of British Hinduism that it is fair to talk of a contemporary process of 'Iskconization'. It is likely that ISKCON's greatest impact will continue to be on Asians born and raised in this country. Carey (1983: 481) foresees this because 'the enthusiastic preaching of the devotees, backed up by an abundance of pamphlets outlining the need for vegetarianism and the perils of drink, and good English-language translation of classical texts, all go a long way in providing a clear set of moral and ethical directives and a robust religious sensibility'. Such a development underscores the importance of representations directed particularly at young people.

Formal religious nurture

Over 40 per cent of Indians in Britain are born in the United Kingdom. Because they are growing up in Britain, instead of in an Indian context steeped in Hindu religious traditions, Robert Jackson (1985:71) suggests:

many Hindu youngsters are confused because they lack an adequate conceptual framework within which to set their practical knowledge and experience in such a way that they can make sense of Hinduism both to themselves and to outsiders. This state of affairs partly explains the rise of more formal methods of transmitting Hindu values and ideas which have emerged in recent years among various Hindu organizations including caste and sectarian associations.

Heightened awareness of this situation led, at one point, to an unsuccessful campaign among some British Asians to establish their own, state-supported, Hindu school (Kanitkar 1979). Its suggested name – Vivekananda Hindu High School – and proposed ethos surrounding the approach and message of Vivekananda interestingly reflects unitary and universalist 'neo-Hindu' assumptions which, as we have seen, arose in the recent history of India and have become of central importance to many throughout the diaspora.

The year 1992 saw the opening of the independent (self-funding) Swaminarayan School in Neasden, west London. The school is located across the street from the spectacular Shri Swaminarayan Mandir. While the school is completely supported and managed by the mandir, its accompanying ashram and school-focused boards of trustees and governors, the British National Curriculum is taught there so it is open to both local and national school inspectors. At its opening the Swaminarayan School had but 70 students; currently there are some 350 in its preparatory (ages 3–11) and senior (ages 11–16+) levels. In addition to National Curriculum subjects, the school offers Gujarati language (compulsory from age 11, along with French) and two lessons per week on Hinduism. Indian classical music and folk dance is also taught. Daily assemblies drawing on sacred scriptures, daily prayers, the celebration of yearly religious festivals and a vegetarian cafeteria contribute to an encompassing Hindu ethos. All teaching is in English.

The meaning of 'Hinduism' conveyed at the Swaminarayan School – despite the fact that the institution is founded and managed by a specific *sampradaya* – is rather broad. Students gain a view that Hinduism encompasses many teachings and values, that God had many incarnations and that other religions were founded by messengers of the same God. However, Vaishnavism is presented as central to the meaning of Hinduism, and of course Swaminarayan teachings are described as an important part of this. The teaching materials for the courses on Hinduism, at all ages, are extremely varied – mostly arising from the *sampradaya* itself or other sources all in India. These include comic books, videos, Bollywood films and translated epics. Not least, much of the curriculum on Hinduism is influenced by the textbook *Explaining Hindu Dharma: A Guide for Teachers*, produced by the Vishwa Hindu Parishad UK (Prinja 1996).

Supplementary classes for young Hindus are offered by numerous Hindu organizations around Britain. Taking place in temples, community centres, schools and private homes, these have become the major source of 'formal religious nurture' among Hindus (Jackson 1987; Dwyer 1988; Jackson and Nesbitt 1986, 1993). Usually the nature and content of the classes differ considerably due to the given organization's sectarian emphasis as well as its main members' region of origin in India, caste composition, general level of formal education and migration history. Prayers, devotional songs, sacred texts, dances and dramas comprise the main elements of teaching in Hindu supplementary schools. Often this takes place alongside Indian language teaching (usually Gujarati, Punjabi or Hindi). Yet while regional, sectarian, and caste traditions are being reproduced in such classes as well as through informal religious nurture at home,

> some of those communities which provide formal Hindu nurture for children – whether they are conscious of it or not – seem to be presenting young people with a more conceptual and unitary view of Hinduism than that gained less formally.
>
> Sometimes this view seems to sit uncomfortably with the picture of the tradition gained elsewhere. Other times the two pictures appear complementary, with various formal approaches providing a conceptual framework and a clear set of moral guidelines which, for young people spanning two cultures, provides the means to give intelligibility to the Hindu tradition.
>
> (Jackson 1985: 73)

Young British Asians, together with their white peers, are also influenced by the picture of 'Hinduism' taught within Religious Education courses in state schools. Since the mid-1970s, most Local Education Authority (LEA) Agreed Syllabuses for Religious Education have come to place a strong emphasis on increasing pupils' knowledge and understanding of several 'world faiths', including 'Hinduism'. Although in many cases such efforts were somewhat ill-conceived at first, by the mid-1980s considerable thought had gone into sensitively portraying 'Hinduism' in the classroom. This has included efforts to recognize the great variety of traditions within the rubric, as well as to be aware of the fact that the version of 'Hinduism' taught in school may differ significantly from the regional, sectarian and caste traditions in which Asian children participate at home and at the temple (Jackson 1984; Killingley *et al.* 1984). Nevertheless, differences among and between LEAs, schools and teachers has meant that, across the country, RE teaching is very uneven. The result is often a picture of 'Hinduism' which is over-simplified, over-generalized, and riddled with factual errors (Jackson 1987, Logan 1988).

Public representation

A singular and rather stereotyped view of 'Hinduism' and 'Hindus' in British society is often found, with a range of consequences, in other spheres as well. For example, Knott (1986b: 53) points out:

> The South Asian population in this country is generally identified in two ways by the government, the press, the Church and community relations bodies. One is as 'Indians, Pakistanis and Bangladeshis' (commonly called 'Asians'), and the other is as 'Hindus, Sikhs and Muslims'. In Leeds, local bodies use this second system of classification for their interactions with the South Asian population, and as a result it is the representative religious bodies which have been authorised to receive local government urban aid and deprivation grants for the ethnic groups.

Such an assumption, by state administrations, of communal unity among ethnic groups has been seen to generate a host of conflicts which can be ultimately dysfunctional for a group in terms of the use of resources, leadership, and collective mobilization (Werbner 1991a; Vertovec 1996b).

Yet it is largely simplified and generalized representations of 'Hinduism' which are formulated and promoted by many British Asian organizations themselves. These representations are often symbolized in the names of institutions themselves: of the 737 associations reported, 105 (14 per cent) have generalized 'Hindu' names. In cities around Britain these include names such as: Sanatan Mandal, Shree Sanatan Dharma Sabha, Bhakti Mandal, Bharat Sevashram

Sangha, Bharat Hindu Samaj, Hindu Religious and Cultural Society, or simply Hindu Temple, Hindu Society, or Hindu Centre. Such names, of course, may mask the actual regional-linguistic or caste composition of an association. For instance, Bowen (1987: 24) learned that Bradford's Shree Hindu Temple was founded and largely maintained by Gujarati Prajapatis. Nonetheless, the choice of such a name remains significant with regard to how they choose to see themselves and/or depict themselves to others – Asian and white.

In addition, many organizations (even those with clearly regional or sectarian orientations) publish circulars, newsletters, pamphlets and booklets that are filled with articles and statements regarding what 'Hinduism' is and what 'Hindus' believe. Virtually all of these are drawn from, or are reformulations of, the '-ism' which emerged in the nineteenth and early twentieth centuries (as described in Chapter 1, including its rationalized neo-Vedanta combined with Puranic understandings, Sanskritic deities – with an emphasis on Vaishnavism – approached through *bhakti* yet linked with monotheism, and so on). This is also evident in the common use of, interchangeably with 'Hinduism', the Sanskrit term 'Sanatan Dharm' (or 'Sanatana Dharma', depending on transliteration). In this context 'Sanatan Dharm is stripped of the socio-political connotations it gathered in India during the late nineteenth and early twentieth centuries; instead, it is employed as a wholly "neutral term"' (Knott 1986b: 78). Kim Knott's (1987: 163–4) study in Leeds exemplifies much regarding processes of representing Hinduism throughout Britain:

> In the temple 'Sanatana Dharma' is held to be a system which incorporates all Hindus, irrespective of ethnic or sectarian divisions. It symbolizes temple religion: it is hailed in one of the final verses of the *arti* service with the phrase 'Sanatana Dharma *ki jay*' ['victory to']; it is the focus of dialogue with other faiths . . . The content of those religious practices which take place in the temple – which form part of 'Sanatana Dharma' – reveals the dynamics of this process, the development towards this new and standardized form of Hinduism.

As noted throughout this book, the growing prominence of a generalized 'Hinduism' or 'Sanatan Dharm' is found throughout the diaspora.

Like the 'Hinduism' which emerged in India, that of Indians in diaspora settings such as Britain has been formulated and utilized *vis-à-vis* 'an Other' – or more correctly, in the latter case, 'Others'. It is this development in contexts abroad that has accented the emergent 'Hinduism' as an ethnic phenomenon.

Conclusion: 'ethnic Hinduism' in Britain

The identifications, status attributions, and practices of groups *vis-à-vis* one another, by way of both self- and other-ascribed criteria, essentially amount to what we often describe as 'ethnic' dynamics. What we might call '*vis-à-vis* dynamics' entail an increasing collective self-consciousness, as members of groups become aware of how others see them, and as they come to realize and to articulate how they wish to see themselves (as socio-cultural, economic, and political actors) in new or changing contexts. As we have seen in both the Indian and British contexts, notions of 'Hinduism' and 'Hindu community' have arisen through such dynamics and their stimulation of collective self-consciousness.

Throughout most daily interactions with whites in Britain, '*vis-à-vis* dynamics' usually entail self-consciousness in terms of 'Black' and 'Asian' criteria (while within the 'Asian' populations, there are also '*vis-à-vis* dynamics' relating to a host of segmentary identities surrounding Indian language and region, caste, extended family group, village and so forth). Yet among Hindus and other Asian people with devout religious inclinations in Britain, there is a further, important '*vis-à-vis* dynamic' stimulated by facets of an environment at once oddly both religiously plural by way of harbouring numerous religious communities, and overwhelmingly secular in terms of its public institutions, culture and ethos.

Thus in the course of Logan's (1988: 124) research, 'many adults reported that they had become more aware of their religion in Britain, as a result of belonging to a minority group in a predominantly irreligious society. They could no longer take their religion and their children's assumption of it for granted.' Their collective self-awareness '*vis-à-vis*' Christianity and secularism, as it were, takes precedence over their regional, sectarian and caste '*vis-à-vis* dynamics'. Therefore, 'In becoming a self-conscious tradition in a new location,' Knott (1987: 165) writes, 'the vernacular has given way to the pan-Indian, diversity has given way to a unified system of belief and practice, and ethnic [regional] identity has given way to "community".' It is a process compounded through being approached as a single 'community', by various state, educational, religious (Christian and inter-faith) and other public bodies – and by common understandings of white British. British Hindus are being represented, and are increasingly representing themselves, as a single 'faith': at the same time they are moving (albeit at differential paces) towards reproducing themselves as a 'community' (cf. Baumann 1996). Hence, Burghart (1987b: 233) concludes, 'The cultural awareness of Hindus has been sharpened in an alien cultural milieu, and they are ready to believe – as many non-Hindus do – that Hinduism is an ethnic religion.' Still, however, it is regional, sectarian and caste-specific traditions that are continuing to be reproduced in domestic and local community spheres: therefore, conflict and confusion persist. This will likely give way as new generations are inculcated with the generalized representations of 'Hinduism' promulgated by broad-based associations and state schools.

Religion supplies criteria wholly unlike other criteria (social actions, cultural forms, economic activities) to which groups refer by way of positioning themselves in relation to one another. For the social scientist, religious phenomena are approached as historically conditioned socio-cultural constructs open to re-definition, re-configuration, and re-institutionalization of symbols and social forms in light of shifting contexts. For the religious adherents, transcendent, sacred notions concerning cosmology and soteriology are regarded as a-historical in content and ultimate in authority. Therefore we should not lose sight of the fact that although 'Hinduism' appears largely to be a relatively recent construct in India and Britain, for those who regard themselves as Hindus this by no means diminishes any of its personal and collective power. Its reformulated symbols and institutions have taken on new roles, in different times and places, as ultimate reference points for identity.

5

CATEGORY AND QUANDARY
Indo-Caribbean Hindus in Britain

To be an Indian or East Indian from the West Indies is to be a perpetual surprise to people outside the region.

(Naipaul 1972: 33)

The great majority of Britain's best-known group of South Asian 'twice migrants' – people of Gujarati and Punjabi origin who came to Britain from East Africa during the late l960s and early 1970s – swiftly took advantage of the social networks and cultural institutions already established by their counterparts who had migrated directly from India to Britain. Besides ensuring that the newcomers tended to cluster in places where settlers with regional and religious origins similar to themselves were already established, these patterns also ensured that the 'twice migrants'' links with the subcontinent would continue to influence the subsequent course of their adaptation and identification.

However, a second group of 'twice migrants' arrived in Britain at much the same time by way of the Caribbean. Indo-Caribbeans, whose very existence is still often overlooked, faced – and still face – a much more perplexing situation. They had lived long as a community away from India, their regional and linguistic origins in the subcontinent were different and they had had some distinctive experiences as overseas settlers (Chapters 2 and 3). As a result, they felt they had no connection with, and indeed were often discouraged from participating in, the networks and institutions dominated by direct migrants from India. Their almost complete severance from the subcontinent, which had been initiated in the middle of the nineteenth century, meant that their 'Indian-ness' often seemed open to question. This chapter explores these and other aspects of the unique ethnic quandary in which Indo-Caribbeans, particularly Hindus, have found themselves since settling in Britain.

The roots of this problem can be found in a confusion of categories surrounding social boundaries, cultural practices and racial traits. Whites, taking no cognizance of distinctive accents, styles and mannerisms, tend to lump Indo-Caribbeans into the generalized category labelled 'Asian'. Even when aware of Indo-Caribbeans' differing backgrounds, most white people still make the generalization that Indo-Caribbeans are 'Asian' because this is how they look. Yet there are other circumstances in which Indo-Caribbeans fall into a quite different social category. Not least, for official purposes they may well be 'West Indians' because the West Indies was where they were born.

Meanwhile those South Asian settlers who have come to Britain either directly or by way of East Africa also tend to perceive Indo-Caribbeans as an enigmatic group. Though physically similar to themselves, Indo-Caribbeans often talk, dress and act in unexpected ways. Hence for many Indians from India, confrontation with a hitherto unknown but unremarkable fact – that some people of Indian descent have lived for generations in the Caribbean – initiates confusion about how one should react to long-lost cousins. This is highlighted in V.S. Naipaul's (1972: 30) description of an encounter in an airport lounge:

There was another Indian in the lounge
'You are coming from –?'
I had met enough Indians from India to know that this was less a serious inquiry than a greeting, in a distant land, from one Indian to another.
'Trinidad,' I said. 'In the West Indies. And you?'
He ignored my question. 'But you look Indian.'
'I am.'
'Red Indian?' He suppressed a nervous little giggle.
'East Indian. From the West Indies.'
He looked offended and wandered off to the bookstall. From this distance he eyed me assessingly.

While Indo-Caribbeans are regularly identified as 'Asians' by most whites – and similarly regularly subjected to racial discrimination – they are often simultaneously excluded (or at best regarded as a low-status, adjunct group) on social and cultural grounds by most

other 'Asians'. This leads, in turn, to many Indo-Caribbeans recip-
rocally dissociating themselves from subcontinental Indians. Yet if
most Indo-Caribbeans have strong reservations about unam-
biguously identifying themselves as 'Asian' or Indian in a British
context, most have even less wish to be identified as 'West Indians'
despite their heritage in Trinidad and Guyana.

Most Indo-Caribbeans regard the term 'West Indian' as having
strong Afro-Caribbean connotations, and, quite apart from negative British stereotypes about this group, there is, in the Caribbean
itself, a long history of Indian antipathy towards people of African
descent (see Brereton 1979). Some scholars have suggested that
Indo-Caribbean attitudes towards Blacks can be traced to the association of dark skin with low caste: hence, perhaps the first Africans
encountered in the Caribbean may have been considered to be highly
polluting in traditional Hindu conceptions (Moore 1977). Other
observers of Indian–African antipathy in the Caribbean place most
emphasis on racialized political competition (Ryan 1972; Hintzen
1989) and the former's experiences of structural inequality at the
hands of the latter (see Cross 1978). In any case, there is mutually
little desire for Afro-Caribbeans and Indo-Caribbeans to co-identify
in Britain – except, interestingly, when England plays the West Indies
at cricket. (A trickier matter arises, of course, when India plays the
West Indies!)

How, then, do Indo-Caribbeans in Britain see themselves? To
address this question it is necessary to recall their background,
described in Chapter 2, and to look at the process of immigration
to Britain and subsequent patterns of settlement and adjustment.

Indians in the Caribbean

Indian cultural patterns in the Caribbean have evolved largely in
response to local conditions, in which scale, geography and poverty
have often militated against the successful maintenance of pre-
migration practices (see, for instance, Jayawardena 1968; Ehrlich
1971; Vertovec 1992b). In Jamaica and the smaller islands where
Indians are both widely dispersed and few in number, recognizably Indian phenomena have seldom been retained. Meanwhile in
Trinidad, Guyana and Surinam, where there have long been large
Indian enclaves, recognizably Indian social and cultural features
are much more widespread. Even so, these 'Indian' patterns – which
vary somewhat between the three territories – are the outcome of

processes of inadvertent permutation as well as of conscious manipulation which have taken place over the course of three to five generations. Indian socio-cultural phenomena in the Caribbean therefore tend to be distinctive.

The rites, texts and calendar of Caribbean Hinduism are clearly derived from India's 'Great Tradition', local styles and procedures have acquired a distinctive pattern of their own. The cultural identity of Indo-Caribbean Hindus has thus been forged in an ethnically plural society that has fostered the growth of communal sentiments. While Trinidadian and Guyanese Hindi is now little used by younger people, most of whom have also been heavily influenced by British and American popular cultural styles, Indo-Caribbeans have been strongly influenced by the cultural and linguistic styles of their Afro-Caribbean neighbours, despite the fact that they retain a strong sense of ethnic distinctiveness. This consciousness of Hindu ethnicity has become steadily more politicized since the early 1950s, when rival Indian and African-backed political parties were formed in both Guyana and Trinidad.

In Guyana, the Indian- (mainly Hindu-) dominated People's Progressive Party (PPP) enjoyed two brief periods of power (1953, 1957–64) over the People's National Congress (PNC) – dominated by people of African descent and often backed by Indian Muslims – before being toppled by pressure from the British and US governments. After race riots in 1963 and 1964 in which 150 people were killed, the PNC again assumed power and in 1966 led Guyana to independence. The party remained in control of the state and was known to use intimidation and vote-rigging to consolidate its power. In 1992 the PNC was finally defeated in fair elections, and the PPP eventually came into power under Janet Jagan, wife of the party's founder Cheddi, in 1997.

In Trinidad the Indian-dominated People's Democratic Party (PDC, later the Democratic Labour Party, DLP) was all but indistinguishable from the Sanatan Dharma Maha Sabha, or national Hindu organization. It never tasted governmental power, for the Black- and Indian Muslim-backed People's National Movement (PNM) retained total control from the mid-1950s, through independence in 1962, until 1986. Since 1995 the United National Congress or UNC, considered an Indian party, has been in power under Prime Minister Basdeo Panday. Even today, Indian perceptions of social and economic changes and opportunities in both Guyana and Trinidad have been heavily influenced by long-standing racial-political confrontations.

111

Certainly from independence in Trinidad and Guyana through the 1980s, Indo-Caribbean fears were not groundless. Heavily concentrated in rural areas where poverty and underemployment were rife, Indians in Trinidad and Guyana had the lowest incomes of any ethnic group throughout the 1950s and 1960s, as well as the highest number of unskilled workers and the fewest professionals. Lacking patronage, they were under-represented in the civil service and subjected to blatant discrimination in many other sectors of the job market (Harewood 1971; Graham and Gordon 1977). Since the 1950s they increasingly concentrated on education as a means of achieving social mobility (Cross and Schwartzbaum 1969; Nevadomsky 1983). This particular combination of a strong sense of ethnic identity, a powerful commitment to upward mobility, and a perceived experience of socio-economic and political exclusion and oppression helps to explain the patterns of migration and community development that have emerged among Indo-Caribbeans in Britain.

Migration and settlement in Britain

Indo-Caribbean migrants arrived in Britain as part of the much larger inflow of Caribbean people in the late 1950s and early 1960s. This movement was largely in response to the employment opportunities then available in the United Kingdom (Peach 1968). But although there are many parallels between Indo- and Afro-Caribbean migratory patterns, they differ in several important ways. Despite the disadvantages in Trinidad and Guyana outlined above, Indo-Caribbean migrants tended to have achieved high levels of education and of occupational skill before their migration (cf. Boodhoo and Baksh 1981). Highly motivated Indians often chose to come to Britain to work and study at levels that they perceived as not being available in Guyana and Trinidad because of either a lack of facilities or deliberate racial discrimination. Many migrants claim that their original intention was to move to Britain, work, then return to the Caribbean once they had gained additional educational and professional credentials and had saved some capital.

The 1991 census data provide figures of 17,620 people in the UK who were born in Trinidad and Tobago and 20,478 born in Guyana. Cross-tabulation with stated ethnicity indicates 1,375 Indians born in the former and 2,707 Indians born in the latter. Following the pattern demonstrated in the Labour Force Survey which shows that the total West Indian population is normally about twice that of West Indians by place of birth, we obtain figures of roughly 2,750 Indo-

Trinidadians in Britain and 5,414 Indo-Guyanese, or just over 8,000 Indo-Caribbeans. However, this figure takes no account of unknown numbers of illegal immigrants or of the unknown (albeit very small) number of Indo-Caribbean migrants from Jamaica, Grenada, and St Vincent.

Around three-quarters of this estimated British-Indo Caribbean population lives in the London region. But despite their small numbers, they have not gathered together in a single residential area but are widely spread across the whole region, although with modest concentrations in the south London areas of Balham and Tooting and smaller ones in Brixton and Catford. While most seem to have moved many times since arriving in Britain, nearly all interviewed had simply moved from one part of London to another.

Since the bulk of British Indo-Caribbean migrants came as young adults intending to work and study, most did not have established families back in Trinidad and Guyana whom they planned to support with remittances. Most married only after living in Britain for some time. Their children – unlike those of many other early Asian settlers in Britain – are almost exclusively British-born and -raised.

The early pioneers

Very few of the earliest Indo-Caribbean pioneers came directly to Britain from rural backgrounds. Most had lived for some years in the urban environment of Port of Spain or Georgetown, where they gained higher levels and quality of education than most of their rural compatriots and were able to accumulate the funds needed to finance the journey. Early settlers invariably found it far more difficult to obtain accommodation than a job, for in the mid-1950s 'No Coloureds' signs were still often displayed in the windows of lodging-houses. A number of such houses in the Notting Hill Gate, Earls Court and Hammersmith districts of London were rather more liberal. Due to this fact, or because in these places there were many houses owned by members of other immigrant groups, many of the early Indo-Caribbean migrants initially settled there. Nevertheless racial discrimination was still a major problem at all but the most menial levels of the employment market: 'You couldn't get a civil servant's job,' recalls one Indo-Caribbean early migrant, 'or any job, in fact, that was commensurate with your education.' Hence trained teachers, accountants and administrators often washed dishes, worked on assembly lines or swept the streets.

Nevertheless the pioneers quickly came to act as contacts for subsequent migrants, and were thus at the centre of rapidly growing migrant networks. Potential emigrants in Guyana or Trinidad needed no more than a name and an address in London and the knowledge that it belonged to someone from their neighbourhood, the friend of a friend, a sister-in-law's cousin and the like, to feel that it was as good as an invitation. Having received a letter announcing that so-and-so would arrive on a certain date, pioneer settlers would dutifully meet new immigrants off the boat train, put them up for a few nights and give them tips on making their way in a new and hostile society. Such a process is entertainingly portrayed among Afro-Caribbeans in Sam Selvon's (1956) novel *The Lonely Londoners*.

Many of the earliest Indo-Caribbean migrants felt socially isolated. One recalls that he 'lived in a shell', circulating between work, school and studying while knowing only a few kindred souls. Some began to frequent, along with increasing numbers of Afro-Caribbeans, the West India Student Centre in Earls Court. There they had meals and 'limed' (hung around joking and chatting) in a more familiar West Indian way. Even so, in the Centre Indo-Caribbeans often met ignorance and exclusion from small islanders of the Caribbean (for instance, Barbadians) who, because their island never received indentured Indians, had not encountered Indo-Caribbeans before.

Before long, however, small groups of Indo-Caribbean Hindus began to meet in 'bedsits' to conduct *puja* (ritual offerings to a deity). In the absence of a priest, they simply used whatever *mantras* (Sanskrit prayers) and other ritual procedures they happened to know. *Murtis* (representations of deities) were no more than pictures brought over from Guyana and Trinidad, and all other ritual accoutrements were equally makeshift since 'in those days there was no Southall [densely Asian-populated area of west London] where you could buy things'. News of their meetings spread rapidly – not least among the non-Indo-Caribbean Hindus who by then were settling in London.

By 1956 Lambeth Town Hall in south London was regularly being hired by Indo-Caribbeans, and ceremonies were held under the supervision of a priest from Guyana and attended by Hindu immigrants from many parts of the world, including India, the Caribbean, East Africa and Mauritius. In 1957 this group established the Hindu Dharma Sabha, which raised funds and continued to rent public halls for the celebration of major festivals such as Shivratri, Navratri and Diwali.

The Sabha represented a significant stage in the evolution of Hindu institutions in Britain. It was possibly the first such body established among Hindu immigrants, and the forms of worship it employed were ecumenical since they had to cater for Hindu immigrants from such a diverse range of backgrounds. Indo-Caribbean rites are of generalized North Indian origin and thus rather 'basic' in character. As described in Chapter 2, such rites are directed towards 'Sanskritic' rather than regional or sectarian deities, and employ English rather than any of India's regional languages as a *lingua franca*. Indo-Caribbean Hinduism therefore provided a convenient framework for the mutual congregation of Hindus from many places. This fusion did not last long, however. The rapid growth of the Hindu presence in London in the late 1950s caused organizational fission into region-ally-based groups, so that Punjabis and Gujaratis (and caste groups within their ranks) set up organizations to facilitate the celebration of their own rituals in their own tongue and in their own manner (see Chapter 4).

As the others peeled off, Indo-Caribbeans organized themselves more exclusively too. In the early 1960s the Hindu Dharma Sabha renamed itself the Caribbean Hindu Society, while continuing to organize the same events. As one founder member explained:

> We thought that if we could make it specifically Caribbean, it could go out and attract people who came from the Caribbean, because they were in greatest need for this kind of cultural contact. If a person from Guyana just saw the name 'Hindu Dharma Sabha', he would think it was some-thing more for people from India, and that he wouldn't feel quite welcome.

Indo-Caribbean Hindus thereby established an institutionalized basis for meeting socially as a distinct ethnic community, as well as for congregating religiously for the practice of distinct ritual activities. But their place in British society was shifting at the same time.

Just as the majority of Indo-Caribbean immigrants had made fre-quent moves around the London area since their first arrival, so they also frequently changed occupation. This is particularly striking amongst those who arrived in the late 1950s and early 1960s: they often took unskilled or semi-skilled jobs while studying for creden-tials (in law, nursing, accounting, engineering, etc.) to which they hoped British employers would be more responsive than to those they had gained in the West Indies. Many of the later arrivals, often already with degrees from the University of Guyana or the University of the West Indies, studied for advanced degrees from one of London's universities. They were in a rather better position and usually did not have to make their initial step into the job market at such a low level as their forerunners.

Indo-Caribbeans, having now achieved a high degree of upward social mobility, today can be characterized as a largely middle-class group with a range of professional, administrative and white-collar occupations: informants include teachers, lawyers, civil servants, accountants, clerks, nurses, a hospital technician, a health visitor, an economist, a maths lecturer and a master tailor. Yet although neither geographically nor occupationally clustered, British Indo-Caribbeans still form a distinct community socially, culturally and religiously.

Some current characteristics

Though obviously of Indian origins, Indo-Caribbean social and cultural styles seem, at least outwardly, much more 'Western' than those of first-generation immigrants from India. This is particularly evident among middle-aged women, who tend to sport salon hairdos and department store dresses; only at major religious events are saris and Indian jewellery normally worn. But it is in their language that the Indo-Caribbean background is most evident.

John R. Bickford (1987) describes the linguistic complexities of Guyanese Creole and also provides lengthy examples and translations of Indo-Guyanese Creole. These include utterances such as '*mii granfaada bin gat plees a filisiti bilid*' ('my grandfather had a place at Felicity village') and '*wails abii tuu o kom nou wi dis boot, mi tel am, mi se, naanaa. a somting an yu na waan tel mii. tel mii a waa!*' ('while the two of us were coming along now in this boat, I told him, I said, Nana, something is wrong, and you don't tell me. Tell me what it is!'; ibid.: 147–9).

Like their Afro-Caribbean peers, Indo-Caribbeans are fluent speakers of local Creole speech-forms which, though based on English, are marked by distinct features of grammar and pronunciation (see Drummond 1980). To those unfamiliar with them, Caribbean Creole styles of speech are often difficult to understand. The fact that they are based on English often makes the task of communication equally frustrating for the speaker and the unaccustomed listener, especially when both feel that it should be straightforward. Context matters, of course, and having lived in Britain for decades, most Indo-Caribbeans now use standard English when talking with non-West

Indians. When they socialize together, however, Creole grammar, dialect, turns of phrase and forms of humour come to the fore.

Due to linguistic changes in the earliest years of their presence in the Caribbean, Indo-Caribbeans' use of Hindi is limited, and their pronunciation of Indian personal names is distinctive. It is these unique, creolized forms of English and Hindi that other British Asians find so confusing. Indo-Caribbean Hindus are also identifiable by their preferred form of greetings – 'Ram-Ram' for the Guyanese, and 'Sita-Ram' for the Trinidadians – both of which also attest to a heritage grounded in the traditions of North Indian Vaishnavite *bhakti* Hinduism.

Other Indo-Caribbean features which may be considered distinct in varying degrees from those of their Gujarati and Punjabi peers include: devotion to a smaller pantheon (largely limited to Rama, Hanuman, Durga and Lakshmi), heavy emphasis on popular lore backed up by a few key Vaishnavite texts (especially the Ramayana and Bhagavata Purana), use of a simplified sacred calendar, and above all the use of more congregational forms of worship in which prayers are often participatory and sermons are given in English (Chapter 6). Yet despite its condensed repertoire of ritual activities, Indo-Caribbean Hinduism still has its own characteristics, such as celebration of the Hanuman *puja*, which is still uniquely concluded by the raising of coloured *jhandi* (prayer flags). Hence amongst Guyanese Hindus in Britain and the Caribbean alike, 'having a *jhandi*' is regarded as synonymous with 'performing *puja*'. Such practices are well rooted in the Hindu tradition, so however unorthodox the details may be, direct migrants from India rarely have much difficulty in making sense of the symbols and practices in Indo-Caribbean temples. Indo-Caribbeans, by contrast, are often confused by the much greater intricacy of religious belief and practice amongst their Gujarati and Punjabi Hindu peers.

Similarly, while the Indo-Caribbeans' culinary practices are discernibly of Indian origin – involving as they do the preparation of various types of *roti* (flatbread), *dal* (lentils), rice and curried vegetables – long years of residence in the Caribbean has led them to evolve a cuisine of their own. So if the curries themselves are milder than many Indian ones, home-made West Indian hot pepper sauce accompanies most dishes as a condiment. Curries prepared in this regionally unique way are always served at the Caribbean Hindu Society, and have the effect of uniting the community socially. Many Indo-Caribbeans, and especially their British-born children, claim that they do not particularly like the 'Indian food' served in local

Asian-run restaurants. Further, true to their West Indian heritage, Indo-Caribbean men often have a strong penchant for rum.

The music many Indo-Caribbeans prefer is Indian: Hindi film music and playback singers singing *bhajans* are regularly heard on home stereos and car cassette-players. Language is a problem, however, and although they often watch Hindi films, they usually take care to select videos with English subtitles. And although Indo-Caribbeans tend publicly to disdain calypsos – the hallmark music of Trinidad – on the grounds that they are associated with Afro-Caribbeans, many can both hum the tunes and recite some of the most popular lyrics.

It is also striking that a whole range of unarticulated values, mannerisms and dispositions are expressed in the subtlest aspects of Indo-Caribbean culture, and these are clearly of Indian origin (see Vertovec 1992b). Thus there is a tendency to be fastidious over matters of bathing and the brushing of teeth, and to display an aversion to spittle – and therefore to talking near food in preparation, and to sharing a bottle or glass (see Khan 1994). There are also certain characteristic hand and arm gestures, such as a gentle rocking of the head when signalling agreement or attention when listening to another person.

While Indo-Caribbean kinship networks in Britain are attenuated, thanks largely to their particular history of migration and settlement, their social networks tend to be extensive. Indo-Caribbean settlers tend to be acquainted with many others of their community; and when Indo-Trinidadians or Indo-Guyanese meet for the first time, it is not unusual for them within minutes to have not only placed each other's original part of the country and village, but also to have discovered some common acquaintance or even a common relative in these parts. Although return visits to the Caribbean tend to be rare, most people have kept in close touch with local and national developments 'back home'.

Formal and informal associations facilitate the maintenance of those networks. In addition to the (largely Guyanese) Caribbean Hindu Society, a (predominantly Trinidadian) temple has been set up by a Brahmin pandit at his home in Catford (South-east London), while a further temple run by a Guyanese swami in Shepherd's Bush (West London) is frequented by Indo-Trinidadians and Indo-Guyanese alike. Indo-Caribbean Muslims account for most of the membership of a body called the United Islamic Association. Meanwhile in the secular sphere the Indo-Caribbean Cultural Association publishes a newsletter, organizes social events and works to promote

118

knowledge of Indo-Caribbean heritage and culture, especially among members of the community. Many Indo-Caribbeans in Britain are also actively involved in Caribbean politics as overseas members of most of the region's major political parties. Recreational groups also flourish, such as the Guyana Sports and Cultural Association which fields largely Indo-Caribbean cricket teams, and a league of card-players who take part in annual tournaments of 'All Foes', a team game played especially by Trinidadians.

These activities serve to integrate Britain's far-flung Indo-Caribbeans. Yet it is ultimately their white and British Asian fellow-citizens' perceptions of them which provide them with the most powerful incentive towards maintaining their ethnic distinctiveness.

Inter-ethnic experiences and attitudes

Drawing on my own interviews, the most revealing statements about those experiences are naturally those made by Indo-Caribbeans themselves. Hence this section contains a selection of brief but typical statements made by over forty people of both sexes, from both Guyana and Trinidad.

On British whites, and experiences of their reaction to them as Indians from the Caribbean:

> 'Initially they think that only blacks live in the West Indies. Most of them have never heard of Guyana. They're usually quite interested in knowing more, and most of them want to go there for a holiday.'

> 'Very surprised – some were interested.'

> 'They just could not care, so we were all classified as Pakis or Sikhs.'

> 'Nice to your face, but not in their minds.'

> 'Ignorance – they ask, "What part of Africa is Guyana?"'

> 'Surprised that Indians from India and from the Caribbean share the same traditions.'

> 'Surprised by my English.'

> 'They make no distinctions – everybody's Paki.'

On Indians from India, especially their experience of the reactions of Indians from India towards them as Indians from the Caribbean:

'I don't think they knew Indian Caribbeans shared their culture.'

'Some very good, some snobbish.'

'They don't see me as one of them.'

'As an Indian from the Caribbean, they look on you as an oddity, mostly as an ignorant cousin to mould.'

'Amazement at our fluency in English, rum-drinking, cricket.'

'In their eyes we're classed as second-hand Indians.'

'Indians don't know what to think of us but are sometimes surprised we have retained the culture.'

'Their attitude toward me is one of surprise and nearly always confusion.'

'That I'm not "pure" Indian because I can't understand their language, the difference in food preparation, etc.'

'I believe people from India know we're Indian by origin, but we're not regarded as true Indian.'

'I haven't experienced negative attitudes – but I haven't met many of them.'

Finally on their own attitudes towards Indians from India whom they have encountered in Britain, I was told such things as:

'Some are very nice, most are very arrogant and self-centred.'

'Perhaps like an Indian would be to another Indian from a distant part of India where traditional activities are different.'

'My attitude towards Indians from India who are living here is negative. I don't quite understand how they can be so prejudiced towards Indians from the West Indies. I think they consider me as being mixed with negroes. I don't know if they have any idea that the West Indies have Indians at all.'

'We are of the same stock, having the same features, culture, etc.'

'I admire the Indians from the subcontinent.'

'We get on very well.'

'On the whole we get along fine. There is always a language barrier.'

'Not much contact – otherwise good.'

'They are my brothers and sisters.'

'No special affinity.'

'I personally feel that I'm one of them when it comes to racial discrimination and would hope that they feel the same towards me.'

There is clearly no consensus of inter-ethnic experiences or attitudes. On the whole, however, a sense of separateness is apparent. Immigrants from India who have had contact with Indo-Caribbeans tend to convey no overtly negative stereotypes of them, and to be impressed by their success in maintaining their cultural traits and sincere religious devotion. One Bengali man hoped his British-born descendants would be able to maintain traditions as well as the Indo-Caribbeans have done despite generations of separation from the subcontinent, while an elderly Gujarati woman was deeply moved at the celebrations at an Indo-Guyanese wedding, which reminded her of her childhood back in village India. Another Gujarati woman, a librarian in Balham and Tooting (South London) who has had much contact with Indo-Caribbeans, describes them in Gujarati as '*trishanku*', a colloquialism for 'dangling' or 'floating in the air'. Other Gujaratis, she said, did not look upon them as Hindus, while the Indo-Caribbeans themselves 'realized they were not part of us'. Yet she also reasons that this has caused the Indo-Caribbeans 'to take more energetic steps' to preserve their ethnicity, because 'they ended up learning Hindi [referring to classes on offer at the Caribbean Hindu Society]; our children haven't bothered'.

What is perhaps more important than the attitudes of other Indians towards them is the Indo-Caribbeans' perceptions (or projections) of themselves. It is common to find a kind of inferiority complex towards subcontinental Indians, due mainly to the inability to converse in an Indian language. Thus Indo-Caribbeans may misattribute to sub-continental Indians an arrogance or negative attitude which is not there. Others are more convinced of the reality of Indian assumptions of social superiority, gladly citing all sorts of unambiguous examples. In yet other instances, Indo-Caribbeans express their own superiority to Indian immigrants (cf. Naipaul 1972: 38). They refer, for example, to the 'peasant' background or behaviour of the latter compared to their own westernized, middle-class habits, and to Indians' 'backward' caste sentiments in contrast to the almost complete absence of caste phenomena in the Indo-Caribbean social tradition. They also claim that Indians 'cringe in the presence of whites' while Indo-Caribbeans are confident enough to treat them as equals. Some suggest, too, that present-day Indians have degraded many Hindu devotional practices which Indo-Caribbeans themselves claim to have kept pristine over 150 years. Either way, perceptions of 'exclusion' – according to either their own Indo-Caribbean criteria or those of others – remain strong.

Conclusion: Indo-Caribbean identifications

How, then, do the Indo-Caribbeans identify themselves? Ethnicity is related to a person's situation and gives rise to level upon level of identification. Thus, while British Indo-Caribbeans are identified as 'Asian' by most members of the dominant white majority, they are by no means fully accepted as belonging in that category by other South Asians. Indo-Caribbeans in Britain are not unique in being faced by such a quandary: a wide range of other post-indenture, twice-migrant groups are in a similar situation, including Indo-Fijians in Vancouver (Buchignani 1980), Indo-Caribbeans in Toronto (Ramcharan 1983), Indo-Caribbeans in The Netherlands (van der Veer 1987), and Indo-Mauritians in London (Lingayah 1987). Hence it is no surprise that many Indo-Fijians and Indo-Mauritians in Britain have also gravitated towards Indo-Caribbean social and religious organizations and activities, rather than linking up with groups that have migrated directly from the subcontinent.

The longer-term future of the British Indo-Caribbean community is far from certain. Organizations like the Caribbean Hindu Society and the Indo-Caribbean Cultural Association do their utmost to foster and preserve a unique sense of identity – thereby expressing cultural resistance to the exclusionist tendencies of both British whites and British Asians. Yet internal fission among the Indo-Caribbeans themselves is already well established, whether between Muslims and Hindus (a pre-migration phenomenon) or between Trinidadians and Guyanese (intra-Caribbean fissioning is quite common in Britain, after all; see Peach 1984). How these even smaller groups will maintain Indo-Caribbean activities remains to be seen.

The orientation of British-born Indo-Caribbeans is at present unpredictable: current trends indicate lack of identification with either the Caribbean or with India. Many seem, instead, to be adopting a generalized British Asian youth culture (symbolized by *bhangra* music), which cuts across the cultural divide which faced their West Indian-born parents. Moreover in sharp contrast to their parents, many young Indo-Caribbeans are almost equally at home in British Afro-Caribbean cultural contexts. Young Indo-Caribbeans therefore represent an important set of people who are successfully 'being multi-cultural' in Britain.

What seems clear is that while British Indo-Caribbeans feel themselves to be very 'Western' and 'British' in class and habit, they are also very conscious that other South Asian settlers may regard them as a kind of pariah group. Hence they are somewhat alarmed by the prospect of being subsumed into a single overarching 'British' or 'Asian' cultural identity or categorization. Instead, Indo-Caribbeans see themselves as forming an important but neglected part of the South Asian/Indian/Hindu diaspora, and as one that should remain unique and unforgotten. These sentiments are exemplified in comments by one of the leaders of the Caribbean Hindu Society, who underscores the communal importance of the organization:

> We's swallowed up by the Asian community because we is so small. But that is why a place like this is so important. A number of times people have raised the question 'Why don't you change the name back to something that's wider?' It will serve in some years to show that there was a Caribbean element, a presence here, that contributed to the larger Asian presence . . . It's not being parochial – it's a historical fact.

In these ways, we might say that Indo-Caribbean Hindus in Britain are conscious of – indeed making a significant point of – being a kind of diaspora of a diaspora.

6

COMMUNITY AND CONGREGATION

Hindu temples in London

Hindu temples in Britain, like Muslim mosques and Sikh gurdwaras, have rapidly grown in number over the past two decades. Their role within the British Hindu population has been generally recognized as being of great social and cultural, as well as religious, value. 'In Britain Hindus are in a diaspora situation,' Ursula King (1984: 6) writes, 'so that the temple has acquired a new significance because it has become an important centre and meeting place for an ethnic and religious minority.' In the UK, 'The temple is no longer just a centre for devotion, but is an oasis of Indian culture in an alien environment' (Jackson 1981: 66). Despite various kinds of modification affecting religious practice among Hindus in Britain, Kim Knott (1986b: 100) points out that overall, 'Participant attendance at the temple . . . is important at the level of both the individual and the group. On the one hand, it is an expression of the performance of duty and, on the other, it is a portrayal of religious and cultural solidarity and the retention of tradition.'

That temples ultimately function as such for many British Hindus is without question. However, ethnographic accounts reveal rather different patterns of social and cultural development among a variety of regional, sectarian and caste-based groups within the British South Asian population (see Ballard 1994b). Similarly, as described below, comparative examination of the use of temples among different British Hindu groups indicates some divergent trends surrounding their assumed role as 'community' centres. In each of three cases discussed here, what has been critical to the unfolding of such trends are the relationships between: the composition and settlement history of the local Hindu population, pre-migration factors relevant to the temple's current religious ideology and modes of ritual practice, and the degree to which certain activities in the temple may be characterized as 'congregational' (and therefore, the extent to which patterns of use have shifted from predominant patterns in India).

A general discussion of temple use among Hindus in India is followed by ethnographic accounts of temple use among three different groups of Hindus in London. The conclusion of the chapter examines the divergent socio-religious trends evident in these British examples, calling into question the description of UK temples as 'community' centres.

Hindu temple use in India

Hindu temples are not of a single kind, and their use does not parallel that of places of worship in Judaeo-Christian and Islamic traditions. Hindu temples exhibit considerable variety in size, structure and focus, and among most Hindus in India, their importance for undertaking accepted forms of worship and for routinely expressing feelings of spiritual devotion is, more often then not, tangential. Instead, as Chris Fuller (1988: 50) emphasizes, 'Much Hindu religious practice takes place in the house, or in the fields or on the riverbanks; some Hindus hardly ever visit temples at all and many certainly engage in as much religious activity outside temples as in them.'

In India, the category 'Hindu temple' refers to 'a vast range of institutions' (ibid.: 49). It basically denotes a structure housing an image of a deity – an image, in turn, which serves as a kind of receptacle into which the deity's power or presence is believed to manifest itself. Beyond this, discussion of general characteristics of temple use is enormously complicated by differences of scale, regional histories and cultures, and myriad styles of worship, devotional orientations and philosophical schools within the loose framework of beliefs and practices of what has come to be designated 'Hinduism'. What follows, then, is but a broad characterization (cf. Basham 1954; Mitchell 1977; Fuller 1979, 1984, 1988).

Hindu temples in India include a range of phenomena in terms of architecture, ideological focus and social complexity. On the most parochial level are small, single room structures often devoted to a specific (and sometimes, only locally recognized) supernatural being – one possibly worshipped, moreover, by only a certain kinship or caste group or single village. A middle range of temples includes moderately sized buildings (devoted to more widely popular deities) whose use and organization are deeply enmeshed with the social, economic, and political dynamics of towns and cities – not least since they require donors. On a grand level are enormous, ancient complexes housing numerous deities and attracting tens of thousands of pilgrims from across the subcontinent. The smaller temples are usually under the care of local sponsors (families, castes, villages) or lone spiritual renouncers, while the medium-sized ones have come to be managed by elected boards of trustees, and the largest temples are often maintained by complex bureaucracies along with special kinds of Brahman priests.

Temples larger than a single room are usually constructed so as to set off, as one enters, concentric zones of increasing purity and sanctity culminating in the innermost, the *garbha grha* or 'womb chamber', where the power of the deity is believed to be present. Given the conceived spiritual purity of these inner zones, members of certain castes (especially untouchables and non-Hindus) are often denied access to them. Further, the *garbha grha* is normally only large enough to accommodate some priests and/or a small party of worshippers.

Although Hindu temples are public places, the presence of an assembled body of devotees generally matters little to the course of rites conducted. Instead, 'The efficacy of public worship is thought to depend mainly on its regular and correct performance by the priests, and its attendance by devotees is unimportant' (Fuller 1979: 461). Such regular rites are conducted in order to please the deity and seek its blessings for the entire world – or, in the case of sponsored rites, for the sponsor and his family. Thus, though continuously visited by significant numbers of Hindus, temples in India have tended to be known for their lack of group-oriented, participatory or what might be called 'congregational' ritual activity. In his historical overview of Indian civilization, A.L. Basham (1954: 336) made a crucial distinction in this regard, noting that 'In the greater temples the acts of worship performed by regular officiants might be watched by a larger number of people, but they were rather an audience than a congregation.' Similarly, John Brockington (1981: 202) has stressed that traditionally in most Hindu temples:

> there is no element of congregational worship. A worshipper would go to the temple alone or with his family to make his own particular act of homage, just as pilgrimage is essentially an individual activity, even if at times large numbers congregate.
>
> The regular acts of worship carried out by the officiants might well be observed by many in the larger temples but as an audience rather than as direct participants.

Such a lack of 'congregational' activity is questionable with reference to certain calendrical rites centred on village temples. For such rites, sponsorship, organization and participation may be rotated, shared out, or collectively undertaken by a number of caste or kin-based groups for the benefit of the village as a whole. One example from Bengal is provided by Ralph Nicholas (1981: 183), who underlines in such ritual activity the sharing of *prasad*, the food blessed by virtue of having been offered to a deity:

> The men who organized the worship divide this food into small parcels, one of which is carried to each house in the village – including the houses of the highest and lowest castes – so that all who are fellow villagers may share in the divine favour won through collective worship. This sharing symbolizes the unity of otherwise decentralized and often strife-torn villages by concretely enacting it; everyone embodies some of the same divinely tainted substance.

In northern India, however, Ursula Sharma (1969: 166) observed that 'The occasions on which a village shrine acts as the venue of any kind of religious concourse are few and far between. Village shrines are more commonly used for private acts of worship than for any other purpose.'

The activities occurring at the temples of certain sects or *sampradayas* – where membership is often specific to dedicated devotees and relationships are close-knit – often tend to be of a more participatory and congregational nature (for instance, activities of the followers of Vallabha; Brockington 1981). These kinds of religious activity, afforded by highly localized social contexts or formal religious bodies, do not generally pertain to the majority of temples in towns, cities and major ceremonial complexes throughout India.

The most common pattern of temple use among the Hindu 'laity', then, is one of individual motivation and practice. For instance, in the course of his research in South India, Milton Singer (1972: 113) found:

> The *gurukkal* [Shaivite temple priest] was not familiar with the Western notion of a religious congregation . . . [T]here did not seem to be a fixed religious community for a particular temple. Worshippers come according to their religious urge; they are under no obligation to come or not to come. Even if a person does not come, he is not considered irreligious or bad.

127

As pointed out above by Fuller, much if not most religious practice is undertaken by Hindus outside of the temple. When a Hindu does choose to visit a temple due to the 'urge' (perhaps to give thanks, to acquire *punya* or spiritual merit, or simply to demonstrate devotion), out of duty (usually to fulfil a promise made to a deity) or because of need (to seek the deity's favour or help in any sort of matter), the practices and related meanings usually involve the following (cf. Babb 1975; Fuller 1984; Knott 1986b). Individuals and their families make their way (locally or through arduous pilgrimage) to temples in order (a) to receive the *darshan*, or direct 'vision' or presence of the deity, and subsequently; (b) to show obeisance, *pranam*, especially through the gesture of bowing with hands pressed together or through prostrating themselves before the image; (c) to demonstrate devotion through *seva* or *puja*, the making of offerings as to an honoured guest or member of royalty (from basic, sometimes idiosyncratic gestures with simple tokens like flowers, to complicated rituals with an elaborate set of offerings and the assistance of a Brahman priest); further, such honorific offering may include *arati*, the 'gift of light' (waving a small flame in front of an image) and/or – especially in Arya Samaj influenced parts of Punjab and Uttar Pradesh – *homa* or *hawan*, an oblation of special substances into a sacred fire; and finally, (d) to obtain *prasad*, food blessed by virtue of having been offered to the deity.

While the enactment and meaning of these individual and familial practices have changed little among Hindu migrants and their offspring in Britain, the nature of the relationship between the temple and the local Hindu population has changed considerably, and in more ways than one.

The growth of Hindu temples in Britain

For the first decade or more of large-scale Hindu settlement in Britain, formal Hindu temples were wholly absent from the scene. Much Hindu ritual activity, however, still took place. Domestic worship, not surprisingly, provided the dominant religious activity of the migrants, just as it had in their places of origin. Collective forms of worship, however, increased as the numbers of Hindus in local areas grew, as they gained in wealth, as their social networks were extended and strengthened, and as they grew in experience and confidence in organizing themselves, making use of public facilities and services, and dealing with British rules, regulations and government bodies.

Since the late 1950s, town halls and other public premises were often rented, and celebrations of major Hindu holy days were organized and well attended. More important in forging local community identities, however, were groups which regularly assembled in homes, 'serving in a sense as congregations without temples' (Burghart 1987a: 9) for the purpose of conducting informal religious rites and a variety of other devotional activities. Many of these evolved into local Hindu organizations many of which, in turn, raised funds with a view to obtaining property in order to establish a temple.

A Hindu Temple in Coventry that opened in 1967, is purported to be Britain's first. One temple after another was founded in rapid succession, often with the substantial contributions of wealthy Hindu businessmen (Bryant 1983). The tide of immigrants from East African countries in the late 1960s and early 1970s did much to hasten the organization of local Hindus and the establishment of temples, for they had gained useful experience in doing just these things during their prior experience of diaspora (Jackson 1981; cf. Morris 1968). Depending on the type of building converted, there were sometimes considerable problems to be sorted surrounding official requirements for registering a temple as a place of worship (Menski 1987). Nonetheless, within ten years following the opening of the first temple, eighty-two Hindu temples across the country had been founded. Now the number of temples stands at over 300.

Some Hindu temples in Britain serve local populations comprised of Hindus from two or more cultural traditions (see Knott 1986b, 1987; Nye 1995), while others are used predominantly by Hindus from one background (in terms of region of origin and history of migration and settlement). The Hindu temples described below are essentially of the latter type. Each has developed some kind of organizational structure (mostly involving a Board of Trustees and a Management Committee) appropriate to the number of regular temple users and the extent of the temple's resources. Moreover, each has experienced internal conflicts of varying degrees of severity. Most of these conflicts have stemmed fundamentally from personality clashes among prominent members, politicking within the local Hindu 'constituency' for support of rival would-be leaders, and arguments over the proper means of collecting and spending finances – all phenomena, indeed, which are known to almost any kind of public organization in control of resources of one kind or another. All of the temples described observe the same special days within the 'all-India' Hindu calendar, though a few additional holy days or periods are recognized by certain groups, and the means of celebrating them are often somewhat different.

The commonly recognized religious occasions among the three Hindu communities in question are: Maha Shivratri, Holi (although it is the Indo-Caribbeans, and to a lesser degree the Punjabis, who celebrate Vasant Panchmi 40 days prior to Holi), Janashtami, Diwali and Navratri (a nine-day period which occurs both in Spring and Autumn; since the former includes Ramnavmi, it sees more emphasis towards the worship of Rama and reverence towards the Ramayana, while during the latter, greater attention is displayed towards the Mother Goddess since this period is associated with Durga ashtami; Gujaratis tend to celebrate only the Autumnal Navratri – this, by way of gatherings characterized by their well-known dances, *garaba* and *ras*). The Indo-Caribbean Hindus, in addition, celebrate both Hanuman jayanti and Ganesh jayanti, while the Punjabis recognize Baisakhi.

A comparison of the ways these temples are used by their members indicates that divergent trends have developed whereby the temples have come to reflect different things among Hindu populations drawn from distinct social and historical backgrounds.

Gujaratis in Balham and Tooting

The Borough of Wandsworth (1991 population 252,425) in South London is not one of Britain's more renowned areas of migrant settlement, despite the fact that over 20 per cent of its residents were born outside the United Kingdom. This is largely because Wandsworth's ethnic minorities are so diverse in origin and pattern of settlement. There are nearly 8,000 Indians in the Borough, plus 4,500 'Other Asians', a category which likely includes a large proportion of East African Asians. Indians have major concentrations in the Balham and Tooting areas (respective total populations 11,426 and 13,319 in 1991): they account for 4 per cent of Balham's population and over 10 per cent of Tooting's. Most are Hindu Gujaratis, whose numbers represent a substantial mixture of Lohanas, Patidars, and Brahmans among others.

A local Hindu Society in Wandsworth sponsors occasional Hindu functions of a mainly 'ecumenical' sort, but it is particularly associated with a small number of Punjabis in the area. Also, there are a few local homes that house shrines and serve as gathering places for socio-religious networks devoted to specific deities or schools of Hindu religious thought. In terms of visible presence and public use,

however, the Radha-Krishna Temple in Balham is the most prominent Hindu institution in the Borough, one especially known to serve
Gujaratis (all notices posted inside on the temple's bulletin board are
written only in Gujarati).

The Radha-Krishna Temple was established in 1975 along with
the Shyama Ashram. The former occupies the ground floor of a
remodelled shop while the latter is on the first floor of the building,
and is home to three *sannyasins* or female spiritual renouncers, two
male devotees, and occasionally other women (given their personal
circumstances or their desire to help during festival periods in the
temple). The temple/ashram is the successful result of efforts by an
elderly woman known as Mother Shyama, a conscientious advocate
of *bhakti* (loving devotion to a deity) whose followers regard her
as a kind of living saint (they have produced a booklet describing
the miraculous and exemplary aspects of her life). Her organizational
skills were well exercised over the past thirty years, during which
she established in India a temple, ashram and school complex
in Vrindaban, a hospital in Govardhan, and a temple in Surat,
as well as outside of India with temples in Zambia (founded in
the mid-1960s) and in Leicester (founded in 1969; see Bryant
1983). Mother Shyama continues to visit all these locations from
time to time, while each institution is wholly funded through local
donations.

In many ways, the structure and use of the Radha-Krishna Temple
in Balham resemble the general Indian pattern, outlined above. It is
primarily devoted to one deity (Radha-Krishna being in effect, a dual
deity) whose image is recessed and secluded in a kind of *garba grha*
into which only the *sannyasins* generally enter. In the rear of the
building, a smaller, separate temple has been constructed to house
a shrine to Ambamata (the Mother Goddess) and a Shiva *linga* (representation of the god), over which there is a dome, much like such
structures associated with the *linga* in temples of India.

Five times each day the doors of the *garba grha* are opened, when
the deity is attended to ('woke', dressed, 'put to rest', etc.) and given
offerings by the *sannyasins*. At these times, members of the public
can see the image (that is, to have *darshan*) and show obeisance
(*pranam*). Each evening *arati* is conducted, when different families
– never consisting of more than a handful of people – sporadically
attend the temple. Overall, little worship occurs here which can
be considered 'congregational'. There is never any kind of sermon
or *katha* (religious lesson drawing from stories concerning deities),
no communal meals are provided for devotees, and *arati* and

131

bhajan-kirtan (hymn) singing takes place with only a few people who happen to be in the temple at such times when the *sannyasins* undertake these. On the few annual occasions when Mother Shyama is present at the temple, a group of her devotees (largely women) tend to spend much time there, collectively singing devotional hymns written by her.

By and large the predominant pattern of temple use is one whereby individuals and families come into the temple on their own at different times in order to conduct their own modes of worship (essentially consisting of *darshan*, *pranam*, private prayer, and the collecting *prasad* in the form of small sweets). Only on major holy days is the temple attended by large numbers of Gujaratis, who observe *arati*, sing *bhajan-kirtan* and dance during Navratri. Many of those interviewed at these Navratri celebrations, however, said that for some if not each of the period's nine nights, they often went to a different Gujarati temple or gathering elsewhere in London. Thus their attendance at the Radha-Krishna Temple was not out of any kind of special identification or allegiance.

The Radha-Krishna temple has probably not developed a strong 'community' identity, and has maintained more of an Indian pattern of use for the following, related reasons. First, Mother Shyama, who is not a settled immigrant herself, has had a solitary role in structuring the use and even architecture of the temple, unlike other Hindu temples in Britain which have developed through negotiations among committees comprised of settled immigrants; her personal focus and style of worship set the mode for the temple as a whole, and thus a rigorous focus on a particular deity/shrine and highly personal style of *bhakti* predominates. Second, the local Gujarati population is socially rather fragmented such that no real sense of community has emerged. Gujaratis throughout Britain have roots in a variety of districts in Gujarat, and a large number have long experience living in parts of Kenya, Tanzania and Uganda. For a host of reasons, Gujaratis now resident in Britain – particularly those connected with East Africa – seem to have maintained and sometimes institutionalized, more than their counterparts from other places in India, specific group identities based on regions and castes of Gujarat (see Chapter 4).

Further, the devotional orientations of Hindu Gujaratis also seem to be more multiform than those of other immigrant Hindu groups. Sometimes this may reflect propensities of entire castes. Among Lohanas, for instance, Maureen Michaelson (1987: 32) suggests temple-based worship is rather peripheral:

Although the study of Hindu temple rituals and temple-going is not without its importance, such a study for the Lohanas ... would be largely uninformative and misleading. The Lohanas, like other Gujarati castes, are involved in an intensive weekly round of religious activities, but in the Lohana case these activities are organized by family and kin, the local caste associations, and various devotional congregations (satsang) in the neighbourhood. Formal temple attendance is sporadic, with some caste members never going at all, even though they might consider themselves to be 'very religious'.

Gujarati Hindus sometimes follow rather different devotional orientations (cf. Pocock 1973), many actually belonging to one or another *sampradaya* (see Barot 1987b). Many of the Gujaratis of Balham follow Pushtimarga, the 'path of divine grace' which entails a highly devotional – sometimes even puritanical – focus on Krishna (especially in the form of veneration towards Shri Nathji, Vallabhacharya, and Jamunaji). The Radha-Krishna temple is indeed devoted to Krishna and has an (albeit, secondary) image of him in his form of Shri Nathji. Activities there follow many of the correct ritual procedures concerning such images as set forth in Pushtimargi tradition (Jindel 1976). However, informants have mentioned that strict Pushtimargis would not visit the Radha-Krishna Temple because of its attached Ambamata-Shiva temple, which the Pushtimargis consider inappropriate or even spiritually rather base. Instead, virtually round the corner from the temple, a woman has set up a more 'orthodox' Pushtimargi temple in her home. Other Pushtimargis travel to East London, where there is a formal Shri Nathji temple. In the same way, many Gujaratis belong to rival Swaminarayan groups; they forego worship in the Radha-Krishna temple in order to travel from Balham to North London, where their own temples have been founded including the massive one at Neasden.

There are also, in the Balham area, Hindus from Fiji, Trinidad and Mauritius who occasionally, also as individuals or families, visit the temple since it is in their neighbourhood. Yet they have obviously developed no sense of community or congregation here either, due to their small numbers and to the considerable linguistic-cultural gap with the Gujarati majority. Instead, many Fijians and Mauritians in Balham – as well as the Indo-Caribbeans – feel more affinity to the congregation attending the Caribbean Hindu Society in Brixton (see below).

133

The Radha-Krishna Temple retains, overall, an individualistic pattern of use. There is not much evidence of truly 'congregational' activities, defined as ones collectively participated in by and for a recognized social 'community'. This is, in one important way, due to the rather socially and religiously fragmented nature of the local Gujarati population. Elsewhere in London, more truly collective patterns of temple use among wholly different Hindu populations are to be found.

Punjabis in Southall

Because of its pronounced South Asian presence, Southall is an area well known for Indian cultural and religious activity (see Peggie 1982; Bhachu 1985; Baumann 1996). Located in West London's Borough of Ealing (1991 population 281,800), Southall's population stood at just over 60,000 people in 1991, 37,000 of whom are of South Asian origin (about 14,000 born in India, 4,000 born in East Africa, and the balance comprising individuals belonging to households headed by persons born in India or East Africa). Within a two square mile area straddling the Uxbridge road, it has been estimated that the population is 90 per cent South Asian. Southall's residents are predominantly Punjabis (and mostly Sikhs, at that), both among the Indian- and East African-born population. Indian culture and language – especially Punjabi – dominate the area's large number of groceries, clothing and jewellery shops, cinemas and video shops, newspapers and magazines as well as temples and gurdwaras.

In 1965, over a decade after Punjabi immigration to Southall commenced, a Hindu Cultural Society was formed (with notable efforts by a few East African Arya Samajis, who had much prior organizational experience) to coordinate various Hindu religious functions. The group originally met in members' homes, but eventually rented public places as its membership and popularity grew. By 1972 the Hindu Cultural Society split, largely over conflicts of personality and political control, into two organizations which became the Hindu Temple Trust and the Vishwa Hindu Kendra. Within a few years, each body eventually purchased its own premises and converted them to temples. Finance came mostly by way of donations (though the Vishwa Hindu Kendra was successful in obtaining a large grant from the Greater London Council). The two organizations have different constitutions and organizational structures, one holding frequent elections with separate functions for its Board of Management and Trustees, the other primarily run by a core set of Trustees who look after most functions and managerial tasks.

The structure and use of both temples are much the same. The main part of each building is a large hall with numerous images lined up along one end, with no kind of *garba grha* (although the images are recessed from public space so that devotees cannot actually touch them). Rama-Sita occupy the central position in the Hindu Temple Trust's building (called the Shri Ram Mandir), while an image of Vishnu is the central image in that of the Vishwa Hindu Kendra. Ambamata (equivalently called Durga or simply Mataji), Radha-Krishna, Shiva, Ganesha and Hanuman are the other prominent deities in each temple.

Both temples are open throughout the day with Brahman priests in attendance, so that individuals and families can enter and freely undertake *darshan, pranam*, individual prayer and offerings, or prayers and offerings with the assistance (in Sanskrit) of a priest, following all of which *prasad* is received. However, each temple conducts a number of congregational services as well, including a Sunday service consisting of *bhajan-kirtan* and *arati*, a lengthy and enjoyable *katha* in Hindi and Punjabi at the Vishwa Hindu Kendra, and communal meals usually sponsored by different families each week (both temples have kitchens, and the Kendra has a huge dining area on its first floor). Other communal activities at the temples include Hindi language classes for young people, and large-scale celebrations of holy days (which often include famous guest singers from India or around Britain).

In addition, the Vishwa Hindu Kendra has a large library of Punjabi books and newspapers which attract visitors throughout the day. It also sponsors a citizens' advice centre dealing largely with immigration questions. The Shri Ram Mandir, in turn, is a favourite place for a number of older women to meet and socialize from day to day. Patterns of membership at each of the temples is attributed to different reasons. Some in Southall say they attend one or the other temple because of their relationship to or approval of the temple's management (or dislike of the other's), while others say it is more parish-like – that is, that the Vishwa Hindu Kendra serves Hindus of northern Southall while the Shri Ram Mandir does so for those in the southern part of town.

While the congregational modes of worship are of increasing popularity and social importance, both temples continue to perpetuate the Indian pattern of individually performed worship. People with or without their families drop by the temple during the day, while collective participation is undertaken at specific times. Indeed, it is interesting to observe that even when the collective activities are taking place – such as *bhajan* singing, the priest's *katha*, and the meal – individuals and families walk past or through the seated crowd to approach the deities for their own personal *darshan*, *pranam*, etc.

The combined pattern of congregational plus individual use can be attributed to the following factors: first, both organizations and their activities have developed through years of committee negotiation, such that, as Knott (1986b: 80–1) has observed in Leeds, the expectations and attitudes of a large number of people are expressed. In this way, a more generalized Punjabi corpus of belief and activity has come into prominence. Second, compared to Gujaratis in places like Wandsworth, the Punjabi Hindus in Southall have the advantage of greater social and cultural homogeneity, by virtue of deriving largely from a more localized area (mainly Jullundar and Hoshiarpur, with others from Ludhiana and Amritsar), so that common practices are easier to sustain. Also, caste differentiation does not play as divisive a role, in terms of religious organization, among the Punjabis in Britain as compared to Gujaratis (with the exception of low caste Punjabi Chuhras and Chamars, who have their own temples in Southall devoted to the Valmiki and Ravidasi religious traditions, respectively). It has been suggested that in the northern Punjab/ Himachal Pradesh region, social and ritual distance between castes is less rigid than in other parts of India (Sharma 1969, 1970). Among Punjabis in Britain, although caste sentiments continue to determine many marriages, and higher castes seem to maintain sway in the management of temple affairs, caste has not been seen to militate against congregational forms of worship (most evident in the preponderance of communal meals).

The Punjab has been the locus of a long-standing rivalry between the Arya Samaj and what has come to be known as Sanatana Dharma (see Chapter 1). Consequently, it has been especially in the Punjab that the latter – a rather broad (albeit Vaishnavite), less caste-divisive, simple and easily adaptable set of Hindu beliefs and practices – came into being.

The Vishwa Hindu Kendra and the Shri Ram Mandir both exhibit individual and congregational patterns of temple use, even, at times, simultaneously. These are patterns that well serve a residentially concentrated, more culturally homogeneous population with large numbers of first-generation settlers. A final example of Hindu temple use in London demonstrates yet another emergent set of temple practices linked to the specific nature of a British Hindu community.

Indo-Caribbeans in Brixton

The South London Borough of Lambeth (1991 population 256,600), particularly the Brixton area, is largely associated with a West Indian presence, and even more specifically with a Jamaican one. However, this and other parts of nearby South London are home to the smaller, virtually 'hidden' Indo-Caribbean population (see Chapter 5). Conjunct with Hinduism's history in the Caribbean through which a common egalitarian forms of religious observance evolved (see Chapter 2), Caribbean Hindu temples developed as structures wholly dedicated to congregational activity. Many even took an architectural form similar to Christian churches (Vertovec 1992b). Individual modes of worship were confined to certain practices at home. These beliefs and practices, developed and practised by generations of Hindus in the Caribbean, have fully continued among Indo-Caribbeans in Britain.

As outlined in the previous chapter, the Caribbean Hindu Society lays proud claim to being the first migrant Hindu organization in Britain, having been established in 1958 (then calling itself the Hindu Dharma Sabha). In its earliest years, it functioned primarily to organize religious events surrounding holy days (events which at the time also involved numerous Hindus from the subcontinent) and to broaden and serve the network of Indo-Caribbean people as they settled throughout London. As the number of Indo-Caribbean immigrants and their families grew by the early 1970s, the Society saw it appropriate to purchase a building and convert it to a temple exclusively for rites and celebrations performed in the manner they knew in the Caribbean (whereas those previously conducted together with subcontinent Hindus had been negotiated towards 'lowest common denominator' forms).

The Society's building, previously a Boy Scout hall, has an office/ library, a small room upstairs which houses the deities' images. Rama-Sita-Lakshman, Hanuman, Lakshmi, Shiva, Durga, Krishna are all placed on a large altar allowing devotees to touch, anoint and directly give offerings to the images. A large hall with a stage is situated on the ground floor, where the images are moved for large-scale celebrations. There is another large room in which classes of many kinds are on offer weekly (from religious education to maths tutoring), as well as a kitchen and other rooms for storage.

While its doctrines and priests espouse individual *bhakti*, the Caribbean Hindu Society's temple is used in a wholly congregational manner. The temple is not open during weekdays for individual and family-based worship, and *darshan* is a term never raised in most Caribbean Hindu religious parlance. The temple usually opens its doors only for some form of collective worship. Each Friday there is Ramayan *satsang*, on Sunday services are held for *bhajan* singing, *arati* and a collectively chanted *hawan* (at the end of which individuals are invited to offer flowers at the feet of the images – a personal mode of worship nonetheless completely regulated by its congregational format), and periodically there occur individually- or family-sponsored *pujas* and collectively organized *yagnas*.

At all of these activities, Caribbean variants of Indian cuisine are served both as *prasad* and as communal meals. Sanskrit prayers are recited in harmony by the congregation: these Sanskrit *mantras* are transliterated into Roman letters, photocopied and distributed like prayer books in Christian churches. Priests give sermons or explanations of texts in English, and they even exhort 'the power of collective prayer' to call down help for the organization, members' needs and other community causes (including the dire political and economic situation in Guyana). Hindi classes, Indian music and dance classes, maths lessons, and discos are also held to attract young, second-generation Indo-Caribbeans.

Perhaps the most important reasons for these wholly congregational uses of the temple are as follows. First, essentially, this was the socio-religious pattern that emerged over generations in Trinidad and Guyana, a pattern itself conditioned by many factors. A 'homogenized' form of Hinduism was forged from the local 'little traditions' whence the Indian migrants to the Caribbean came. Coupled with such a common form of belief and practice, the almost complete attenuation of the caste system in this context allowed for new, collective modes of worship. Further, Hindus were relegated to the bottom of each of these colonial Caribbean societies' social structure; congregational worship provided for mutual moral support and the maintenance of self-esteem among members of a severely downtrodden ethnic group. That is, their collective religious practices in the Caribbean were among the most prominent focuses of demonstrating and reinforcing their ethnic identity.

Second, not only was it natural for the Indo-Caribbean immigrants in Britain to carry on their traditions as they had been developed in Trinidad and Guyana, but their unique ethnic quandary in this country has bolstered the tendency to congregate (see Chapter 5). Indo-Caribbean people in Britain find themselves in an unfortunate position where the white British population thinks they are subcontinental Indian or 'Asian' while on paper they are 'West Indian' (although they usually seek to socially distance themselves from Afro-Caribbeans, recalling well the discrimination they suffered in the Caribbean), and the South Asians here often treat them as a kind of pariah group.

Consequently, Indo-Caribbean Hindus have decided to socio-religiously segregate themselves by establishing their own temple and engaging in their own modes of worship. Although they are residentially dispersed throughout London, their sense of 'community' is very strong, sustained by the experience of exclusion by British Asians as well as British whites, facilitated by a shared set of unique Indian traditions, and manifested in wholly congregational use of the temple.

Conclusion

In the examples provided here, we have seen three different types of temple use, each linked intrinsically to the nature of the main Hindu population who visit the places in question. It can be argued that each of the temples indeed functions as a 'community centre' in that it is a public place serving certain social, cultural and religious needs of Hindus. But, as we have seen, the nature of each local Hindu population calls into question the use of the term 'community', as the composition and migration history of each population examined show differing characteristics. Among Gujaratis in Balham, 'community' refers only to a linguistic commonality among those in a geographic area. For the Punjabis in Southall, linguistic commonality combines with residential concentration and shared religious activities so that 'community' is truly evident socially and geographically. For the Indo-Caribbeans, 'community' has nothing to do with residence (as most are scattered throughout London) and everything to do with cultural habits and mutual experiences of exclusion. 'Congregational' religious activities both draw from and reinforce 'community' sentiments in the latter two examples, while in the former, such activities have not arisen due to the fragmented nature of the local Hindu population, as well as to the predominant – and perhaps more 'traditional' – style of temple use instituted by its founder.

These are certainly not the only possible trends regarding the nature of local Hindu 'communities' and their patterns of temple use in the Hindu diaspora (compare, for instance, Aveling 1978; Jayawardena 1980; Rayaprol 1997). What they underscore, as throughout this book, is the need to account for differential patterns of Hindu activity by way of the complex social and cultural make-up of Hindu groups, compounded by their specific migration histories and trajectories of development throughout the world.

7

THREE MEANINGS OF
'DIASPORA'

While previous chapters have provided a look at some of the kinds of social and cultural processes affecting Hinduism and Hindu communities *in* diaspora (that is, in a generalized context outside of a place of origin), this chapter explores some of the meanings of the concept 'diaspora' itself, illustrated by examples surrounding Hindu phenomena outside India.

'Diaspora' is the term often used today to describe practically any population which is considered 'deterritorialized' or 'transnational' – that is, whose cultural origins are said to have arisen in a land other than that in which they currently reside, and whose social, economic and political networks cross the borders of nation–states or, indeed, span the globe. To be sure, such populations are growing in prevalence, number and self-awareness. Several are emerging as (or have historically long been) significant players in national, regional or global political economies (see Sheffer 1986; Kotkin 1992; Cohen 1997).

In recent years, intellectuals and activists from within these populations have increasingly begun to utilize the term 'diaspora' to describe themselves. James Clifford (1994: 311) notes that we have witnessed the emergence of 'Diasporic language [which] appears to be replacing, or at least supplementing, minority discourse'. Among academics, transnational intellectuals and 'community leaders' alike, 'diaspora' has become a loose reference conflating categories such as immigrants, guest-workers, ethnic and 'racial' minorities, refugees, expatriates and travellers. The current over-use and under-theorization of the notion of 'diaspora' threatens the term's descriptive usefulness (cf. Safran 1991; Tatla 1993; Cohen 1995).

Mixed meanings of 'diaspora'

Within a variety of academic disciplines, recent writing on the subject conveys at least three discernible meanings of the concept 'diaspora'. These meanings refer to what we might call 'diaspora' as *social form*, 'diaspora' as *type of consciousness*, and 'diaspora' as *mode of cultural production* (Vertovec 1997a). By way of but a few respective examples, it is further suggested that these rather different meanings each have certain utility for conceptualizing, interpreting and theorizing processes and developments affecting South Asian religions like Hinduism outside of South Asia.

'Diaspora' as social form

'The Diaspora' was at one time a concept referring almost exclusively to the experiences of Jews, invoking their traumatic exile from a historical homeland and dispersal throughout many lands. With this experience as reference, connotations of a 'diaspora' situation were usually rather negative as they were associated with forced displacement, victimisation, alienation, loss. Along with this archetype went a dream of return. These traits eventually led by association to the term's application to populations such as Armenians and Africans.

Martin Baumann (1995) indicates three quite different referential points with respect to the historical Jewish experience 'in the diaspora': these are (a) the *process* of becoming scattered; (b) the *community* living in foreign parts; and (c) the *place* or geographic *space* in which the dispersed groups live. Useful as it is to realize, at any time, to which of these reference points a discourse refers, for the purposes of this chapter I nevertheless suggest that these distinctions all ultimately concern 'diaspora' as a social form in that the emphasis remains upon an identified group characterized by their relationship-despite-dispersal.

Other common traits attributed to a general social category of diaspora, drawing upon yet going beyond the classic Jewish model, can be compiled from a range of descriptive and theoretical works (Armstrong 1976; Sheffer 1986; 1995; Safran 1991; Clifford 1994; Cohen 1995, 1996). These traits include:

- specific kinds of *social relationships* cemented by special ties to history and geography. These see diasporas broadly as:

142

created as a result of voluntary or forced migration from one home location to at least two other countries;

consciously maintaining collective identity, which is often importantly sustained by reference to an 'ethnic myth' of common origin, historical experience, and some kind of tie to a geographic place;

institutionalizing networks which transcend territorial states and creating new communal organizations in places of settlement;

maintaining a variety of explicit and implicit ties with their homelands;

developing solidarity with co-ethnic members in other countries of settlement;

unable to be, or not wishing to be, fully accepted by 'host society' – thereby fostering feelings of alienation, or exclusion, or superiority, or other kind of 'difference';

- a unique *way of life* produced by the above relationships, including the ability or necessity to 'live in several societies simultaneously' (Glick Schiller *et al.* 1992: 11);
- a tension of *political orientations* given that diasporic peoples are often confronted with divided loyalties to homelands and host countries. Individual immigrants may be significant actors, or collective associations may be powerful pressure groups, in the domestic politics of their host countries as well as in the international political arena by way of interests in the political plight of a country of origin (the Jewish and Irish lobbies in the USA are obvious examples). Sheffer (1995) underscores the growing role of 'new nongovernmental trans-state political organizations' in the global political arena. For example, groups such as Armenian organizations linked together in the USA, France and the Middle East demonstrate how transnational communities 'are among the world's most sophisticated political lobbyists, according to western political analysts and diplomats' (*Financial Times*, 16 September 1994);
- the *economic strategies* of transnational groups represent an important new source and force in international finance and commerce. This domain comprises the focus of Joel Kotkin's (1992) portrayal of how ethnic collectivism on a world-wide scale provides a key to success in the new global economy.

Economic success of diasporic groups is seen to result from the mutual pooling of resources, transfer of credit, investment of capital and provision of services among family, extended kin, or co-ethnic members.

Finally, in all of these domains – particularly in the contemporary period characterized by relative ease of transportation and communication – 'diaspora' as social form is characterized by a 'triadic relationship' (Sheffer 1986; Safran 1991) between (a) globally dispersed yet collectively self-identified ethnic groups; (b) the territorial states and contexts where such groups reside; and (c) the homeland states and contexts whence they or their forebears came.

Practically all of the general texts concerning South Asian communities (including specifically religious groups) outside South Asia concentrate, in one way or another, on 'diaspora' as social form, particularly by way of the kinds of *social relationships* noted above (see especially the Hugh Tinker trilogy 1974, 1976, 1977, as well as Kondapi 1951; Clarke *et al.* 1990b; Vertovec 1991c; Ballard 1994b; van der Veer 1995). Therefore it is not particularly necessary to recapitulate this large body of information here. Features of diaspora as a *way of life* appear implicitly in many such studies; it is described more explicitly by Ballard (1994a: 29) when he portrays the contemporary diasporic condition of South Asians in contexts outside South Asia, like Britain, as '*Desh Pardesh*' ('home from home' or 'at home abroad') – a term which he suggests as 'the embodiment of the self-created worlds of Britain's South Asian settlers'.

The homeland *political orientations* of South Asian religious groups are ever rapidly evolving and, in some quarters, intensifying. Arjun Appadurai (1990: 301) suggests that the process of deterritorialization among diasporic groups sometimes creates 'exaggerated and intensified senses of criticism of or attachment to politics in the home-state'. Further, he writes:

> Deterritorialization, whether of Hindus, Sikhs, Palestinians or Ukrainians, is now at the core of a variety of global fundamentalisms, including Islamic and Hindu fundamentalism. In the Hindu case for example . . . it is clear that the overseas movement of Indians has been exploited by a variety of interests both within and outside India to create a complicated network of finances and religious identifications, in which the problems of cultural reproduction for

Hindus abroad has become tied to the politics of Hindu
fundamentalism at home.

(ibid.: 301–2)

Right-wing Hindu nationalist organizations are known to gain much
support from overseas populations. Most notably, these include the
Rashtriya Swayamsevak Sangh (RSS), the Vishwa Hindu Parishad
(VHP) and the Bharatiya Janata Party (BJP). Such organizations
gain considerable support (financial not least) from Hindus in Great
Britain and the United States (see Bhatt 1997; Rajagopal 1997;
Kurien 1997; Raj 1999).

In the sphere of *economic strategies* involving diaspora populations, the government of India has recently enacted measures to
attract the intellectual and financial resources of 'NRIs' (non-resident
Indians), especially by way of salary incentives for return migrants,
special financial packages and favourable rates for non-resident
Indian investors in a range of enterprises (Lessinger 1992). For
example, in 1998 the government of India launched a Resurgent India
Bond to acquire foreign reserves in the wake of economic sanctions
wrought by India's nuclear tests (see Rogers 1998b). With an attrac-
tive 7.75 per cent interest rate and the facility for return payment
after five years in US dollars, British pounds or German marks, the
bonds 'illustrate perfectly how the ties between immigrants and
their homeland are exploited for mutual economic gains' whether
the investors are BJP government supporters or not (Sengupta 1998).
Working through a hired agency, the State Bank of India initially targeted around 3 million NRIs. Within the first two weeks of launching
the bond, $2 billion were raised; in just one month, the total was
$4.1 billion.

With regard specifically to the economic strength of overseas
religious groups, Kotkin (1992: 201–32) details examples of intra-
group business connections respectively between Sikhs, Parsis, Jains,
Ismailis, and Gujerati Hindus. These are usually incidental, Kotkin
suggests, to the promotion of any kind of religious 'cause'. On the
other hand, there are purported transnational financial flows of
considerable size co-ordinated by the World Hindu Congress (a VHP
institution), while the Hindu Heritage Endowment (which supports
the diaspora-oriented newspaper *Hinduism Today*) manages an
annual budget of over $1 million devoted to the global propagation
of Hinduism.

The above-mentioned examples of political and economic links
support the notions of 'triadic relationships' within the South Asian

religious diaspora. Two specific events also demonstrate modalities of traidic relationship. One surrounded the destruction of the Babri Masjid in Ayodhya in December 1992 (Kundu 1994; Burlet and Reid 1995; see also Rai 1995). Prior to this act, there had been much campaigning throughout the UK, including the wide circulation of a video about Ramjanmabhoomi (the birthplace of Rama), by Hindu organizations calling for the removal of the mosque and for the creation of a temple devoted to Rama. These campaigns were importantly advocated by the RSS and VHP (Bhatt 1997). Following the masjid's destruction in India, in Britain there were several incidents of damage to Hindu temples and cultural centres (plus a few mosques and, curiously, one Sikh gurdwara), numerous local government-organized forums for inter-community dialogue, and much leafleting of the South Asian population by Hindu and Muslim organizations. In the wake of these activities, there was established the Alliance against Communalism and for Democracy in South Asia (which holds various kinds of public events and distributes information with the aim of combating all forms of religious communalism among South Asians in Britain).

Another example of emergent forms of relationship between India and the diaspora was the 'milk miracle' of September 1995. As reported by many news agencies, religious images or *murtis* in Hindu temples around Britain (London, Leicester, Birmingham and Leeds) and around the world (including New York, Delhi, Hong Kong and Bangkok) were observed to 'drink' substantial quantities of milk. News of one such 'miracle' in one location was rapidly heard at another, where milk was subsequently offered: if 'drunk' by the *murti*, the news was immediately relayed elsewhere. Practically in the course of a day, news of similar incidents spread around the world. A South Asian religious diaspora, now connected through advanced global telecommunications, had wrought 'the age of the instant miracle' (*The Guardian*, 23 September 1995). As Chetan Bhatt (1997: 252) describes it, however, 'The VHP and RSS were quick to mobilize their international networks to generate the miracle globally.'

'Diaspora' as type of consciousness

Another approach to 'diaspora' in current literature puts greater emphasis on features concomitant with a variety of experience, a state of mind and a sense of identity. 'Diaspora consciousness' is a particular kind of awareness said to be generated among contemporary transnational communities (Safran 1991; Clifford 1994). Its particularity is described as being marked by various dimensions of *dual or paradoxical nature*. This nature is constituted negatively by experiences of discrimination and exclusion, and positively by identification with a historical heritage (such as 'Indian civilization') or contemporary world cultural or political forces (such as 'Islam'). James Clifford (1994: 312) suggests that:

> Experiences of loss, marginality, and exile (differentially cushioned by class) are often reinforced by systematic exploitation and blocked achievement. This constitutive suffering coexists with the skills of survival: strength in adaptive distinction, discrepant cosmopolitanism, and stubborn vision of renewal. Diaspora consciousness lives loss and hope as a defining tension.

With a direct allusion to W.E.B. Du Bois's notion of 'double consciousness', Paul Gilroy (1987, 1993a, b), too, describes a kind of duality of consciousness characterizing diasporic individuals' awareness of decentred attachments. Gilroy describes the diaspora condition as living with the sense of being simultaneously 'home away from home' or 'here and there' or British and something else. Similarly Clifford (1994: 322) proposes that 'The empowering paradox of diaspora is that dwelling here assumes a solidarity and connection there. But there is not necessarily a single place or an exclusivist nation . . . [It is] the connection (elsewhere) that makes a difference (here).'

The *awareness of multi-locality* also stimulates the need to conceptually connect oneself with others, both 'here' and 'there', who share the same 'routes' and 'roots'. For Stuart Hall (1990), diaspora is comprised of ever-changing representations that provide an 'imaginary coherence' for a set of malleable identities. Robin Cohen (1996: 516) develops Hall's point with the observation that

> transnational bonds no longer have to be cemented by migration or by exclusive territorial claims. In the age of cyberspace, a diaspora can, to some degree, be held together or re-created through the mind, through cultural artefacts and through a shared imagination.

In this way, Cohen points out, 'An identification with a diaspora serves to bridge the gap between the local and the global' (ibid.).

In addition to awareness of multi-locality and links of the imag-ination, some writers have described diaspora consciousness by way of other functions of the mind. Arjun Appadurai and Carol Breckenridge (1989: i), for example, state that whatever their form or trajectory, 'diasporas always leave a trail of collective memory about another place and time and create new maps of desire and of attachment'. Yet these *collective memories* and 'new maps' do not always serve to consolidate identities. Rather, Appadurai and Breckenridge note:

> More and more diasporic groups have memories whose archaeology is fractured. These collective recollections, often built on the harsh play of memory and desire over time, have many trajectories and fissures which sometimes correspond to generational politics. Even for apparently well-settled diasporic groups, the macro-politics of reproduction trans-lates into the micro-politics of memory, among friends, relatives and generations.
>
> (ibid.)

Compounded by the awareness of multi-locality, the 'fractured memories' of diaspora consciousness produce a multiplicity of histo-ries, 'communities' and selves. Yet instead of being represented as a kind of schizophrenic deficit, such *multiplicity* is being redefined by diasporic individuals as a source of adaptive strength. Nina Glick Schiller, Linda Basch and Cristina Blanc-Szanton (1992: 11) explain:

> Within their complex web of social relations, transmigrants draw upon and create fluid and multiple identities grounded both in their society of origin and in the host societies. While some migrants identify more with one society than the other the majority seem to maintain several identities that link them simultaneously to more than one nation. By maintaining many different racial, national, and ethnic iden-tities, transmigrants are able to express their resistance to the global political and economic situations that engulf them, even as they accommodate themselves to living conditions marked by vulnerability and insecurity.

Diaspora consciousness is further considered to be the source of resistance through *engagement with*, and consequent *visibility in, public space.* Here, Cohen (1995: 13) comments: 'Awareness of their precarious situation may also propel members of diasporas to advance legal and civic causes and to be active in human rights and social justice issues.' This is especially witnessed today in the ever more effective and organized expressions of group concerns (often described as ethnic mobilization, identity politics, or the politics of recognition).

A further kind of diaspora consciousness is specific to religious groups. This occurs through a particular kind of *self-questioning* stimulated by conditions of 'diaspora' coupled with religious pluralism. Under such conditions, believers are often compelled to realize that the routine habitual practice, rote learning and 'blind faith' underpinning previous contexts (where their faith may have been homogeneous or hegemonic) are no longer operational. Emblematic of such a shift in religious self-consciousness, Clifford Geertz (1968: 61) has described ways in which, in Morocco and Indonesia (representing two margins of the Islamic world) 'the primary question has shifted from "What shall I believe" to "How shall I believe it?" ' This shift has entailed, further, 'a distinction between "religiousness" and "religious-mindedness", between being held by religious convictions and holding them' (ibid.). As a minority in a situation of pluralism, the believer may now be in a position of having to rationalize and justify elements of belief and practice to members of other faiths. In these ways, we must even speak of 'religious diaspora consciousness'.

Bhikhu Parekh has alluded to a kind of change in consciousness among Hindus living in overseas contexts. By way of such contexts, Parekh (1994: 617) conjectures, 'The diasporic Hindu was no longer a Hindu happening to live abroad, but one deeply transformed by his diasporic experiences.'

Aspects of *multi-locality* affecting members of Hindu communities outside India are perhaps indicated most readily by the high degree of pilgrimage which still takes place among diasporic persons travelling back to the subcontinent to visit shrines and other holy places. Another, related yet somewhat obverse, example of this is provided in an anecdote by Arjun Appadurai (1991), who describes a trip (with his American-raised son) from his current home in the United States back to his childhood home of Madurai. There, Appadurai was surprised to learn that a particular priest, who had long served in the temple devoted to the goddess Meenaksi, was now a priest in Houston, Texas. This unexpected development stimulated Appadurai (ibid.: 202) to reflect upon 'the globalization of Hinduism, the transformation of "natives" into cosmopolites of their own sort, and the fact that the temple is now not only a magnet for persons from all over the world but also itself reaches out. The goddess Meenaksi has a living presence in Houston.'

Both *duality* and the modifications of mind which Appadurai and Breckenridge have described as *fractures of memory* and attachment are perhaps evident in the statement by the President of Bradford's Hindu Cultural Society who, following the bloody aftermath of events in Ayodhya in December 1992, claimed that 'What has happened in India has nothing to do with us' (in Kundu 1994: 28). Either this was a case of denial in order to deflect the media, or the 'triadic relationship' of homeland–country of settlement–diaspora had been broken conceptually.

There is ample evidence with regard to members of South Asian religions seeking to establish a legitimate place in *public space*, largely through engagement in political mobilization around specific causes or civic domains (Vertovec 1995, 1996a, 1997b; Vertovec and Peach 1997). These have included calls for public resources for 'community' associations, acceptance of group-specific values and practices – including safeguarding these in law – and a range of accommodations in the education and social service systems. As Pnina Werbner (1991a, b) demonstrates, the 'multiple realities' of life among diasporic groups (in the case of her research, Pakistani Muslims in Manchester) are importantly contested, negotiated and revised in the course of engaging the public sphere. Such processes sharpen, in an evolutionary way, the agendas and identities with which ethnic minorities engage the state. Iris Kalka (1991) similarly shows how processes and institutions for consultation established by the local Council affected the ways Hindus in Harrow, North London (particularly their 'ethnic brokers') developed and concretized notions of 'difference' and 'community'.

In a superb ethnography of Southall, West London, Gerd Baumann (1996) describes how the dominant discourses of 'culture' and 'community' – both reified as notions connoting homogeneity, fixity and boundedness – are reproduced in the everyday classification' of residents. The combined context of ethnic pluralism and conditions of diaspora, impacted upon by the dominant discourse, instils a 'culture consciousness' that Baumann describes as a

> heightened awareness that one's own life, as well as the lives of all others, are decisively shaped by *culture* as a reified heritage . . . an awareness that whatever one, or anyone, does and thinks is intrinsically and distinctively *culture-*

bound, and defined in relation to both one's own culture and the *cultures* of others.

(ibid.: 98, 107)

Moreover, while everyone in the social field that is Southall is readily identified in terms of culture-community, 'religion continues to function as the local *community* marker *par excellence*' (ibid.: 181).

However – and here lies the crux of Baumann's argument – despite an exacerbated 'culture consciousness' and the construction of reified 'communities' (namely 'Sikhs', 'Hindus', 'Muslims', 'Afro-Caribbeans' and 'Whites') in Southall, at the same time Southallians maintain a contrasting 'demotic discourse' surrounding their own *multiplicity*. This latter type (differentially patterned among groups) also makes use of notions of 'culture' and 'community', but in open-ended ways which recognize the complex ties, overlapping affiliations, sub-differentiations and multiple identities sustained in everyday practice.

> Yet this process is not one of simple segmentary fission, of a 'majority *community*' falling apart. Rather, it increases the institutional repertoire while leaving intact the multiplicity of cross-cutting cleavages. One may picture, for instance, an East African Punjabi Sikh of the Tharkan caste. He or she can speak to certain Muslim and Hindu Southallians as a fellow East African; they may do likewise with former East Africans who are Gujarati, rather than Punjabi; they may similarly speak to fellow Sikhs of the Raj or Lohar caste as fellow Ramgarhia, whether they hail from the subcontinent or from East Africa. Which of these mutually independent identifications they draw upon or stress will depend on the perceived context, the strategies of everyday life, and the classificatory choices deemed appropriate between the various parties.
>
> (ibid.: 115)

Just as such identifications shift contextually, a 'dual discursive competence' allows Southallians to engage in dominant or demotic discourses of 'culture' and 'community' depending upon their judgements of situation and purpose.

The heightening of awareness with regard to 'culture' is paralleled by new kinds of *self-awareness* with regard to religious belief and practice. Concerning Hindus in Britain the process has been exemplified in Chapter 1 with reference to David Pocock's (1976) discussion of Bochasanwasi Shri Akshar Purushottam Sanstha of the Swaminarayan movement and their dilemma of 'emulating the Jews' by consciously 'dis-embedding' their 'religion' and 'Gujarati culture'.

Processes of self-consciously distinguishing elements of religion/culture are bound to have differing results in various domains (in temples, in religious or cultural associations, in homes, in the workplace). Such processes have been part of a long historical trajectory in some parts of the Hindu diaspora (as described in Chapter 2) whereas they have relatively recently commenced in others.

Such modalities of 'sharpening awareness' seem to be a prominent development, in one form or another, throughout many Hindu communities overseas. Again, it is a trend common to diasporas and fostered by self-reflection stimulated amongst minorities in contexts of ethnic and religious pluralism. Hence Ninian Smart (1987: 295) writes:

> [D]iaspora reinforces contact with major world cultural forces. This factor underlines the need for the faith to express itself in the face of universal religions and secular values . . . Each such religion needs to give a universal account of itself, and to articulate its teachings, perhaps under some general principle.

Such a universalizing or ecumenical trend parallels that under way in America, which Raymond Williams (1988: 54) describes as 'the redefinition of boundaries through the manipulation of symbols and the expansion of their cultural contextualization so as to include as many Asian Indians as possible under a single religious identity'. Baumann (1996) observed a similar phenomenon is Southall which he calls processes of perceived encompassment and convergence of religious traditions. Ashis Nandy (1990: 104), however, provides a somewhat different twist to the notion that self-consciousness is a catalyst for transformation:

> I suspect that the diaspora has created identities which do not open up the older Indian identities but narrow them. Hinduism in the diaspora, for example, is much more exclusive and homogenic. Out of feelings of inferiority, many Hindus have tried to re-define Hinduism according to the dominant Western concept of religion. The result has been a more globalized, more Brahmanic – even a more semiticised

152

– version of Hinduism which endorses some of the most atavistic elements in Indian politics.

The foremost questions to arise, then, will likely revolve around the status and 'legitimacy' of the emergent and evolving diaspora religious traditions that claim global recognition, or indeed, 'authority'.

'Diaspora' as mode of cultural production

This final set of meanings that various writers have attributed to the notion of 'diaspora' is usually conveyed in discussions of globalization. In this sense globalization is examined in its guise as the world-wide flow of cultural objects, images and meanings resulting in variegated processes of creolization, back-and-forth transferences, mutual influences, new contestations, negotiations and constant transformations (see, for instance, Appadurai and Breckenridge 1988; Appadurai 1990; Hannerz 1992). In this way 'diaspora' is described as involving the *production and reproduction of transnational social and cultural phenomena* (see especially Appadurai 1991; Kearney 1995; Hannerz 1996). Glick Schiller, Basch and Blanc-Szanton (1992: 11) point to the logic of transnational activity of sending and receiving involving both material items and persons:

> [T]he constant and various flow of such goods and activities have embedded within them relationships between people. These social relations take on meaning within the flow and fabric of daily life, as linkages between different societies are maintained, renewed, and reconstituted in the context of families, of institutions, of economic investments, business, and finance and of political organisations and structures including nation-states.

Also with reference to questions of globalization, an interest in 'diaspora' has been equated with anthropology's now commonplace anti-essentialist, constructivist, and processual approach to *ethnicity* (see, for instance, Baumann and Sunier 1995). In this approach, the fluidity of constructed styles and identities among diasporic people is emphasized. These are evident in the production and reproduction of forms (increasingly the focus of interests in Cultural Studies) which are sometimes called syncretic, creolized, translated or hybrid. Regarding the creation of such forms, Stuart Hall (1990: 235) writes:

[D]iaspora does not refer us to those scattered tribes whose identity can only be secured in relation to some sacred homeland to which they must at all costs return, even if it means pushing other peoples into the sea. This is the old, the imperializing, the hegemonizing form of 'ethnicity' . . . The diaspora experience as I intend it here is defined not by essence or purity, but by the recognition of a necessary heterogeneity and diversity; by a conception of identity which lives with and through, not despite, difference; by hybridity. Diaspora identities are those which are constantly producing and reproducing themselves anew, through transformation and difference.

The production of such hybrid cultural phenomena and 'new ethnicities' is especially to be found among diasporic *youth* whose primary socialization has taken place with the cross-currents of differing cultural fields. Among such young people, facets of culture and identity are often self-consciously selected, syncretized and elaborated from more than one heritage.

An increasingly key avenue for the flow of cultural phenomena and the transformation of diasporic identity is, not surprisingly, *global media and communications*. Appadurai and Breckenridge (1989: iii) comment, 'Complex transnational flows of media images and messages perhaps create the greatest disjunctures for diasporic populations, since in the electronic media in particular, the politics of desire and imagination are always in contest with the politics of heritage and nostalgia' (cf. Appadurai 1990). Gayatri Spivak (1989: 276) also highlights 'the discourse of cultural specificity and difference, packaged for transnational consumption' through global technologies, particularly through the medium of 'microelectronic transnationalism' represented by electronic bulletin boards and the Internet.

Most anthropological studies regarding South Asian religions outside South Asia have broadly concerned issues of *cultural production and reproduction* (particularly surrounding religious aspects of family and kinship, caste, and ritual practice; see especially Bharati 1976; Jayawardena 1980; Burghart 1987b; Vertovec 1991a, 1992b, 1995; Ballard 1994b; van der Veer 1995). These include purported processes of cultural 'homogenisation' (Vertovec 1989, 1992b), 'retraditionalization' (Knott 1986b), complexification and increased conspicuous consumption (Werbner 1990; Ballard 1994a).

A less studied, but growing field of study concerns cultural production and reproduction of religious belief and practice among

South Asian *youth* (see Drury 1991; Jackson and Nesbitt 1993; Ballard 1994a; Baumann 1996; Vertovec and Rogers 1998). Key findings here generally indicate young people adapting their own interpretations of belief and consciously taking decisions as to the nature of their religious values and modes of participation in 'religious community' activities.

The examination of *media and communications* in the South Asian religious diaspora is very new. In this field, Marie Gillespie (1995) has produced a valuable ethnographic study of the role of transnational television and film in the formation and transformation of identity among young Punjabi Londoners. Reminiscent of the already-mentioned notions of 'triadic relationship', multi-locality, fractured memory and desire, Gillespie looks at the transformational ties such media create between India and persons throughout the diaspora.

> The connections and relations of 'absence' between these places are greatly strengthened by modern communications systems, which have augmented a sense of diasporic awareness among the Punjabi families in Southall. The connections may be as simply symbolic links between viewers of the same blockbuster Bombay movies; or they may be more concrete links between kin and friends in the form of 'video letters' and home videos of weddings and other rites of passage, especially coming-of-age celebrations.
>
> (ibid.: 7)

'It is clear', Gillespie (ibid.: 87) observes, 'that the VCR is being used for the purposes of reformulating and "translating" cultural traditions in the Indian diaspora.' This occurs not least in the viewing of 'sacred soaps', when 'Religious or "mythological" films are viewed for devotional purposes, particularly (but not only) in Hindu families, and their viewing is often integrated into daily acts of worship' (ibid.). When watching episodes of the *Ramayana* or *Mahabharata* made for TV in India, Hindus in Britain may light incense, perform 'devout salutation' when a deity appears on screen, conduct *puja* before or after viewing, and establish that, once commenced, the video must be watched in its entirety 'out of respect'. Gillespie demonstrates ways in which patterns surrounding the consumption of transnational media – including the modes through which it is viewed and discussed – both serve to secure the conservative valuing of 'traditional' South Asian culture among older South Asians in the

UK, and to prompt cosmopolitan admixtures of South Asian and other cultural streams among younger, British born-and-raised Asians.

By way of 'microelectronic transnationalism', Amit S. Rai (1995) examines contested modes of constructing Hindu identity in diaspora via electronic bulletin boards and Internet discussion groups (such as *alt.hindu*, and *soc.culture.indian*). Indeed, a casual surf of the Internet reveals myriad home pages and hypertext links to sites dedicated to the world-wide maintenance and propagation of Hinduism (including local temple sites across the United States, the National Hindu Students Forum in the UK, Hinduism Today's Electronic Ashram, vhp.org, and Hindunet). As mentioned at the end of the previous section, it is likely that the 'legitimacy' and 'authenticity' of such new constructions of Hinduism will continue to be hotly contested in the future.

Conclusion

In this chapter there have been suggested various ways of thinking about 'diaspora' and, thereby, different ways of considering what is happening among Hindus outside India, particularly in the United States and Britain. The discussion raised methodological questions of history, structure and agency.

Throughout his introduction to the edited volume entitled *Desh Pardesh*, Roger Ballard (1994a) invokes the notion of 'adaptive strategies' to emphasize how diverse South Asian groups in the UK follow their own distinctive dynamics. 'From this perspective the members of each colony are best understood as being in the midst of a vigorous process of adaptation, and thus busily engaged in deploying their own particular set of cultural, linguistic, religious and kinship resources to plot a better future for themselves' (ibid.: 29). From such a perspective we are also able to realize, Ballard (ibid.: 8) states, that 'the new minorities have become an integral part of the British social order, and they have done so *on their own terms*' (emphasis in original). Such a perspective is a significant corrective to a long-standing 'deprivationist' view of ethnic minorities as rather helpless and passive pawns whose life courses are wholly determined by the whims of a racist society (see Ballard 1992).

Although I wholly concur with Ballard with regard to the general perspective, I would raise a *caveat*. Too much emphasis on own-term strategies and the like can sound very much like functionalism (i.e. people do such-and-such because it does something else, perhaps unconsciously, for them). More disturbingly, it can sound like rational choice theory, which presumes that among social actors the 'selection of a course of action is rational and will be the most effective means of realising their preferred goal' (Hechter 1986: 264). Complete with overly economistic notions of 'rational trading', 'benefit/cost calculation', 'probability of success', 'profit-sharing' and 'group rewards', rational choice theory suggests that social actors are ever aware of what they are doing, and do so for maximum individual benefit. Although he certainly would not back such a view, Ballard's statement that 'adaptive strategies' involve conscious, logical choices and deployment can sound a lot like these assumptions within rational choice theory.

Elsewhere in the same piece, Ballard makes an important analogy between cultural and linguistic practice (drawing on Drummond 1980). 'Just as individuals can be bilingual', Ballard (1994a: 31) emphasizes, 'so they can also be multicultural, with the competence to behave appropriately in a number of different arenas, and to switch codes as appropriate.' Unfortunately, a rational choice-like model is again perpetuated when he goes on to say that such individuals 'must constantly decide how best to behave in any given context' (ibid.). Surely conscious choices affecting individual and group trajectories are frequently and very importantly made. But this is not all there is to it.

If we are to probe further the analogy of cultural and linguistic practice, we must recognize that most often these involve non-conscious processes. This is especially the case surrounding ideas of code-switching and code-mixing. Ben Rampton's (1995) detailed sociolinguistic study of 'language crossing' among youths in an ethnically mixed neighbourhood looks at uses of Punjabi, 'Stylized Asian English' and Caribbean Creole to manifest relationships of 'boundary transgression' as well as to affirm participants' claims to membership of certain self-defined groups. Such phenomena are parallel in many ways, I would suggest, to elements and functions of the 'demotic discourse' described by Baumann (1996).

> The ethnolinguistic boundary transgression inherent in code-crossing responded to, or produced, liminal moments and activities, when the ordered flow of habitual social life was loosened and when normal social relations could not be taken for granted. Code crossing occurred at the boundaries of interactional enclosure . . . Adolescents used language

to cross ethnic boundaries in moments when the constraints
of everyday social order were relaxed.

(Rampton 1995: 281)

Rampton observes that such acts of 'crossing' become ritualized
depending on a number of factors. A significant finding throughout
the study was that 'Members may alternate between codes without
even being consciously aware of it' (ibid.: 282) and that problems
of cultural/linguistic conflict are met with 'solutions which people
improvise together in the arena of intergroup practice itself' (ibid.: 296).

Non-conscious acts of 'crossing' or cultural reproduction were
evident to Bob Jackson and Eleanor Nesbitt (1993) in their research
on the reproduction of beliefs and practices among Hindu children
in Britain. Jackson and Nesbitt conclude that:

> While acknowledging that some practices may reinforce
> boundaries, our studies suggest that the situation is not clear
> cut and is becoming less so. Rather than being individuals
> with a fixed sense of belonging to this group or that, or
> feeling comfortable in only one type of cultural situation, it
> became clear that, in general, the children we were studying
> could move unselfconsciously from one milieu to another.
>
> (ibid.: 174–5)

Such examples of 'crossing' and 'milieu-moving', I believe, are rather
different to the usual notions of 'hybridity' discussed in much
literature within Cultural Studies. While the latter celebrate new
mixtures, the former indicate ways in which individuals not only
create syncretic forms, but are competent in – and can improvise
from – a number of (in some ways discrete, in some ways overlapping) cultural and linguistic systems (see Vertovec and Rogers
1998).

Cultural competence and improvisation are, of course, core
features of Pierre Bourdieu's (1977) notion of *habitus*: a name for
the non-conscious set of dispositions and classificatory schemes
that people gain through experience. The *habitus* provides a kind of
repertoire for situationally competent action, improvisation and
the generation of new practices. Bourdieu describes *habitus* as something historically patterned yet open to adjustment in relation to the
changing conditions of the social field. It is a concept particularly
useful for approaching the subject of agency in diasporic cultural
practice and reproduction. Appadurai (1991: 200) suggests such as

well, yet he believes we must re-work the concept with reference to 'a general change in the global conditions of life-worlds: put simply, where once improvisation was snatched out of the glacial undertow of *habitus*, *habitus* now has to be painstakingly reinforced in the face of life-worlds that are frequently in flux'.

Therefore, in coming back to questions raised in Chapter 1 as to how we can methodologically best grasp, in a comparative manner, myriad changes among diasporic communities such as Hindus outside India, we need systematically to take some account of (a) facets of historically conditioned structure or context, plus (b) agency approached as *habitus* – multiplied, as it were, by the conscious intervention of social actors through mediation, negotiation, and contestation within and between self-defined social groups. All of these complex matters are addressed when we considered together the complementary three meanings of 'diaspora'.

8

CONCLUSION

Many scholars have commented upon how the category 'Hinduism' is a rather artificial or historically constructed one since the beliefs and practices subsumed under it are so variegated. By way of developments outside India, examples described in this book indicate a number of ways in which singular concepts of Hinduism and Hindu identity have been forged, defined, reified and rallied around. In other words, as Ninian Smart (1987: 294) wryly comments on the diaspora, 'Maybe over much of its history there was no such clearly demarcated "-ism" as Hinduism; there is now.'

In the Caribbean we have seen how homogeneous 'official' modes of Hinduism have arisen – sometimes becoming embedded in forms of postcolonial ethnic-political competition (Chapter 2) – and how the formulation of staunch ethnic ideologies can concretize a Hindu identity (Chapter 3). In Britain the studies of Hindus and Hinduism offered in this book point to regional and caste-specific meanings and activities underpinning the reproduction of discrete communities (Chapter 4), the sometimes adverse relations between them (Chapter 5) and their distinct patterns of religious practice (Chapter 6). These developments have arisen in light of given historically and contextually conditioned processes within diasporic settings. So too have the many modalities described in Chapter 7 that inform us much about the notion of 'diaspora' itself.

Beyond methods and accounts that may help us gain an understanding of socio-religious dynamics in settings outside India, in order to get a fuller picture of what's happening – and going to happen – to Hinduism globally we need to turn attention and sharpen social scientific skills on the varieties of interplay between subcontinental and diasporic groups. Today, 'There is a constant flow of persons, goods, and information between India and the rest of the world which now makes Hinduism transnational' (van der Veer and

Vertovec 1991: 164). There are a number of significant forms this takes and reasons why they take place.

One core reason for heightened transnational activity among Hindus in India and the diaspora has to do with certain dynamics of the 'rootedness' noted in the Introduction. Wherever Hindus are, India will have a very deep meaning for them. One aspect of this has to do with religious authority – or perhaps better, religious sanction or legitimacy. For example, Bhikhu Parekh (1993) wonders why the Hindu diaspora has not thrown up one new deity or, for that matter, any religious leader of stature. A likely reason lies in the fact that many diasporic Hindus themselves refer to India as the source of authority (van der Veer 1996). Traditions, sects, schools and *swamis* in India, for all intents and purposes, have precedence and control over presumed orthodoxy primarily because they are presumed 'closer' to the wellsprings of Hinduism itself (sacred geography, art and architecture, philosophical traditions, spiritual milieu, and such). That some arguably new things could be 'invented' in Trinidad Hinduism is attributable to the legitimacy provided by local Brahmans, who established themselves as the nearest replacement thing to a direct India connection due to their caste lineage (see Vertovec 1991a; van der Veer and Vertovec 1991).

These points do not contradict the statements made in the Introduction surrounding the call for researchers to resist the temptation always to measure diaspora Hinduism against forms found in India. It is one thing for social scientists to assume Indian Hinduism as the 'authentic' norm (an assumption which degrades belief and practice in the diaspora), and another for Hindus in diaspora themselves to attribute 'authoritative' status to India (which is more to do with privileging a presumed continuity and intensity of heritage).

Another significant reason for the current augmentation of transnational ties between diaspora and India surrounds the transmission and reproduction of religious tradition among young, diaspora-born Hindus. Raymond Williams (1992a) has outlined the four primary media for the transmission of Hindu traditions between generations. These are temples, rituals, texts and exemplary persons. As we have seen in a number of examples in this book, these media exist in myriad forms and continue to serve their purposes in a number of divergent settings. Such media themselves often become shaped by their diasporic contexts. As John Hinnells (1997b: 829–30) explains, 'The means of transmission, and what is being transmitted, are therefore changing. Institutional forms are also subject to change in order to meet the perceived needs of members in a Western setting, for example youth groups and camps, weekend seminars, social and welfare committees and functions.' In order that the changes in diaspora do not go too far, however, the leaders of many Hindu organizations seek to tap the more 'authoritative' sources of India to ensure that the next generations stay in line and stay connected to the wellsprings. Hence throughout the diaspora (but particularly in Britain and the USA, not least where greater financial resources are at hand) there are calls for leaders of religious foundations, *sadhus* or saintly world-renouncers, and other religious specialists to tour and give lectures, sermons and 'discourses' in English (Lessinger 1995; Williams 1998).

The divergent diasporic developments wrought by history and the contemporary transnational dynamics linking diasporas and India contribute to three overall, and differentially directed, trends affecting Hinduism world-wide. These have been intermittently discussed throughout the book.

The first possible trend is for caste, sectarian and linguistic/regional traditions and communities to remain more or less intact. This has been a tendency in East Africa and Great Britain. Transnational links such as lecture tours by spokespersons and *sadhus* from India or the distribution of vernacular literature and videos may help sustain this pattern. But this is a path increasingly hard to sustain in the diaspora where caste identities are waning, linguistic skills are decreasing (in favour of English) and regional identities are becoming rather meaningless to people born, raised and dwelling outside India. Sectarian versions of Hinduism are facing increasing competition from the other two trends, Hindutva 'universalism' and 'ecumenical' Hinduism.

In India attempts to consolidate the meaning of Hinduism have been in motion for the past two hundred years. Today, singular definitions of Hinduism are the hallmark of the Hindutva movement. A foremost agent of this is the Vishwa Hindu Parishad, which is remarkably active throughout the Hindu diaspora. In this definition of Hinduism, all varieties are formally welcomed and understood as permutations of the same, ultimately unitary thing. In this sense it is presented as a kind of universal Hinduism. It is of course the core of a modern – and to many, a rigid and intolerant – religious nationalism. The appeal of this movement to diasporic Hindus is interesting, perhaps curious; in India, the support gained from the diaspora is significant and potentially transformative. 'By now the VHP is probably the strongest transnational movement among Hindus all over the world,' Peter van der Veer (1994: 134) observes:

'There is, then, an interesting interplay of "foreignness" and "native-ness," of "nationalism" and "transnationalism" here. I would suggest that the marginality felt by migrants in other parts of the world make them into important agents of innovation at home.' Van der Veer's analysis is shared by Arvind Rajagopal (1997). Rajagopal probes the question as to why the VHP has acquired such popularity among well-educated elite Hindus in the United States. He concludes:

> A redefined cultural nationalism is the answer for most expatriates as they distance themselves from the political problems of their homeland, and selectively embrace aspects of the U.S. environment. Rightwing Hindu nationalism, as embodied in the VHP, has capitalized on this tendency to its immeasurable advantage, defining its work in the United States largely in terms of religion and culture, offering ways of belonging and means of acculturation for later generations of Indian immigrants. The focus on religious identity serves to deflect the awkward questions of race and provides the VHP with a genteel multicultural presence. At the same time, VHP's vision of a strong Hindu state offers compensatory gratification for the experience of exile and marginality and promises redemption.
>
> (ibid.: 47)

The third trend is towards the (usually localized) development of an 'ecumenical' kind of Hinduism (Williams 1988). In this, a variety of kinds of Hinduism are recognized. Separate modes of worship co-exist while certain organizations, activities and celebrations occasionally bridge the distinct communities and traditions. The potentials for this trend are themselves shaped by contexts of dias-pora. Thus Martin Baumann (1998: 122) notes that 'In Europe, in contrast to the United States, eclectic pan-Hindu or "ecumenical" associations and temples are so far rather the exception than the rule.'

Among many Hindu communities in many places, it is likely that aspects of all three of these trends exist. Each is of significance to Hindus, each raises important questions that Hindus everywhere probably have to face, and each may lay claim to being the most valid or appropriate response to the condition of diaspora. And since each may link itself to some 'authoritative' source in India, 'The lines of authority in the global network of South Asian religions may well become complex, if not conflicting' (Hinnells 1997b: 834).

Perhaps yet another trend is emerging, however, that is in

some ways capable of mediating all three options – communal, universal/nationalist, and ecumenical Hinduism. That is, in some quarters of the diaspora we may be witnessing the emergence of what Peter van der Veer (1999) has called a 'cosmopolitan Hinduism'. Taking van der Veer's cue, we might say that cosmopolitanism (a) represents a capacity or skill to live in multiplex environments, and (b) recognizes that individuals have co-existing multiple identities, one or another of which can come to the fore in any particular setting. In this way, the three trends outlined above are not 'either/or' but 'also/and' options.

One example of this general approach is represented by the Swaminarayan movement (see Pocock 1976; Barot 1980; Williams 1984). With firm ties to Gujarati identity, Swaminarayanis are said to have strong connections with the Hindutva movement. At the same time, as Raymond Williams (1998) describes, Swaminarayanis have the diaspora critically in mind. They have established at least one centre in India for training *sadhus* from a range of backgrounds to go out to diasporic settings and teach, in English, Hinduism for young people living outside India. The aim, Williams relates, is to create 'a transnational sect with a cosmopolitan corps of *sadhus* [that] makes new types of transnational ethnicity possible' (ibid.: 859).

Diasporas and transnationalism constantly create forms and expressions of cosmopolitanism (cf. Cheah and Robbins 1998). Diasporic phenomena and processes of transnationalism among Hindu Indians, too, are fostering novel configurations of cosmopolitanism. Building upon historical patterns of definition and change, a new cosmopolitanism is beginning to be reflected in yet further evolving conceptualizations of Hinduism and Hindu identity.

BIBLIOGRAPHY

Aberle, D. (1962) 'A note on relative deprivation theory as applied to millennarian and other cult movements', in 'Millennial Dreams in Action', S. Thrupp (ed.), *Comparative Studies in Society and History*, Supplement II, The Hague: Mouton, pp. 209–14.

Angrosino, M.V. (1983) 'Religion among overseas Indian communities', in G.R. Gupta (ed.), *Religion in Modern India*, New Delhi: Vikas, pp. 357–98.

Appadurai, A. (1990) 'Disjuncture and difference in the global cultural economy', in M. Featherstone (ed.), *Global Culture: Nationalism, Globalization and Modernity*, London: Sage, pp. 295–310.

—— (1991) 'Global ethnoscapes: notes and queries for a transnational anthropology', in R.G. Fox (ed.), *Recapturing Anthropology: Working in the Present*, Santa Fe: School of American Research Press, pp. 191–210.

Appadurai, A. and Breckenridge, C. (1988) 'Why public culture?', *Public Culture* 1: 5–9.

—— (1989) 'On moving targets', *Public Culture* 2: i–iv.

Arasaratnam, S. (1979) *Indians in Malaysia and Singapore*, Kuala Lumpur: Oxford University Press.

Armstrong, J.A. (1976) 'Mobilized and proletarian diasporas', *American Political Science Review* 70: 393–408.

Arya, U. (1968) *Ritual Songs and Folksongs of the Hindus of Surinam*, Leiden: E.J. Brill.

Ashby, P.H. (1974) *Modern Trends in Hinduism*, New York: Columbia University Press.

Aveling, M. (1978) 'Ritual change in the Hindu temples of Penang', *Contributions to Indian Sociology* 12: 173–93.

Babb, L.A. (1974) 'Hindu mediumship in Singapore', *Southeast Asian Journal of Social Science* 2: 29–43.

—— (1975) *The Divine Hierarchy: Popular Hinduism in Central India*, New York: Columbia University Press.

Ballard, R. (1986) 'Changing life styles among British Asians', *New Community* 13: 301–3.

—— (1990) 'Migration and kinship: the differential effect of marriage rules on the processes of Punjabi migration to Britain', in C. Clarke, C. Peach and S. Vertovec (eds), *South Asians Overseas: Migration and Ethnicity*, Cambridge: Cambridge University Press, pp. 219–49.

—— (1992) 'New clothes for the emperor? The conceptual nakedness of the race relations industry in Britain', *New Community* 18: 481–92.

—— (1994a) 'Introduction: the emergence of *Desh Pardesh*,' in R. Ballard (ed.), *Desh Pardesh: The South Asian Presence in Britain*, London: C. Hurst, pp. 1–34.

—— (1994b) (ed.) *Desh Pardesh: The South Asian Presence in Britain*, London: C. Hurst.

Banks, J.A. (1972) *The Sociology of Social Movements*. London: Macmillan.

Barot, R. (1973) 'A Swaminarayan sect as a community', *New Community* 2: 34–7.

—— (1980) 'The social organization of a Swaminarayan sect in Britain', PhD thesis, University of London School of Oriental and African Studies.

—— (1987a) 'Religion and community among Bristol Hindus: the case of Sanatan Deevya Mandal', paper presented at the Colston Research Symposium on Religious Pluralism, Bristol.

—— (1987b) 'Caste and sect in the Swaminarayan movement', in R. Burghart (ed.), *Hinduism in Great Britain*, London: Tavistock, pp. 67–80.

Barrett, D.B. (ed.) (1982) *World Christian Encyclopedia*, Oxford: Oxford University Press.

Basham, A.L. (1954) *The Wonder That Was India*, London: Sidgwick & Jackson.

Bassier, W.M.Z. (1987) 'Kali Mai worship: a quest for a new identity', in I.J. Bahadur (ed.), *Indians in the Caribbean*, London: Oriental University Press, pp. 269–93.

Baumann, G. (1996) *Contesting Culture: Discourses of Identity in Multi-Ethnic London*, Cambridge: Cambridge University Press.

Baumann, G. and Sunier, T. (1995) 'De-essentializing ethnicity,' in G. Baumann and T. Sunier (eds), *Post-Migration Ethnicity: Cohesion, Commitments, Comparison*, Amsterdam: Spinhuis, pp. 1–8.

Baumann, M. (1995) 'Conceptualizing diaspora: the preservation of religious identity in foreign parts, exemplified by Hindu communities outside India', *Temenos* 31: 19–35.

—— (1998) 'Sustaining "Little Indias": Hindu diasporas in Europe', in G. Ter Haar (ed.), *Strangers and Sojourners: Religious Communities in the Diaspora*, Leuven: Peeters, pp. 95–132.

Bellah, R.N. (1965) 'Epilogue: religion and progress in modern Asia', in R.N. Bellah (ed.), *Religion and Progress in Modern Asia*, New York: Free Press, pp. 168–229.

Bentley, G.C. (1987) 'Ethnicity and practice', *Comparative Studies in Society and History* 29: 24–55.

Berreman, G.D. (1967) 'Caste as social process', *Southwestern Journal of Anthropology* 23: 351–70.

Bhachu, P. (1985) *Twice Migrants: East African Sikh Settlers in Britain*, London: Tavistock.

Bharati, A. (1970) 'A social survey', in D.P. Ghai and Y.P. Ghai (eds), *Portrait of a Minority: Asians in East Africa*, Nairobi: Oxford University Press, pp. 15–67.

—— (1971) 'Hinduism and modernization', in R.F. Spencer (ed.), *Religion and Change in Contemporary Asia*, Minneapolis: University of Minnesota Press, pp. 67–104.

—— (1972) *The Asians in East Africa: Jayhind and Uhuru*, Chicago: Nelson-Hall.

—— (1976) 'Ritualistic tolerance and ideological rigour: the paradigm of the expatriate Hindus in East Africa', *Contributions to Indian Sociology* 10: 317–39.

Bhardwaj, S.M. and Rao, M. (1990) 'Asian Indians in the United States: a geographic appraisal', in C. Clarke, C. Peach and S. Vertovec (eds), *South Asians Overseas: Migration and Ethnicity*, Cambridge: Cambridge University Press, pp. 197–217.

Bhatt, C. (1997) *Liberation and Purity: Race, New Religious Movements and the Ethics of Postmodernity*, London: UCL Press.

Bickford, J.R. (1987) *Dimensions of a Creole Continuum: History, Texts, and Linguistic Analysis of Guyanese Creole*, Stanford, CA: Stanford University Press.

Bilimoria, P. (1985) 'The Arya Samaj in Fiji: a moment in Hindu diaspora', *Religion* 15: 103–29.

—— (1997) 'The Australian South Asian diaspora', in J.R. Hinnells (ed.), *A New Handbook of Living Religions*, Oxford: Blackwell, pp. 728–55.

Boodhoo, M.J. and Baksh, A. (1981) *The Impact of Brain Drain on Development: A Case Study of Guyana*, Georgetown: University of Guyana.

Bourdieu, P. (1977) *Outline of a Theory of Practice*, Cambridge: Cambridge University Press.

Bowen, D. (1981) 'The Hindu community in Bradford', in D. Bowen (ed.), *Hinduism in England*, Bradford: Bradford College, pp. 33–60.

—— (1987) 'The evolution of Gujarati Hindu organizations in Bradford', in R. Burghart (ed.), *Hinduism in Great Britain*, London: Tavistock, pp. 15–31.

Brear, D. (1986) 'A unique Hindu Festival in England and India, 1985: a phenomenological analysis', *Temenos* 2 21–39.

Brennan, L. and Lal, B.V. (1998) (eds) 'Across the Kala Pani: Indian overseas migration and settlement', special issue, *South Asia* 21: 1–237.

Brereton, B. (1979) *Race Relations in Colonial Trinidad, 1870–1900*, Cambridge: Cambridge University Press.

—— (1981) *A History of Modern Trinidad 1783–1962*, London: Heinemann.

Brockington, J.L. (1981) *The Sacred Thread: Hinduism in its Continuity and Diversity*, Edinburgh: University of Edinburgh Press.

Bronkhurst, H. V. P. (1883) *The Colony of British Guiana and Its Labouring Population*, London: T. Woolmer.

—— (1888) *Among the Hindus and Creoles of British Guiana*, London: T. Woolmer.

Bryant, M.T. (1983) 'A way to God: a study of some of the beliefs and practices of Hindus in Leicester and Leicestershire', MPhil thesis, University of Leicester.

Buchignani, N. (1980) 'The social and self-identities of Fijian Indians in Vancouver', *Urban Anthropology* 9: 75–97.

Burghart, R. (1987a) 'Introduction: the diffusion of Hinduism into Great

Britain', in R. Burghart (ed.), *Hinduism in Great Britain*, London: Tavistock, pp. 1–14.

—— (1987b) 'Conclusion: the perpetuation of Hinduism in an alien cultural milieu', in R. Burghart (ed.), *Hinduism in Great Britain*, London: Tavistock, pp. 224–51.

—— (ed.) (1987c) *Hinduism in Great Britain*, London: Tavistock.

Burlet, S. and Reid, H. (1995) 'Cooperation and conflict: the South Asian diaspora after Ayodhya', *New Community* 21: 587–97.

Carey, S. (1983) 'The Hare Krishna movement and Hindus in Britain', *New Community* 10: 477–86.

—— (1987) 'The Indianization of the Hare Krishna movement in Britain', in R. Burghart (ed.), *Hinduism in Great Britain*, London: Tavistock, pp. 81–99.

Cheah, P. and Robbins, B. (eds) (1998) *Cosmopolitics: Thinking and Feeling Beyond the Nation*, Minneapolis: University of Minnesota Press.

CIA (1997) *The World Factbook*, Washington, DC: Central Intelligence Agency.

Clarke, C. (1986) *Indians in a West Indian Town: San Fernando, Trinidad, 1930–70*, London: Allen & Unwin.

Clarke, C., Peach, C. and Vertovec, S. (1990a) 'Introduction: themes in the study of the South Asian diaspora', in C. Clarke, C. Peach and S. Vertovec (eds), *South Asians Overseas: Migration and Ethnicity*, Cambridge: Cambridge University Press, pp. 1–29.

—— (1990b) (eds) *South Asians Overseas: Migration and Ethnicity*, Cambridge: Cambridge University Press.

Clifford, J. (1994) 'Diasporas', *Cultural Anthropology* 9: 302–38.

Cohen, R. (1995) 'Rethinking "Babylon": iconoclastic conceptions of the diasporic experience', *New Community* 21: 5–18.

—— (1996) 'Diasporas and the nation-state: from victims to challengers', *International Affairs* 72: 507–20.

—— (1997) *Global Diasporas: An Introduction*, London: UCL Press.

Collens, J.H. (1888) *A Guide to Trinidad*, London: Elliott Stock.

Comins, D.W.D. (1893) *Note on Emigration from India to Trinidad*, Calcutta: Bengal Secretariat.

Coward, H. (1997) 'The religions of the South Asian diaspora in Canada', in J.R. Hinnells (ed.), *A New Handbook of Living Religions*, Oxford: Blackwell, pp. 775–95.

Crissman, L.W. (1967) 'The segmentary structure of urban overseas Chinese communities', *Man* 2: 185–204.

Crooke, W. (1886) *The Tribes and Castes of the North-Western Provinces and Oudh*, 4 vols, Calcutta: Central Printing Office.

Cross, M. (1973) *The East Indians of Guyana and Trinidad*, London: Minority Rights Group.

—— (1978) 'Colonialism and ethnicity: a theory and comparative study', *Ethnic and Racial Studies* 1: 37–59.

Cross, M. and Schwartzbaum, A.W. (1969) 'Social mobility and secondary school selection in Trinidad and Tobago', *Social and Economic Studies* 18: 189–207.

Crowley, D. (1957) 'Plural and differential acculturation', *American Anthropologist*, 59: 817–24.

Dahya, B. (1974) 'The nature of Pakistani ethnicity in industrial cities in Britain', in A. Cohen (ed.), *Urban Ethnicity*, London: Tavistock, pp. 77–118.

Deshpande, S. (1998) 'Hegemonic spatial strategies: the nation-space and Hindu communalism in twentieth-century India', *Public Culture* 10: 249–84.

Dew, E. (1978) *The Difficult Flowering of Surinam*, The Hague: Martinus Nijhoff.

Diesel, A. (1990) 'Hindu firewalking in Natal', *Journal for the Study of Religion* 3: 17–33.

—— (1998) 'The empowering image of the Divine Mother: a South African Hindu woman worshipping the Goddess', *Journal of Contemporary Religion* 13: 73–90.

Drummond, L. (1980) 'The cultural continuum: a theory of intersystems', *Man* (N.S.) 15: 352–74.

Drury, B. (1991) 'Sikh girls and the maintenance of an ethnic culture', *New Community* 17: 387–400.

Durbin, M.A. (1973) 'Formal changes in Trinidad Hindi as a result of language adaptation', *American Anthropologist* 75: 1290–304.

Dwyer, J.H. (1988) 'The formal religious nurture in two Hindu temples in Leicester', PhD thesis, University of Leicester.

Eck, D.L. (1996) 'American Hindus: the Ganges and the Mississippi', paper presented at conference on 'The Comparative Study of the South Asian Diaspora Religious Experience in Britain, Canada and the USA', School of Oriental and African Studies, November.

Ehrlich, A.S. (1971) 'History, ecology and demography in the British Caribbean: an analysis of East Indian ethnicity', *Southwestern Journal of Anthropology* 27: 66–88.

Eisenstadt, S.N. (1968) 'Introduction', in M. Weber [Selected Papers, S.N. Eisenstadt (ed.)], *On Charisma and Institution Building*, Chicago: University of Chicago Press, pp. ix–lvi.

Emmer, P. (1984) 'The importation of British Indians into Surinam (Dutch Guiana) 1873–1916', in S. Marks and P.D. Richardson (eds), *International Labour Migration*, London: Frank Cass, pp. 90–111.

Eriksen, R. (1984) '"Indians" and "Africans" in a Hindu Gujarati community', unpublished ms, Dept. of Social Anthropology, Cambridge University.

Fitzgerald, T. (1990) 'Hinduism and the "world religion" fallacy', *Religion*: 20: 101–18.

Forbes, R.H. (1984) 'Arya Samaj in Trinidad: an historical study of Hindu organisation process in acculturative conditions', PhD dissertation, University of Miami.

Freitag, S.B. (1980) 'Sacred symbol as mobilizing ideology: the North Indian search for a "Hindu" community', *Comparative Studies in Society and History* 22: 597–625.

—— (1989) *Collective Action and Community: Public Arenas and the Emergence of Communalism in North India*, Berkeley, CA: University of California Press.

Froude, J.A. (1888) *The English in the West Indies*, London: Longmans, Green & Co.

Frykenberg, R.E. (1989) 'The emergence of modern "Hinduism" as a concept and as an institution: a reappraisal with special reference to South India', in G.D. Sontheimer and H. Kulke (eds), *Hinduism Reconsidered*, Delhi: Manohar, pp. 29–49.

—— (1990) 'The construction of "Hinduism" as a "public" religion: looking again at the role of the Company Raj in South India', paper presented at the 11th European conference on Modern South Asian Studies, Amsterdam.

Fuller, C.J. (1979) 'Gods, priests and purity: on the relation between Hinduism and the caste system', *Man* (N.S.) 14: 459–76.

—— (1984) *Servants of the Goddess: The Priests of a South Indian Temple*, Cambridge: Cambridge University Press.

—— (1988) 'The Hindu temple and Indian society', in M. V. Fox (ed.), *Temple in Society*, Winona Lake: Eisenbrauns, pp. 49–66.

Gambhir, S.K. (1983) 'Diglossia in dying languages: a case study of Guyanese Bhojpuri and Standard Hindi', *Anthropological Linguistics* 25: 28–38.

Gamble, W.H. (1886) *Trinidad; Historical and Descriptive*, London: Yates & Alexander.

Gans, H.J. (1999) 'Symbolic ethnicity: the future of ethnic groups and cultures in America', in S. Vertovec (ed.), *Migration and Social Cohesion*, Aldershot: Edward Elgar, pp. 392–410.

Geertz, C. (1968) *Islam Observed: Religious Developments in Morocco and Indonesia*, Chicago: University of Chicago Press.

—— (1973) 'Religion as a cultural system', in C. Geertz, *The Interpretation of Cultures*, New York: Basic Books, pp. 87–125.

Geoghegan, J. (1873) *Notes on Emigration from India*, Calcutta: Government Printery.

Gillespie, M. (1995) *Television, Ethnicity and Cultural Change*, London: Routledge.

Gilroy, P. (1987) *There Ain't no Black in the Union Jack*, London: Hutchinson.

—— (1993a) *The Black Atlantic: Modernity and Double Consciousness*, London: Verso.

—— (1993b) *Small Acts: Thoughts on the Politics of Black Cultures*, London: Serpent's Tail.

Glick Schiller, N., Basch, L. and Blanc-Szanton, C. (1992) 'Transnationalism: a new analytic framework for understanding migration', in N. Glick Schiller, L. Basch and C. Blanc-Szanton (eds), *Toward a Transnational Perspective on Migration*, New York: New York Academy of Sciences, pp. 1–24.

Goa, D.J., Coward, H.G. and Neufeldt, R. (1984) 'Hindus in Alberta: a case study', *Canadian Ethnic Studies* 16: 96–113.

Gombrich, R. (1992) 'Traditional Hinduism', presentation in Modern History seminar, Oxford University, 28 April.

Graham, S. and Gordon, D. (1977) *The Stratification System and Occupational Mobility in Guyana*, Mona, Jamaica: Institute of Social and Economic Research.

Grierson, G. (1885) *Bihar Peasant Life*, London: Truebner & Co.

Grillo, R. (1985) *Ideologies and Institutions in Urban France: The Representation of Immigrants*, Cambridge: Cambridge University Press.

Hall, S. (1985) 'Religious ideologies and social movements in Jamaica', in R. Bocock and K. Thompson (eds), *Religion and Ideology*, Manchester: Manchester University Press, pp. 269–96.
—— (1990) 'Cultural identity and diaspora', in J. Rutherford (ed.), *Identity: Community, Culture, Difference*, London: Lawrence and Wishart, pp. 222–37.
Hannerz, U. (1992) *Cultural Complexity: Studies in the Social Organization of Meaning*, New York: Columbia University Press.
—— (1996) *Transnational Connections: Culture, People, Places*, London: Routledge.
Hardgrave, R.L. (1970) 'Urbanization and the structure of caste', in R.G. Fox (ed.), *Urban India: Society, Space and Image*, Hillsborough, NC: Duke University Program in Comparative Studies on South Asia, Monograph No. 10, pp. 39–50.
Hardy, F. (1990) 'Hinduism', in U. King (ed.), *Turning Points in Religious Studies*, Edinburgh: T. & T. Clark, pp. 145–67.
Harewood, J. (1971) 'Racial discrimination in employment in Trinidad and Tobago', *Social and Economic Studies* 20: 267–93.
Hechter, M. (1986) 'Rational choice theory and the study of race and ethnic relations', in J. Rex and D. Mason (eds), *Theories of Race and Ethnic Relations*, Cambridge: Cambridge University Press, pp. 264–79.
Hinnells, J.R. (1997a) 'The study of diaspora religion', in J.R. Hinnells (ed.), *A New Handbook of Living Religions*, Oxford: Blackwell, pp. 682–90.
—— (1997b) 'Comparative reflections on South Asian religion in international migration', in J.R. Hinnells (ed.), *A New Handbook of Living Religions*, Oxford: Blackwell, pp. 819–47.
Hintzen, P.C. (1985) 'Bases of elite support for a regime: race, ideology and clientelism as bases for leaders in Guyana and Trinidad', *Comparative Political Studies* 16: 363–91.
—— (1989) *The Costs of Regime Survival: Racial Mobilization, Elite Domination and Control of the State in Guyana and Trinidad*, Cambridge: Cambridge University Press.
Hofmeyr, J. (1983) 'Homogeneity and South African Hinduism', *Journal of Religion in Africa* 13: 139–49.
Hole, E.A. (1996) 'Hindu women of the diaspora: some preliminary notes on the lives of Hindu women in Sweden', paper presented at the 14th European Conference on Modern South Asian Studies, Copenhagen.
Hollup, O. (1993) 'Changing conceptualization of Indian ethnic identity in Mauritius', DrPolit thesis, University of Bergen.
Holy, L. (1987) 'Description, generalization and comparison: two paradigms', in L. Holy (ed.), *Comparative Anthropology*, Oxford: Blackwell, pp. 1–21.
Hutheesing, M.O.L.K. (1983) 'The Thiratee Kalyanam ceremony among South Indian Hindu communities of Malaysia', *Eastern Anthropologist* 36: 131–47.
Ishwaran, K. (1980) 'Bhakti tradition and modernization: the case of Lingayatism', *Journal of Asian and African Studies* 15: 72–82.
Jackson, P. and Smith, S.J. (eds) (1981) *Social Interaction and Ethnic Segregation*, London: Academic Press.

Jackson, R. (1981) 'The Shree Krishna Temple and the Gujarati Hindu community in Coventry', in D.G. Bowen (ed.), *Hinduism in England*, Bradford: Bradford College, pp. 61–85.

—— (1984) 'The concerns of religious education and the characterization of Hinduism', *British Journal of Religious Education* 6: 141–6.

—— (1985) 'Hinduism in Britain: religious nurture and religious education', *British Journal of Religious Education* 7: 68–75.

—— (1987) 'Changing conceptions of Hinduism in "time-tabled religion"', in R. Burghart (ed.), *Hinduism in Great Britain*, London: Tavistock, pp. 201–23.

Jackson, R. and Nesbitt, E. (1986) 'Sketches of formal Hindu nurture: Hindu supplementary classes in England', *World Religions in Education* (Shap Mailing), London: Commission for Racial Equality.

—— (1993) *Hindu Children in Britain*, Stoke-on-Trent: Trentham.

Jaffrelot, C. (1992) 'Hindu nationalism: strategic syncretism in ideology building', paper presented at the British Association for South Asian Studies, Birmingham.

—— (1996) *The Hindu Nationalist Movement and Indian Politics, 1920 to the 1990s*, Oxford: Berg.

Jain, P. (1989) 'Emigration and settlement of Indians abroad', *Sociological Bulletin* 38: 155–68.

Jain, R.K. (1968) 'Religion and morality: a preliminary framework for comparison of beliefs and practices among the Hindu Tamils of India and Malaysia', paper presented at the VIIIth Congress of Anthropological and Ethnological Sciences.

Jayawardena, C. (1963) *Conflict and Solidarity in a Guianese Plantation*, London: Athlone.

—— (1966) 'Religious belief and social change: aspects of the development of Hinduism in British Guiana', *Comparative Studies in Society and History* 8: 211–40.

—— (1968) 'Migration and social change: a survey of Indian communities overseas', *Geographical Review* 58: 426–49.

—— (1971) 'The disintegration of caste in Fiji Indian rural society', in L.R. Hiatt and C. Jayawardena (eds), *Anthropology in Oceania*, Sydney: Angus and Robertson, pp. 89–119.

—— (1980) 'Culture and ethnicity in Guyana and Fiji', *Man* (N.S.) 15: 430–50.

Jha, J.C. (1982) 'The background of the legislation of non-Christian marriages in Trinidad and Tobago', in B. Brereton and W. Dookeran (eds), *East Indians in the Caribbean*, London: Kraus, pp. 117–39.

—— (1989) 'Hinduism in Trinidad', in F. Birbalsingh (ed.), *Indenture and Exile: The Indo-Caribbean Experience*, Toronto: TSAR, pp. 225–33.

Jindel, R. (1976) *Culture of a Sacred Town*, Bombay: Popular Prakashan.

Jones, K.W. (1976) *Arya Dharm: Hindu Consciousness in Nineteenth Century Punjab*, Berkeley, CA: University of California Press.

Kalka, I. (1991) 'The politics of the "community" among Gujarati Hindus in London', *New Community* 17: 377–85.

Kanitkar, H. (1979) 'A school for Hindus?', *New Community* 7: 178–83.

Kapferer, B. (1983) *A Celebration of Demons*, Bloomington: Indiana University Press.

—— (1988) *Legends of People, Myths of State*, Washington, DC: Smithsonian Institution Press.

—— (1995) 'The performance of categories: plays of identity in Africa and Australia', in A. Rogers and S. Vertovec (eds), *The Urban Context*, Oxford: Berg, pp. 55–80.

Kearney, M. (1995) 'The local and the global: the anthropology of globalization and transnationalism', *Annual Review of Anthropology* 24: 547–65.

Kelly, J.D. (1988) 'From Holi to Diwali in Fiji: an essay on ritual and history', *Man* 23: 40–55.

—— (1991) *A Politics of Virtue: Hinduism, Sexuality and Countercolonial Discourse in Fiji*, Chicago: University of Chicago Press.

—— (1995) '*Bhakti* and postcolonial politics: Hindu missions to Fiji', in P. van der Veer (ed.), *Nation and Migration: The Politics of Space in the South Asian Diaspora*, Philadelphia: University of Pennsylvania Press, pp. 43–72.

Khan, A. (1977) 'Kali Mai Puja in Guyana', *Religion* 7: 35–45.

Khan, A. (1994) '*Juthaa* in Trinidad: food, pollution and hierarchy in a Caribbean diaspora community', *American Ethnologist* 21: 245–69.

Killingley, D., Killingley, S.Y., Nowicki, V., Shukla, H. and Simmonds, D. (1984) *A Handbook of Hinduism for Teachers*, 2nd rev. edn, Newcastle-upon-Tyne: Grevatt & Grevatt.

King, U. (1984) 'A report on Hinduism in Britain', Leeds: Community Religions Project Research Papers (New Series) No. 2, Dept. of Theology and Religious Studies, University of Leeds.

Kingsley, C. (1905) *At Last, a Christmas in the West Indies*, (3rd edn.) London: Macmillan.

Kirpalani, M. *et al.* (1945) *Indian Centenary Review*, Port of Spain: Indian Centenary Review Committee.

Klass, M. (1961) *East Indians in Trinidad*, New York: Columbia University Press

—— (1991) *Singing with Sai Baba: The Politics of Revitalization in Trinidad*, Boulder, CO: Westview Press.

Klostermaier, K.K. (1989) *A Survey of Hinduism*, Albany, NY: State University of New York Press.

Knott, K. (1986a) 'Religion and identity and the study of ethnic minority religions in Britain', in V. Hayes (ed.), *Identity Issues and World Religions*, Sydney: Australian Association for the Study of Religions.

—— (1986b) *Hinduism in Leeds: A Study of Religious Practice in the Indian Hindu Community and Hindu-Related Groups*, Leeds: Community Religions Project, University of Leeds.

—— (1987) 'Hindu temple rituals in Britain: the reinterpretation of tradition', in R. Burghart (ed.), *Hinduism in Great Britain*, London: Tavistock, pp. 157–79.

—— (1991) 'Bound to change? The religions of South Asians in Britain', in S. Vertovec (ed.), *Aspects of the South Asian Diaspora*, New Delhi: Oxford University Press, pp. 86–111.

—— (1994) 'From leather stockings to surgical boots and beyond: the Gujarati Mochis of Leeds', in R. Ballard (ed.), *Desh Pardesh: The South Asian Presence in Britain*, London: C. Hurst, pp. 213–30.

Knott K. and Toon, R. (1982) 'Muslims and Sikhs and Hindus in the UK: problems in the estimation of religious statistics', *Religious Research Papers* No. 6, Leeds: Department of Sociology, University of Leeds.

Kondapi, C. (1951) *Indians Overseas 1838–1949*, Bombay: Oxford University Press.

Kotkin, J. (1992) *Tribes: How Race, Religion and Identity Determine Success in the New Global Economy*, New York: Random House.

Kundu, A. (1994) 'The Ayodhya aftermath: Hindu versus Muslim violence in Britain', *Immigrants and Minorities* 13: 26–47.

Kuper, H. (1957) 'An interpretation of Hindu marriage in Durban', *African Studies* 16: 221–35.

Kurien, P. (1997) 'Constructing "Indianness" in the United States and India: the role of Hindu and Muslim immigrants', http://www.usc.edu/dept/LAS/SC2/kurien.html.

Lannoy, R. (1971) *The Speaking Tree: A Study of Indian Culture and Society*, London: Oxford University Press.

Lawrence, K.O. (1971) *Immigration into the West Indies in the 19th Century*, St Lawrence, London: Caribbean Universities Press.

Leach, E.R. (1968) *Dialectic in Practical Religion*, Cambridge: Cambridge University Press.

Lee, R.L.M. (1982) 'Sai Baba, salvation, and syncretism: religious change in a Hindu movement in urban Malaysia', *Contributions to Indian Sociology* 16: 125–40.

Lee, R.L.M. and Rajoo, R. (1987) 'Sanskritization and Indian ethnicity in Malaysia', *Modern Asian Studies* 21: 389–415.

Lessinger, J. (1992) 'Nonresident-Indian investment and India's drive for industrial modernization', in F.A. Rothstein and M.L. Blim (eds), *Anthropology and the Global Factory*, New York: Bergin & Garvey, pp. 62–82.

—— (1995) *From the Ganges to the Hudson: Indian Immigrants in New York City*, Boston: Allyn & Bacon.

Lingayah, S. (1987) *Mauritian Immigrants in Britain: A Study of their Hopes and Frustrations*, London: Mauritius Welfare Association.

Logan, P. (1988) 'Practising Hinduism: the experience of Gujarati adults and children in Britain', unpublished report, Thomas Coram Research Unit, University of London Institute of Education.

McDonald, M. (1987) 'Rituals of motherhood among Gujarati women in East London', in R. Burghart (ed.), *Hinduism in Great Britain*, London: Tavistock, pp. 50–66.

MacNeill, J. and Lal, C. (1914) *Report on the Condition of Indian Immigrants in the Four British Colonies: Trinidad, British Guiana or Demerara, Jamaica and Fiji and in the Dutch Colony of Surinam or Dutch Guiana*, Simla: Government Central Press.

Malik, Y.K. (1966) 'The Democratic Labour Party of Trinidad: an attempt at the formation of a mass party in a multi-cultural society', PhD dissertation, University of Florida.

—— (1971) *East Indians in Trinidad: A Study in Minority Politics*, London: Oxford University Press.

Mangru, B. (1987) *Benevolent Neutrality: Indian Government Policy and Labour Migration to British Guiana 1854–1884*, London: Hansib.

Marriott, M. (1955) 'Little communities in an indigenous civilization', in M. Marriott (ed.), *Village India*, Chicago: University of Chicago Press, pp. 171–223.

—— (1965) *Caste Ranking and Community Structure in Five Regions of India and Pakistan*, Poona: Deccan College.

Mearns, D.J. (1995) *Shiva's Other Children: Religion and Social Identity amongst Overseas Indians*, New Delhi: Sage.

Menski, W. (1987) 'Legal pluralism in the Hindu marriage', in R. Burghart (ed.), *Hinduism in Great Britain*, London: Tavistock, pp. 180–200.

Michaelson, M. (1979) 'The relevance of caste among East African Gujaratis in Britain', *New Community* 7: 350–60.

—— (1983) 'Caste, kinship and marriage: a study of two Gujarati trading castes in England', PhD thesis, University of London School of Oriental and African Studies.

—— (1984) 'Gujarati communities in Britain', paper presented at the Symposium on Gujarati Ethnicity, University of London School of Oriental and African Studies.

—— (1987) 'Domestic Hinduism in a Gujarati trading caste', in R. Burghart (ed.), *Hinduism in Great Britain*, London: Tavistock, pp. 32–49.

Mitchell, G. (1977) *The Hindu Temple: An Introduction to Its Meaning*, London: Paul Elek.

Mitchell, J.C. (1987) *Cities, Society and Social Perception: A Central African Perspective*, Oxford: Clarendon Press.

Modood, T., Berthoud, R., Lakey, J., Nazroo, J., Smith, P., Virdee, S. and Reishon, S. (1997) *Ethnic Minorities in Britain: Diversity and Disadvantage*, London: Policy Studies Institute.

Moore, B. (1977) 'The retention of caste notions among the Indian immigrants in British Guiana during the nineteenth century', *Comparative Studies in Society and History* 19: 96–107.

Moore, R.J. (1970) 'East Indians and Negroes in British Guiana, 1833–1880', PhD thesis, University of Sussex.

Morris, H.S. (1968) *The Indians of Uganda*, London: Weidenfeld & Nicolson.

Morton, S. (1916) *John Morton of Trinidad*, Toronto: Westminster.

Nagar, R. (1997) 'The making of Hindu communal organizations, places and identities in postcolonial Dar es Salaam', *Environment and Planning D: Society and Space* 15: 707–30.

Naidoo, T. (1992) *The Arya Samaj Movement in South Africa*, Delhi: Motilal Banarsidass.

Naipaul, V.S. (1972) *The Overcrowded Barracoon and Other Articles*, London: André Deutsch.

Nandy, A. (1990) 'Dialogue and the diaspora', *Third Text* 11: 99–108.

Nesbitt, E. (1987) 'British Punjabi Hindu children and their religious tradition', *Punjab Research Group Discussion Paper* Series No. 11.

—— (1989) 'Valmiki and Ravidasi children: a spectrum of identity', paper presented at the 15th Symposium on Indian Religion, Oxford.

Nevadomsky, J. (1983) 'Economic organization, social mobility, and changing social status among East Indians in rural Trinidad', *Ethnology* 22: 63–79.

Nicholas, R.W. (1981) 'Understanding a Hindu temple in Bengal', in A.C.

Mayer (ed.), *Culture and Morality*, Delhi: Oxford University Press, pp. 174–90.

Niehoff, A. and Niehoff, J. (1960) *East Indians in the West Indies*, Milwaukee: Milwaukee Public Museum Publications in Anthropology No. 6.

Nye, M. (1991) 'A Hindu community in Edinburgh: regionalism and religion', paper presented at the 5th annual conference, British Association for South Asian Studies, London.

—— (1995) *A Place for Our Gods: The Construction of an Edinburgh Hindu Temple Community*, Richmond: Curzon.

—— (1996) 'The Iskconisation of British Hinduisms', paper presented at conference on The Comparative Study of the South Asian Diaspora Religious Experience in Britain, Canada and the USA, School of Oriental and African Studies, November.

Oddie, G.A. (1987) 'Regional and other variations in popular religion in India: hook-swinging in Bengal and Madras in the nineteenth century', *South Asia* 10: 1–10.

O'Malley, L.S.S. (1935) *Popular Hinduism*, Cambridge: Cambridge University Press.

Parekh, B. (1993) 'Some reflections on the Indian diaspora', *Journal of Contemporary Thought* 3: 105–51.

—— (1994) 'Some reflections on the Hindu diaspora', *New Community* 20: 603–20.

Patel, N. (1976) 'Hinduism outside India: selective retention in Gujarati families', in G.R. Gupta (ed.), *Family and Social Change in Modern India*, New Delhi: Vikas, pp. 233–56.

Patel, P. and Rutten, M. (1999) 'Patels of Central Gujarat in Greater London', *Economic and Political Weekly*, 17–24 April, pp. 952–4.

Peach, C. (1968) *West Indian Migration to Britain: A Social Geography*, Oxford: Oxford University Press.

—— (1984) 'The force of West Indian island identity in Britain', in C. Clarke, D. Ley and C. Peach (eds), *Geography and Ethnic Pluralism*, London: Allen & Unwin, pp. 214–30.

—— (1994) 'Three phases of South Asian emigration', in J. Brown and R. Foot (eds), *Migration: The Asian Experience*, Basingstoke: Macmillan, pp. 38–55.

Peach, C., Robinson, V., Maxted, J. and Chance, J. (1988) 'Immigration and ethnicity', in A.H. Halsey (ed.), *British Social Trends since 1900*, London, Macmillan: pp. 561–615.

Peel, J.D.Y. (1991) 'History, culture and the comparative method: a West African puzzle', in L. Holy (ed.), *Comparative Anthropology*, Oxford: Blackwell, pp. 88–118.

Peggie, A.C.W. (1982) 'Intergenerational differences and minority politics: a study of young Sikhs in Southall', PhD thesis, University of Bristol.

Phillips, L.H.C. (1960) 'Kali-Mai puja', *Timehri* 11: 136–46.

Planalp, J.M. (1956) 'Religious life and values in a North Indian village', PhD dissertation, Cornell University, New York.

Pocock, D.F. (1957) '"Difference" in East Africa: a study of caste and religion in modern Indian society', *Southwestern Journal of Anthropology* 13: 285–300.

—— (1973) *Mind, Body and Wealth*, Oxford: Basil Blackwell.

—— (1976) 'Preservation of the religious life: Hindu immigrants in England', *Contributions to Indian Sociology* 10: 341–65.

Poynting, J. (1985) 'Literature and cultural pluralism: the East Indian in the Caribbean', PhD thesis, University of Leeds.

Prinja, N.K. (1996) *Explaining Hindu Dharma: A Guide for Teachers*, Norwich: Religious and Moral Education Press.

Prins, C.J.M (1994) 'Islamieten en Hindoes in Nederland: herziening van tijdreeks', *Maandstatistiek van de bevolking* (CBS), 42, 2: 22–7.

Rai, A.S. (1995) 'India on-line: electronic bulletin boards and the construction of a diasporic Hindu identity', *Diaspora* 4: 31–57.

Raj, D.S. (1997) 'Shifting culture in the global terrain: cultural identity constructions amongst British Punjabi Hindus', PhD thesis, University of Cambridge.

—— (1999) '"Who the hell do you think you are?" Promoting religious identity amongst young Hindus in Britain', *Ethnic and Racial Studies* 23: 535–58.

Rajagopal, A. (1997) 'Transnational networks and Hindu nationalism', *Bulletin of Concerned Asian Scholars* 29(3): 45–58.

Ramanathan, K. (1997) 'The Malaysian Hindu diaspora and their temples', paper presented at the International Conference on the Hindu Diaspora, Concordia University, Montreal.

Rambiritch, B. and van den Berghe, P.L. (1961) 'Caste in a Natal Hindu community', *African Studies* 20: 217–25.

Ramcharan, S. (1983) 'The social, economic and cultural adaptation of East Indians from the British Caribbean and Guyana to Canada', in G. Kurian and R.P. Srivastava (eds), *Overseas Indians: A Study in Adaptation*, Delhi: Vikas, pp. 51–7.

Ramnarine, T. (1977) 'The growth of the East Indian community in British Guiana, 1880–1920', PhD thesis, University of Sussex.

Rampton, B. (1995) *Crossing: Language and Ethnicity among Adolescents*, London: Longman.

Ramsoedh, H. and Bloemberg, L. (1995) 'The institutionalization of Hinduism in Suriname and Guyana', Surinaamse Verkenningen series, Paramaribo: Leo Victor.

Rayaprol, A. (1997) *Negotiating Identities: Women in the Indian Diaspora*, Delhi: Oxford University Press.

Robinson, V. (1986) *Transients, Settlers and Refugees: Asians in Britain*, Oxford: Clarendon Press.

Rogers, A. (1998a) 'Non-resident Indians', *Traces* 1(1), on-line news digest, http://www.transcomm.ox.ac.uk

—— (1998b) 'India seeks financial help from overseas Indians', *Traces* 1(3), on-line news digest, http://www.transcomm.ox.ac.uk

Ryan, S. (1972) *Race and Nationalism in Trinidad and Tobago*, St Augustine, Trinidad: University of the West Indies, Institute for Social and Economic Research.

Safran, W. (1991) 'Diasporas in modern societies: myths of homeland and return', *Diaspora* 1: 83–99.

Samaroo, B. (1982) 'Missionary methods and local responses: the Canadian Presbyterians and the East Indians in the Caribbean', in B. Brereton and W. Dookeran (eds), *East Indians in the Caribbean*, London: Kraus, pp. 93–115.

Sander, Å. (1997) 'To what extent is the Swedish Muslim religious?', in S. Vertovec and C. Peach (eds), *Islam in Europe: The Politics of Religion and Community*, Basingstoke: Macmillan, pp. 179–210.

Schwartz, B.M (ed.) (1967a) *Caste in Overseas Indian Communities*, San Francisco: Chandler.

—— (1967b) 'Differential socio-religious adaptation', *Social and Economic Studies* 16: 237–48.

Selvon, S. (1956) *The Lonely Londoners*, London: Wingate.

Sengupta, S. (1998) 'India taps into its diaspora: expatriates buy bonds for love of country, and 7.75% interest', *New York Times*, 19 August.

Sharma, K.O. (1989) 'Hindu', in *Virat Hindu Sammelan, Souvenir*, Souvenir Committee.

Sharma, U.M. (1969) 'Hinduism in a Kangra village', PhD thesis, School of Oriental and African Studies, University of London.

—— (1970) 'The problem of village Hinduism: "fragmentation" and integration', *Contributions to Indian Sociology* (N.S.) 4: 1–21.

Sheffer, G. (1986) 'A new field of study: modern diasporas in international politics', in G. Sheffer (ed.), *Modern Diasporas in International Politics*, London: Croom Helm, pp. 1–15.

—— (1995) 'The emergence of new ethno-national diasporas', *Migration* 28: 5–28.

Sims, R. (1981) 'Spatial separation between Asian religious minorities: an aid to explanation or obfuscation?', in P. Jackson and S.J. Smith (eds), *Social Interaction and Ethnic Segregation*, London: Academic Press, pp. 123–35.

Singaravelou (1987) *Les Indiens de la Caraïbe*, 3 vols, Paris: L'Harmattan.

Singer, M. (1966) 'The modernization of religious beliefs', in M. Weiner (ed.), *Modernization*, New York: Basic Books, pp. 55–67.

—— (1971) *When a Great Tradition Modernizes*, New York: Yaeger

Smart, N. (1987) 'The importance of diasporas', in S. Shaked, D. Shulman and G.G. Stroumsa (eds), *Gilgul: Essays on Transformation, Revolution and Permanence in the History of Religions*, Leiden: E.J. Brill, pp. 288–97.

Smith, R.T. (1962) *British Guiana*, London: Oxford University Press.

Smith, W.C. (1964) *The Meaning and End of Religion: A New Approach to the Religious Traditions of Mankind*, New York: New American Library.

Speckman, J.D. (1965) *Marriage and Kinship among Indians in Surinam*, Assen: van Gorcum.

Spivak, G. (1989) 'Who claims alterity?', in B. Kruger and P. Mariani (eds), *Remaking History*, Seattle: Bay, pp. 269–92.

Srinivas, M.N. and Shah, A.M. (1968) 'Hinduism', in D.L. Sills (ed.), *International Encyclopedia of the Social Sciences*, New York: Macmillan, vol. 6, pp. 358–66.

Streng, F.J. (1979) '"Sacred" and "secular" as terms for interpreting modernization in India', *Religious Traditions* 2: 21–9.

Tambs-Lyche, H. (1975) 'A comparison of Gujarati communities in London and the Midlands', *New Community* 4: 349–55.

—— (1990) 'Fundamentalism or secularism? The case of the Swaminarayans of Gujarat', paper presented at the 11th European Conference on Modern South Asian Studies, Amsterdam.

Tatla, D. Singh (1993) 'The politics of homeland: a study of ethnic linkages and political mobilisation amongst Sikhs in Britain and North America', PhD thesis, Centre for Research in Ethnic Relations, University of Warwick.

Ter Haar, G. (ed.) (1998) *Strangers and Sojourners: Religious Communities in the Diaspora*, Leuven: Peeters.

Tewarie, B. (1988) 'Hinduism, nation-building and the state', in S. Ryan (ed.), *Trinidad and Tobago: The Independence Experience 1962–1987*, St Augustine, Trinidad: University of the West Indies, Institute of Social and Economic Research, pp. 207–16.

Thapar, R. (1989) 'Imagined religious communities? Ancient history and the modern search for a Hindu identity', *Modern Asian Studies* 23: 209–31.

Thiara, R. (1994) 'Migration, organization and inter-ethnic relations: Indian South Africans 1860–1990', PhD thesis, University of Warwick.

Thomas, T. (1993) 'Hindu dharma in dispersion', in G. Parsons (ed.), *The Growth of Religious Diversity: Britain from 1945, Vol. I – Traditions*, London: Routledge, pp. 173–204.

Thompson, K. (1986) *Beliefs and Ideology*, London: Tavistock.

Tinker, H. (1974) *A New System of Slavery: The Export of Indian Labour Overseas 1830–1920*, London: Oxford University Press.

—— (1976) *Separate and Unequal: India and the Indians in the British Commonwealth 1920–1950*, London: C. Hurst.

—— (1977) *The Banyan Tree: Overseas Emigrants from India, Pakistan and Bangladesh*, Oxford: Oxford University Press.

Underhill, E.B. (1862) *The West Indies: Their Social and Religious Condition*, London: Jackson, Walford & Hodder.

van der Burg, C. (1993) 'Surinam Hinduism in the Netherlands and social change', in R. Barot (ed.), *Religion and Ethnicity: Minorities and Social Change in the Metropolis*, Kampen: Kok Pharos, pp. 138–55.

van der Burg, C. and van der Veer, P. (1986) 'Pandits, power and profit: religious organization and the construction of identity among Surinamese Hindus', *Ethnic and Racial Studies* 9: 514–29.

van der Veer, P. (1987) 'East Indians from the West Indies in the Netherlands: identity as disposition and instrument', paper given at the Conference on the Dynamics of Ethnicity in Eastern and Western Europe, Utrecht, The Netherlands.

—— (1991) 'Religious therapies and their valuation among Surinamese Hindustani in the Netherlands', in S. Vertovec (ed.), *Aspects of the South Asian Diaspora*, Delhi: Oxford University Press, pp. 36–56.

—— (1994) *Religious Nationalism: Hindus and Muslims in India*, Berkeley, CA: University of California Press.

—— (ed.) (1995) *Nation and Migration: The Politics of Space in the South Asian Diaspora*, Philadelphia: University of Pennsylvania Press.

—— (1996) 'Authenticity and authority in Surinamese Hindu ritual', in D. Dabydeen and B. Samaroo (eds), *Across the Dark Waters: Indo-Caribbean History and Culture*, Basingstoke: Macmillan, pp. 131–46.

—— (1999) 'Cosmopolitanism, secularism and transnational religion', presentation in the ESRC Transnational Communities Programme seminar, Oxford University, 6 May.

van der Veer, P. and Vertovec, S. (1991) 'Brahmanism abroad: on Caribbean Hinduism as an ethnic religion', *Ethnology* 30: 149–66.

Vasil, R.K. (1984) *Politics in Bi-Racial Societies*, New Delhi: Radiant.

Vertovec, S. (1989) 'Hinduism in diaspora: the transformation of tradition in Trinidad', in H. Kulke and G.D. Sontheimer (eds), *Hinduism Reconsidered*, New Delhi: Manohar, pp. 152–79.

—— (1990a) 'Religion and ethnic ideology: the Hindu youth movement in Trinidad', *Ethnic and Racial Studies* 13: 225–49.

—— (1990b) 'Oil boom and recession in Trinidad Indian villages', in C. Clarke, C. Peach and S. Vertovec (eds), *South Asians Overseas: Migration and Ethnicity*, Cambridge: Cambridge University Press, pp. 89–111.

—— (1991a) 'Inventing religious tradition: *yagnas* and Hindu renewal in Trinidad', in A. Geertz and J.S. Jensen (eds), *Religion, Tradition and Renewal*, Aarhus: Universitetsforlag, pp. 77–95.

—— (1991b) 'East Indians and anthropologists: a critical review', *Social and Economic Studies* 40: 125–61.

—— (1991c) (ed.) *Aspects of the South Asian Diaspora*, New Delhi: Oxford University Press.

—— (1992a) 'Community and congregation in London Hindu temples: divergent trends', *New Community* 18: 251–64.

—— (1992b) *Hindu Trinidad: Religion, Ethnicity and Socio-Economic Change*, Basingstoke: Macmillan.

—— (1993) 'Hindu Mother-Goddess cults in the Caribbean', *Etnolog* 54(3): 179–94.

—— (1994a) '"Official" and "popular" Hinduism in the Caribbean: historical and contemporary trends in Surinam, Trinidad and Guyana', *Contributions to Indian Sociology* 28(1): 123–47.

—— (1994b) 'Caught in an ethnic quandary: Indo-Caribbean Hindus in London', in R. Ballard (ed.), *Desh Pardesh: The South Asian Presence in Britain*, London: C. Hurst, pp. 272–90.

—— (1995) 'Hindus in Trinidad and Britain: ethnic religion, reification and the politics of public space', in P. van der Veer (ed.), *Nation and Migration: The Politics of Space in the South Asian Diaspora*, Philadelphia: University of Pennsylvania Press, pp. 132–56.

—— (1996a) 'Muslims, the state and the public sphere in Britain', in G. Nonneman, T. Niblock and B. Sjazkowski (eds), *Muslim Communities in the New Europe*, London: Ithaca Press, pp. 167–86.

—— (1996b) 'Multiculturalism, culturalism and public incorporation', *Ethnic and Racial Studies* 19: 49–69.

—— (1996c) 'On the reproduction and representation of Hinduism in Britain', in T. Ranger, Y. Samad and O. Stewart (eds), *Culture, Identity and Politics: Asians and Afro-Caribbeans in Britain*, Aldershot: Avebury, pp. 77–89.

—— (1997a) 'Diaspora', in E. Cashmore (ed.), *Dictionary of Race and Ethnic Relations*, (4th rev. edn), London: Routledge, pp. 99–101.

—— (1997b) 'Accommodating religious pluralism in Britain: South Asian religions', in M. Martiniello (ed.), *Multicultural Policies and the State*, Utrecht: ERCOMER, pp. 163–77.

—— (1999) 'Three meanings of "diaspora," exemplified among South Asian religions', *Diaspora* 6: 277–300.

Vertovec, S. and Peach, C. (1997) 'Introduction: Islam in Europe and the politics of religion and community', in S. Vertovec and C. Peach (eds), *Islam in Europe: The Politics of Religion and Community*, Basingstoke: Macmillan, pp. 3–47.

Vertovec, S. and Rogers, A. (1998) 'Introduction', in S. Vertovec and A. Rogers (eds), *Muslim European Youth: Re-producing Religion, Ethnicity and Culture*, Aldershot: Avebury, pp. 1–24.

Voigt-Graf, C. (1998) *Asian Communities in Tanzania: A Journey through Past and Present Times*, Hamburg: Institute of African Affairs.

von Stietencron, H. (1989) 'Hinduism: on the proper use of a deceptive term', in G.D. Sontheimer and H. Kulke (eds), *Hinduism Reconsidered*, Delhi: Manohar, pp. 11–27.

Wallace, A.F.C. (1956) 'Revitalization movements', *American Anthropologist* 58: 264–81.

Weightman, S. (1978) *Hinduism in the Village Setting*, Milton Keynes: Open University Press.

—— (1984) 'Hinduism', in J. Hinnells (ed.), *A Handbook of Living Religions*, Harmondsworth: Penguin, pp. 191–236.

—— (1997) 'Hinduism', in J. Hinnells (ed.), *A New Handbook of Living Religions*, Oxford: Blackwell, pp. 261–309.

Werbner, P. (1990) *The Migration Process: Capital, Gifts and Offerings among British Pakistanis*, Oxford: Berg.

—— (1991a) 'The fiction of unity in ethnic politics: aspects of representation and the state among British Pakistanis', in P. Werbner and M. Anwar (eds), *Black and Ethnic Leaderships in Britain: The Cultural Dimensions of Political Action*, London: Routledge, pp. 113–45.

—— (1991b) 'Shattered bridges: the dialectics of progress and alienation among British Muslims', *New Community* 17: 331–46.

Wilkinson, S.M. (1994) 'Young British Hindu women's interpretations of the images of womanhood in Hinduism', PhD thesis, University of Leeds.

Willford, A. (1998) 'Within and beyond the state: ritual and the assertion of Tamil-Hindu identities in Malaysia', paper presented at the conference on 'Globalization from Below', Duke University, North Carolina.

Williams, R.B. (1984) *A New Face of Hinduism: The Swaminarayan Religion*, Cambridge: Cambridge University Press.

—— (1988) *Religions of Immigrants from India and Pakistan: New Threads in the American Tapestry*, Cambridge: Cambridge University Press.

—— (1992a) 'A sacred thread: introduction', in R.B. Williams (ed.), *A Sacred Thread: Modern Transmission of Hindu Traditions in India and Abroad*, Chambersburg: Anima, pp. 3–6.

—— (1992b) 'Sacred threads of several textures', in R.B. Williams (ed.), *A Sacred Thread: Modern Transmission of Hindu Traditions in India and Abroad*, Chambersburg: Anima, pp. 228–57.

—— (1998) 'Training religious specialists for a transnational Hinduism: a Swaminarayan sadhu training center', *Journal of the American Academy of Religion* 66: 841–62.

Wood, D. (1968) *Trinidad in Transition*, London: Oxford University Press.

Zaidman, N. (1997) 'When the deities are asleep: processes of change in an American Hare Krishna temple', *Journal of Contemporary Religion* 12: 335–52.

INDEX

Brereton, B. 70
British Hinduism: and building of temples 96–7; and cultural transmission 93–5; and domestic sphere 94–5; and education 102–4; and institutionalization 95–9; and women 94
British Hindus 29–30, 33–4, 36; background, composition, differentiation 87–93; broad-based organizations 100–1; disparate religious traditions of 92–3; and ethnic Hinduism 106–7; facets of representation 99–106; facets of reproduction 93–9; formal religious nurture 101–4; levels of provenance 88–90; migration patterns 87–8; population by area or origin/religion 88; public representation 104–6; regional-minority communities 93
British Raj 9, 10
Brockington, J. 126, 127
Bronkhurst, H.V.P. 48, 50, 51–2
Bryant, M.T. 129
Buchignani, N. 122
Buddhism 92
Burghart, R. 1, 18, 97, 100, 107, 154
Burlet, S. and Reid, H. 146

Carey, S. 30, 101
Caribbean Hindu Society (UK) 97, 115, 118, 121, 122, 133, 137
Caribbean Hinduism: activities 48–52; alternative official forms 58–9; amorphous/peripheral forms 61; and celebration of festivals 50–1; collective forms 59–60; contemporary 58–61; domestic forms 60; early 47–52; growth of 'official' 52–7; individual forms 60–1; official forms 58; ongoing trends/debates concerning 61–2; organizational development of 54; rites/rituals 51, 53–4; toleration of 48; traditions 46–7

Caribbean Hindus 39, 110–12; arrival of 43–7; conditions of 43–4; descriptive categories 39–42; and diaspora 39–42; differences in socio-religious heritage 44–5; domestic sphere 51–2; as indentured immigrants 44–5; linguistic diversity of 48; numbers of 45–6; origins of 45–6; population 42; traditions of 49; *see also* Indo-Caribbean Hindus
caste system 24–6, 29, 41, 46–7, 52–3, 93, 98, 110, 136, 160
Chaitanya sect 46
Chamars 24, 47, 60, 89
Charotar Patidar Samj (UK) 98
Cheah, P. and Robbins, B. 164
Chovis Gam Patidar Samaj (UK) 98
Clarke, C. 25; *et al* 13, 15, 21, 87, 144
Clifford, J. 19, 141, 142, 147
Cohen, R. 2, 141, 142, 147, 149
Collens, J.H. 51
Comins, D.W.D. 49, 50
Coward, H. 14
Crissman, L.W. 89
Crooke, W. 47
Cross, M. 64, 66, 110; and Schwartzbaum, A.W. 72, 112
Cultural Festival of India (UK) 100–1

Dahya, B. 95
Democratic Labour Party (DLP) (Trinidad) 72, 111
Dew, E. 56
dharma 83, 85
diaspora: adaptive strategies 156; and awareness of multi-locality 147–50; and collective memories 148; community development 23; comparative method for study of 18–20; crossing/milieu-moving 158; cultural 21–2, 150–1, 157–8; as divergent 1; dual/paradoxical nature of 147, 150; as economic strategy 143–4, 145; and